MARK REYNOLDS

A Journey with Strangers

A JOURNEY WITH STRANGERS. Copyright © 2014 by Mark A. Reynolds. *All rights reserved. No part of this publication may be reproduced, distributed, or transmitted without the express consent of the author.*

Although this book is based on true events, the narrative came solely from the author's recollections and should not be considered to be historically accurate. Fictional names were used throughout, and some of the characters are fictional representations of actual persons.

Cover Art. *Front:* photos and design © Mark A. Reynolds. *Back*: photo by Pierre Camateros, "Kelbaker Road in the Mojave Desert" (14 may 2008), design by Mark A. Reynolds.

First Edition.

ISBN: 978-0-692-35973-0

December, 2014

*"I'm not a prophet or a stone age man
Just a mortal with the potential of a superman"*

- David Bowie

For Matthew…

AUTHOR'S NOTE

THIS STORY TAKES PLACE around a hitchhiking adventure that I went on soon after graduating from high school. Although I didn't really keep a journal at the time, the memories described continue to be vivid and dear to me. This was not a safe journey, to be sure, nor was it a linear one. Every person I met along the way had something unexpected to teach me, and some of those things took me years to fully understand. Perhaps that's why it took so long for me to write about them. I decided to use fictional names for my characters. It just seemed the proper way to share my story.

I could never have completed this book without the help and support of family and friends. First, I want to thank my son Matt, who helped refresh these memories by riding along to retrace the journey from New Orleans to Orlando. He took notes on his laptop while I drove and had lots of good suggestions. Second, I want to thank my brother Jeff and wife Laure for suffering with me through numerous rewrites, and for staying patient and enthusiastic the entire way. Finally, I want to thank Brad, Mary Beth, Chuck and my sister Julie for all of your encouragement and for pointing out a number of inaccuracies that I had missed. I'm sure I've still missed a few.

I've tried my best to share these experiences from my eighteen year old perspective since that was my journey. But I understand that we all have different ways of reflecting on our memories, so I'll leave it to the reader to decide if I got it right. Anyhow, it's time for me to go back out and catch another wave...

CHAPTER ONE

LEANING AGAINST A SIGNPOST beside the freeway onramp, I stuck out my thumb. My blue work shirt flapped urgently in a Santa Ana desert wind that was pushing its way into the valley. I was back in 1974, a Sunday morning in June, nine days after high school graduation. I took a deep breath, and then another, settling my mind as I stood there about a mile up the boulevard from my home in Southern California. Although the sun was still low on the horizon, beads of sweat were already trickling down my forehead into my eyes. Today would be a hot one for sure, and I understood this. But I would be okay out there I told myself, the kind of forced calm I'd settle into while paddling ahead of a cresting ocean wave, just before the rush that came from sliding down into the curl. I was heading to Florida to see about a girl.

The peaks of the San Gabriel Mountains were still barely visible through the brown and hazy smog. Although the wind would eventually win this day, shoving it out over the Pacific Ocean to sulk and fume, the smog would probably creep its way back here in a day or two. Tailpipe exhaust from the endless procession of cars and trucks speeding by would lure it back when the winds had settled down, but I wasn't about to hang around for that. School was out and I was ready for an adventure, dammit. And even more, I longed for the desert and bluer sky. The sign I happened to be leaning on said that pedestrians and motor-driven cycles were prohibited beyond this point. I would have to get into one those cars speeding by if I was going to make it out of here.

There was a roadmap of the USA in the outer pouch of my backpack. I would head east on Interstate 10, according to the map.

It was from Shell Oil, funny how they used to hand those maps out for free. I haven't seen one like it since that covers the entire United States. I had traced the route with a yellow highlighter just before leaving the house. I would follow Interstate 10 until I reached Texas and take Interstate 20 through Dallas and Louisiana. From there I wanted to make my way down to the Gulf coast and head east on Interstate 10 again to the Florida panhandle. If I could make it to Tallahassee, I should be able to catch a ride from there down to Orlando. I had a few other possible destinations circled, for example the Carlsbad Caverns in New Mexico since I had heard about them from a girl I met on the beach, but those side trips would depend on how lucky I got with the rides.

My buddy Dean did some hitching the summer before. He claimed to have made it all the way to Canada, which was kind of hard to believe until you listened to his stories. He stayed a few days in a commune just outside of Spokane. Some hippies had taken over Highbridge Park for the summer. Dean said there were naked chicks sitting outside making clothes from foot pedal sewing machines. Some of them were actually living in caves on the other side of the creek. I figured it would be kind of hard to make that stuff up.

The traffic light changed and another bolus of cars queued up the ramp, but their drivers didn't seem to notice me as they accelerated onto the freeway. I thought about Dennis Hopper in the movie *Easy Rider*, straddling his Harley and leaning over to Peter Fonda. "Adventure, man," he would say just before he gunned his Harley and pulled it back out onto some desert highway. Yeah, I was headed that way. Still the sun baked down through the smoggy haze. I shaded my eyes with one hand while trying to get cars entering the freeway to notice my outstretched thumb.

I also had a Polaroid picture of the girl in my pouch, the one from Florida. She was wearing a string bikini in the photo and had this compellingly assured smile, with a lean athletic figure and sun bleached brown hair... A young man who happened to walk by a girl like that on the beach would stumble in the sand for sure.

It felt like my internal compass was spinning when I woke up that morning. Staring at the photo had settled my mind on a destination. And to be honest, I wasn't sure I would want to come back when I got there, even though I had accepted admission to a local college for the coming fall. Stupid I know, but that was me at eighteen. I had no idea what to do at this stage of my life, and I needed some time to sort through my thoughts. There would be plenty of time to do this when I was hitching rides, hence the allure. I was hoping to find some answers along the way.

I met her the previous summer while staying with my father, a father I hadn't grown up with. He was back in the states and it had been really great to see him again. But it still seemed like we barely knew each other; there hadn't been enough time to make up for the lost years. That was another reason why I had charted a course to Florida, I realized. I wanted us to spend more time together.

The reason I happened to be hitching that day was a bit more black and white, it seemed. My blue 1970 Triumph TR6 sports car was still in the shop, the one I had paid cash for by working nights and weekends at the local movie theatre, squeezing in as many hours as I could between school, sports and homework. When I had called the shop on Friday the guy had told me that he was still waiting on a part, but I needed to go right then or not at all since my summer job would be starting two weeks later.

On my high school graduation day, nine days before, I had gotten up early to drive to a local city park and drink cheap sweet wine and eat strawberries with some of my closest friends. It was Teresa's idea that we should meet there that morning, a fitting end to a new beginning she said, because it was our last day as seniors and we would be graduating that afternoon. Teresa was a raven haired Puerto Rican goddess with a killer body and a sharp mind, and had been one of my closest friends since the seventh grade. Somehow I had missed her interest in me during those earlier years, missed all of her cues as we both grew into our post-adolescent bodies. Then Teresa got popular around school, more popular than me, an attractive high energy cheerleader with a possessive football player boyfriend. She had the graceful moves of a professional dancer, and watching her cheerlead down there in front of the bleachers was pretty much all I remembered from the few football games I had managed to attend. She was going to UC Berkeley in the fall and wanted to become a lawyer. Considering how she could put her mind to things, I knew that she would do it. I remember wondering what *I* wanted to "be" exactly while sitting there in mild intoxication, with a full scholarship to one of the Claremont Colleges pulling me forward.

That park had been our staging ground for parties most of those Saturday nights during our senior year. We would stand around in the parking lot blasting rock music from open car doors, and come to a consensus about which parties to crash based on who knew what was happening. Someone would let it slip at school that their parents were going to be out of town that weekend, and word would get around. We brought our own booze and always tried to leave their houses and backyards free of bottles and trash by the time we left. Our code of ethics was always to join in, party-hearty, but don't leave a mess behind, and it worked pretty well most of the time. We made friends with guys and chicks from other schools around the valley at those parties, a growing roster of co-conspirators for future such endeavors. It was kind of cool to bump into them at our favorite beach hangouts over the summer, 15th Street at Newport, or sometimes Huntington Cliffs. We all liked to chase the surf on up the coast.

But we were still groggy from sleep in the early dawn on this particular morning, and there was a foggy mist in the air that muffled out any background noise, so it was exceptionally quiet. Teresa had put our dawn patrol picnic together with the help of some of her girlfriends, and those of us who were lucky enough to be invited could not say no. There we sat atop blankets on the wet grass, underneath a large oak tree that had been there decades before the park had ever been built. The sweet wine would not have been our first choice, but we drank it graciously anyhow. We said our goodbyes, vowing to keep in touch but knowing that our lives would diverge and possibly recombine in a variety of unpredictable ways. It was a good time to breathe deeply and smile at each other, sipping the wine out of disposable plastic cups, knowing that things would never be quite the same. Somehow we made it to our senior breakfast (at least most of us), and then the big graduation ceremony itself, with caps and gowns and family and friends.

I was one of the co-valedictorians and I remember nervously babbling some meaningless crap into the microphone. I just couldn't seem to find the right words when I was writing my speech the day before, afraid to say anything too provocative because frankly, whatever I really wanted to say had not yet made it out of my subconscious mind. So I picked some safe things to say about heading into our future, thanking our parents and teachers, a pretty boring speech actually. I still have it. I remember the audience and students clapping politely at the end, but that's about it.

Some of us declined the bus ride to grad night at Disneyland that evening, having decided instead to gather for one last party. So there I was again with my friends that night, drinking, talking and laughing, and singing with the songs on the stereo like we had written them ourselves. Suddenly I found myself in a shouting match with Teresa's football player boyfriend who was not planning to go to college. Maybe he was just mad that his girl happened to be sitting on my lap at the time, but his belligerence really pissed me off.

"Mickey, just chill out, man, you're being really stupid," Teresa said.

Her soon to be ex-boyfriend Mickey was eager for a fight to release his beer-enhanced melancholy about an uncertain future. He had not received a scholarship to anywhere. Having blown out a knee during one of the last games of the regular season, he was not able to play in that California Interscholastic Federation playoff game where college scouts would be making their selections. I guess he figured I would be an easy target to vent his frustration. He probably didn't expect me to fight back. I was a four-year varsity distance runner, six foot three and 178 pounds of mostly leg muscle who didn't spend much time lifting weights. I decided to keep my hands resting on Teresa's thighs, steadying her on my lap while she continued to yell at Mickey. Mickey didn't like that.

"Get your hands off my girl, shithead!" he said.

Teresa leveled her stare on Mickey. "Brett and I were just talking, shithead!" she said. "We've been friends since the seventh grade." She remembered! I realized as I was talking to her just then that I had been hoping (or wanting to believe) that our relationship might possibly shift to a more intimate level. There seemed to be a mutual attraction brewing, I felt pretty sure of that. But now that spell had been broken. Something extremely unfair had just happened.

Mickey slurred something about me not deserving my scholarship. He had read about it in the local paper announcing our graduation ceremony. I considered putting in a dig about his football career, but that would have been way uncool and frankly I did feel a little sorry for him.

I decided to leave the party early and drive myself home; even though I had made a pact with my buddies that none of us would drive until we had sobered up. Teresa stood up to continue her escalating argument with Mickey. Unfortunately, now that my hands were free, I reached into my pocket and found my car keys. The next thing I remember was starting the engine and shifting gears as I accelerated down Benson Road toward Central Avenue. Monsoon like conditions had been hovering for days and a downpour erupted suddenly. I could barely see through the windshield, my wiper blades were flapping back and forth at full speed. I tried to focus on the road ahead, cranking up the volume on my cassette deck to summon the adrenaline I would need, an album I had recorded from vinyl. David Bowie was singing about *Ziggy Stardust and the Spiders from Mars*.

"Now Ziggy played...guitar!"

The traffic light changed to red as I approached Central Avenue and I stomped on the brakes, but too abruptly it seemed as I swerved into the turn lane and skidded to a stop pointed sideways. A police car happened to be parked at the gas station on the opposite corner and a search light was beaming in my direction. Someone was shouting through a bullhorn directing me to pull into the gas station parking lot *"after the light turned green, not before!"* I waited for the light to change and shifted into first gear, driving slowly and deliberately toward the gas station. But I made a turn into the parking lot too abruptly and my rear tire skidded into the rain gutter, which by now was swollen with rushing rainwater. My wheel slammed hard against the curb and I heard a wrenching metallic snap as my rear axle broke. I opened the door, staggered forward into the parking lot with the rain smacking against my skull, tripped and fell face first onto the drenched asphalt. *Ziggy* wafted from the open door of my little sports car out into the rain.

After answering the policeman's questions as honestly as I could while he shined his flashlight in my face, he looked over to my damaged car and considered what to do with me. It was a very long uncomfortable moment.

"Can you lock it?" he finally asked. The driver's side door was still wide open.

"Yeah, I think so," I said, stepping carefully over to the car and removing my keys from the ignition so I could lock the door.

"Here, give me those," he said, grabbing my keys and thrusting them in his pocket. He studied me for a few seconds and then nodded. "I think I'll drive you home this time," he said. He would not be taking me to jail.

My mom was stunned when she saw us at the door but regained her composure when the policeman handed over my car keys. She invited him in and poured us each a cup of coffee at the kitchen table. Then she listened intently while the policeman explained what had happened, glancing several times in my direction with an expression of disbelief.

"Brett was our high school valedictorian this afternoon," she said. I tried to focus as she spoke to the officer on my behalf.

"But I can't imagine how he could have wound up like this," she continued. "I can see that he has been drinking and I don't think he's done that before." I just sat there, having enough sense left in my foggy brain not to contradict her. I think I just nodded while she spoke.

"And he is going to college in the fall," she continued. "He was accepted with honors. With sports, school, and all of the extra-curricular activities that he was involved in, he didn't have much time for parties. In fact I'm pretty sure this could be the first time he ever tried alcohol, but regardless it's not like him to drink and drive. He's usually very responsible." She was pretty convincing, even to me. The policeman left me in my parent's custody with a warning, quite an amazing escape and I knew I was lucky. Once in a while you get a lucky break, but they're always for a reason, they never come free. My stepfather arranged to have my car towed to the body shop the next day.

The unseasonable rain that had fallen nine nights ago was a distant memory now. The brown and nasty smog had returned by the middle of the week and I was already finding it to be intolerable. I was wasting time in my room listening to my vinyl albums over and over again. My family left in the van last Friday for a camping trip to Utah, but I didn't want to go. I told them I'd see them when they got back in a couple weeks. I would be fine at home. But Saturday was kind of a blur.

So yeah, I was dreaming about that girl in the picture when I woke up this Sunday morning. I hadn't made plans to go out again this coming summer since my stepfather had gotten me a job at the company where he worked, a steel fabrication plant out in Etiwanda. This job would pay a lot more than the movie theatre job I had in high school, and I needed that money for college, but it wouldn't be starting until two weeks from tomorrow. I started thinking about those two weeks... was it enough time for an adventure? Where could I go?

Moved purely by emotion and not thinking about the consequences, I got down my backpack from the upper shelf in the garage, and assembled the equipment and supplies that I thought would need. My modest camping gear amounted to a ground cloth, a goose down sleeping bag, a mess kit, a small first aid kit, a water bottle, a small flashlight, and a poncho. My clothes included leather hiking boots, running shoes and beach sandals, two pairs of Levis, corduroy shorts, some T-shirts from various rock concerts I had attended, a small pile of underwear and socks, a used track sweatshirt in case it got cold at night, and a Hang Ten shirt for special occasions.

I also packed some dried fruit and nuts from my mom's kitchen, a wheel of Edam cheese still wrapped in red wax, and a can of tomato sauce for some reason. I wasn't planning to cook on this trip, but I figured it might come in handy if I happened to encounter some other hitcher along the way who was. Then I reached under my mattress and found the bag of pot I had hidden there after my graduation party. It was still in the glove compartment of my car the next day when my stepfather and I went back for it with the tow truck. I had managed to grab the baggie and stuff it in my pants when no one was looking. I figured it could come in handy when I was hitching rides, "grass for gas" was my preferred version of the phrase. Oh, and I had found the roadmap in our hall closet just off the kitchen. It would guide me on my journey.

There was also the matter of the two hundred dollars I had stashed away to cover expenses, including bus fare if I happened to get stuck somewhere. I wanted to be careful about how much I spent along the way. If I was lucky, I might have enough left at the end of my trip for a one way plane ticket home, assuming I made it to Florida that is. But it certainly wasn't enough to cover a round trip ticket. I knew that since I had checked out the rates in the LA Times earlier that morning, having "borrowed" it temporarily from our neighbor's front yard. So I stood there determined, committed and ready to go. That Sunday would be the first day of my cross country adventure, and I was going to take it mile by mile.

CHAPTER TWO

A KID WITH LONG STRINGY BLOND HAIR pulled over in a faded red Ford Ranchero. He rolled down his passenger window and hollered out, "Well do you want a ride or not?" The guy looked to be about my age but he had bad acne and a cigarette dangling from his lips. The Rolling Stones' *Let it Bleed* album was blaring out from a cassette deck beneath the dash. He didn't look like he would wait long for an answer, so this was it. I tossed my pack into the truck bed and climbed into the cab. His ashtray was filled with joint stubs and the floor boards were littered with crumpled fast food wrappers. As soon as I had shut the door he nodded and floored the Ranchero up onto the freeway.

"Dude you got any pot?" he asked with a grin as we merged into traffic. I decided to say no, not really wanting to get messed up just then. We rode on in silence for several minutes.

"Where you going?" he asked and I said Florida. "Well, I'm heading to Fontana," he said. "Guess that'll get you part of the way there huh?" This ride wouldn't even get me out of the valley, but I was somewhat relieved. I tried to enjoy the next song, *Midnight Rambler*, but wasn't quite in the mood.

"So how come you're heading out to Florida, man? I know they got beaches out there, dude, but not like here," he said. "I hear Cocoa Beach is pretty cool though, crappy surf but tons of bikini babes, or so they say. You surf, yeah?" I hadn't bothered to cut my hair for graduation, just couldn't see the point. It was pretty long and wavy. I thought I looked a bit like Roger Daltrey, actually. And it had that kind of bleached out look that surfers got from spending a lot of time out in the water.

"Yeah, but I just need to go someplace different, you know? Just got to get away, that's all. Out here we all talk the same, think the same. I want to head through Arizona, make my way through Texas, travel down through the South and see how other people live. It's just that I've got all these unfinished thoughts inside my head, you know, can't sort through them. Feels like I need to get some different perspectives to even them out. So man, yeah like I said, I've got to go. Ever read *On the Road* by Jack Kerouac?"

"Who?"

"Never mind."

"Well dude, you're gonna miss a lot of good beach action dying of thirst out there in the desert."

"*Dude*, if I get stuck out there I'll just find me a saguaro cactus, sit down under it and wait for nightfall, and gaze up into the stars. It will be cool. You stay here and have a good summer. And thanks for the ride. This one's my first." He slowed down as we approached an off-ramp just outside of Ontario. There were grape vineyards extending for miles to the north and south of us now.

There had been a few moderately successful wineries in the valley around that time. My friends and I would ride our bikes out into the vineyards to shoot off our bee-bee guns, back when we were maybe eleven or so. This would generally be okay with our folks so long as we got home before dark. Parents back then didn't seem to mind us kids taking off on our bikes for most of the day. There wasn't anything to do inside the house anyway, no computers, nothing but soap operas on the television in the afternoon, and we didn't have cell phones back then either. Your folks expected you to make it home in time for dinner. If that didn't happen, they'd call your friend's parents. We wouldn't want them to start dialing those numbers... one or more of us could get "put on restriction" and that would mean one or two less members of our posse for next time.

"This is where I turn off and head north. Have fun with them coyotes." He pulled over and let me out. "See you later dude." I wondered why guys said that when they knew they probably wouldn't. I stepped out, grabbed my backpack and said thanks. He revved the engine and popped the clutch, peeling rubber back onto the freeway until he was gone.

I hadn't made it very far with this ride, but it would be a long walk home if I gave up now, and I didn't want to do that anyway. The sun was baking down and it would be a scorcher by noon. Somehow the smog always makes it harder to endure the heat. It hurts to breathe a little. The Santa Ana breeze was blowing steady now although it felt almost as hot as the air coming out of a Thanksgiving oven. Anyway, at least the breeze kept my hair from sticking to my face. I would be okay, I told myself again. After saying a mental goodbye to the vineyards, I hiked partway back up the onramp and stuck out my thumb again.

My mind began to wander and my thoughts returned to Florida. My father had moved back there a couple of years before, although he had been stationed overseas with the Air Force during most of my teenage years. He and my mom split up when I was four and Mom decided to move out to California, but he would visit my sister and me whenever his flight schedule allowed for a stopover in LA, which happened about once a year. He usually just stayed for a day or two though. It was enough time to take us to places like Disneyland and Knott's Berry Farm, but there was never enough time to get to know him, ask him questions about girls, things like that.

But two years before, after serving for ten more years in Europe and Southeast Asia, he decided to take early retirement and return to the states with his second wife, my stepmother. He had always wanted to live in Florida, ever since his parents retired there. He would buzz their orange groves in a P58 when he was in flight training at Patrick Air Force Base.

Unfortunately, when he found out that the commercial airlines operating out of McCoy weren't hiring forty-year-old pilots, he was forced to take whatever odd jobs he could find. But after working on several bathroom remodels and room additions, he decided to get a general contractor's license so he could work for himself. He was designing and building custom houses now, and lived in one of them with my stepmother, a master planned subdivision just north of Orlando. I had gone out to see him the previous summer and help out on the job sites, even managed to learn a bit carpentry. My sister came along, somewhat reluctantly though since she had been only two when Dad and Mom split up. But when we got there she quickly figured out who the cute boys were around the neighborhood, and who had cars.

The house my dad lived in now was a short walk down to a lake. There was a small park with a sandy beach there where the local kids would gather after dusk and hang out, at least until the mosquitoes came out and chased us home. My sister and I went down most evenings after dinner to join them. The other kids asked us about California as though this were some sort of competition, Florida versus California, who had the best beaches, who had the best surf, you get the idea. I told them our beaches were better and the surf was always epic. They would yell "naw!" and shake their heads. It got to be a nightly thing. My sister would just nod and let me tell my stories about weekends on the beach.

But really, we were just trying to make some friends. One evening a guy named Jimmy who lived up the street brought his "former" girlfriend Kyla down to the lake. He had wanted to make that "former" part clear when he introduced her to me. I later learned they had had a torrid affair the summer before and Kyla's parents now forbade her from seeing him again, although they still snuck off together occasionally. My sister started flirting with Jimmy so I got to talk with Kyla.

Although she was beautiful in a disturbingly provocative sort of way, Kyla also happened to be a self-proclaimed "intellectual" and this seemed to annoy most of the kids. Still, there was something about her eyes that made me forget about everyone else around. Most of the other kids probably thought she was crazy, and I guess she was in some ways. But I enjoyed listening to her ideas about music, how people reacted to it, and how the rain feels on your face when you look up through it to the sky.

"So are you planning to go to college?" she asked. I said that I probably would, or at least assumed that I was going.

"What do you mean by *assumed*?" No one had come out and asked me this before and I didn't have an answer, so I just shrugged it off and smiled.

"Well I can't wait to get out of high school and go to college," she said. "I'm going to study art history, languages and philosophy, learn about other cultures and religion. It's like I've finally managed to climb the tree and now I can reach the apples."

"Yeah but you still have to pick them one at a time," I said.

"Well right now I just don't care! It's exciting, don't you think?"

I found more and more time to talk with Kyla over the next couple of weeks when my sister and I went down to the lake in the early evenings. My sister made friends with one or two of the other boys who came there regularly.

Kyla had a way of making me forget that the mosquitoes were starting to bite. One time it began to rain and we just kept on talking, nodding and smiling at each other. We decided to walk down Highway 434 to get a soda at the 7-Eleven outside of our custom home community, almost a two-mile walk in the increasing downpour. We were soaked to the skin by the time we got there but didn't care, just walked into the store dripping wet. Talking with Kyla was sensational beyond words, and listening to the way she spoke in her lilting southern accent was an experience unto itself. It had more to do with the way she spoke than what she said exactly, she just had this infectious energy that I wanted to latch onto.

"You know what I think?" she asked. "You're a California boy who has come out here to chase his fantasies. So am I one of your fantasies?" It seemed like she was trying to read my mind and tease me at the same time. I wanted to prove to her that I was real and that she was real, but to be honest my thoughts were piling on top of each other quickly at that young age. I could barely grasp the boundaries between reality and fantasy most of the time.

"I don't think of you as a fantasy; you are fascinating, however."

She smiled.

My sister and I got invited to a party at Kyla's house on the Fourth of July. Her parents were away for the weekend but my dad didn't know that. We arrived to loud music and pot smoke, with kids jumping in and out of the pool, and another light rain was starting to fall. I was thinking it must rain like this every day in Florida, which it almost always did that summer. And then I saw Kyla, with a red white and blue T-shirt that stretched seductively around her ample bosom, made me want to salute them but fortunately I caught myself. There was a beer keg out on the patio near the screened in pool. Thankfully the mosquitoes would be excluded from our evening reverie.

It was legal for kids to buy beer in Florida if they were over eighteen. There had been a political debate on the topic of its legality shortly before the Vietnam War had ended. The soldiers coming back from 'Nam argued that if they were old enough to fight and die for their country, why weren't they old enough to drink when they got home? Apparently booze was a staple of daily management over there. A number of states had decided that this logic made sense and lowered the drinking age to eighteen or nineteen. California was not one of them though, must have had something to do with too many freeways and cars. But the Florida state legislature agreed to make it legal to buy booze when you turned eighteen, as had many of the southern states. It obviously helped increase state tax revenues but much of what was permissible then would probably be unthinkable now. There were drive-thru liquor stores, for example, and it was even legal to have an open container in the car so long as you weren't driving drunk. Despite the liberal idealistic beliefs I held at that young age, I still found that distinction a bit hard to grasp. I would learn a hard lesson on that score by the following summer though.

When the keg was half gone we all took a dip in the pool and toweled off. Then we went back into the house and started dancing around the sparsely furnished living room, without any structure to it really, just moving around together with the music. Kyla was over in a corner dancing alone and I tried to get her attention, but she didn't seem to notice. Then a guy I hadn't seen before walked into the room and waved Kyla over to him. She rested her arms on his shoulders and gave him a kiss. The guy had long brown hair, wire rim glasses, and appeared a bit older than the rest of us.

Kyla's younger sister Annie danced over to me, apparently trying to distract me away from Kyla. "Hey Brett," she shouted, seeing my forlorn look. "That's Kyla's boyfriend John. He must have just come home from college." My heart sank.

I was just about to leave when the doorbell rang and Annie went to answer it, and then it happened: a strikingly beautiful girl with sandy brown hair walked in to the living room with Annie and they were approaching me. Kyla and the new guy had gone off somewhere.

"Brett, I'd like you to meet my friend Michelle," she said. "Michelle, this is my friend Brett. He's from California and has been visiting his dad here in Sweetwater." It felt like I was being set up, but I didn't mind. Michelle extended her hand and I took it, enjoying the feel of her soft skin and firm grip. She was as attractive as Kyla, I realized, getting the pleasant idea now that Florida must have a lot of pretty girls. Standing six foot three myself, I felt an immediate attraction to her slender five foot eleven body and captivating hazel eyes.

When Michelle's eyes met mine, there was just the hint of a smile. I took her hand and asked if she wanted to dance. This was probably the first time I heard a KISS album played loud and it seemed to energize both of us. Their self-titled album had just come out earlier in the year. Dancing can be a really great ice breaker.

When the music stopped Michelle shouted out "Let's go out to Cocoa Beach and dance in the sand!" Everyone seemed to think this was a good idea, and so fifty minutes later, after driving down a darkened Route 50 with our music blaring out into the night, four carloads of us drove over the causeway and down onto the sandy beach. We kicked off our sandals and flip flops and chased around in the shiny black surf. And then, with everyone panting for breath, we spread out blankets and passed a joint around while we watched a full moon rise up over the horizon, casting a furrow of lively silver reflections on the ocean water.

"I remember watching the last Saturn V rocket take off from over there on the cape," someone said. "We could see it from our house fifty miles away. I still remember how brightly it glowed while climbing skyward, how amazingly loud it was even from our house." While listening to him, I thought about the time I had watched Neil Armstrong step out onto the moon's surface for the first time. What must it be like to survive the violence of liftoff and escape earth's gravity, and then to bound around on the moon with ease wearing a 350 pound space suit? I settled next to Michelle and exhaled, trying to imagine all of that.

"My dad took us out here to watch the launch of Apollo 7," Michelle said. "It was the coolest thing I've ever seen. I could actually feel the sound waves as they hit my clothing. The rocket lifted up very slowly at first, but it was extremely loud, and it was very bright. Soon it was just a tiny speck of light against the bright blue sky. I watched until it was gone.

"We watched Apollo 11 take off from clear across Florida," she continued. "We were on vacation in St. Petersburg when that one took off. We could see the first rocket stage separate, even from out there on the Gulf Coast, it was that big. And we could even hear the distant rumble of the rocket engines. I could hardly believe it."

My mind often wandered to thoughts of Michelle after that night. I would think about her during the day while I was working with my dad, hanging doorframes or hammering trim work, tacking drywall or laying sod. I had an image of her inside my head that had been nicely drawn and colored onto a clean slate. No history had passed between us until then, yet somehow it felt like we were destined to be together. This seemed like a chance to create the kind of relationship I was yearning for, or at least I thought so in my mind, with no preconceived notions or expectations holding us back. I must have known those thoughts were more fantasy than reality. I would be returning to California in September and had no idea whether I would be coming back. But still, I wanted to get closer to her.

Michelle invited me to her house on a Saturday afternoon about a week after that, just the two of us since her family was on vacation but she had to stay home for work. We went swimming in the pool and listened records on the stereo in her living room. It felt like sparks of electricity when our lips touched for the first time. That kiss even gave me a charley horse in my left calf muscle. And then it started to rain. When I got back to my dad's house, I decided to go out for a jog in the growing downpour and felt more alive than I could remember.

So that was Michelle, the girl in the photo that I kept in my pack.

A grey haired couple pulled over to offer me a ride. They said they were heading to Palm Springs, so evidently I would make it out of the valley today after all. Grandpa smiled back at me from the rearview mirror and muttered that they didn't usually pick up hitchhikers, but apparently they had decided that I looked alright. He nodded over to his wife, and then turned his head back to the road with his hands firmly planted on the wheel, driving exactly 55 miles an hour. I said I had just graduated from high school, feeling the need to justify myself somehow. Grandpa smiled again and confided that he used to do a lot of hitchhiking after he got home from the Second World War. I returned the smile and nodded.

We reached the Palm Springs exit and grandpa pulled over to let me out. "There's a rest area just up ahead," Grandpa said. "You ought to be able to catch another ride from over there." I thanked them both, grabbed my backpack and hiked down toward it.

I hadn't gotten their names and they hadn't asked for mine, but that ride had solidified my journey. I had managed to catch my first ride, and I had just caught another one. I could do it again.

After using the restroom and refilling my water bottle from the drinking fountain outside, I hiked back to the onramp and waited there about a couple hours with no one stopping. A tumbleweed rolled by as the Santa Ana wind increased its intensity. Finally I decided to hike against the gale back down to the rest area to try hitching from there, just as folks were returning to the highway. A man in a wheelchair was palming his way from the restroom back to the parking lot and I asked if he needed any help. He ignored me at first, but then he saw my backpack leaning over against the restroom wall.

"You need a ride?" he asked. "Frankly I could use the company." A bumper sticker on the back of his wheelchair read "POWs and MIAs: We Remember". I told him I was hitching to Florida and yes, I would definitely appreciate the ride.

"Must be nice to just up and go like that," he said, "now that the war is over I mean." I told him I wouldn't know since I had turned eighteen shortly before the Vietnam War ended. The now meaningless draft card was still in my wallet. There was a low lottery number printed beneath my name, a good thing the war stopped before my number came up. I hadn't thought about it much until now.

"Yeah, I'm just lucky I guess. It must have been tough over there, for you I mean."

"Boy you got no idea. Well anyway, toss that pack of yours in the trunk and let's get them levers off the pedals so you can drive. I'm hoping to make it to Phoenix by night fall so let's go; we can talk more when we're underway. You don't mind driving, do you?" The late model Cadillac had handles fastened to the floor pedals so he could drive. I understood why he had decided to bring me along. He showed me how to unfasten the handles and had me set them on the back seat. Then I helped him into the passenger's seat and folded up the wheelchair, lowering it in down into the cavernous trunk next to my pack.

I settled into the driver's seat and made sure the pedals still worked. The ashtray was stuffed with cigar butts. After checking the brakes and accelerator, I headed up the onramp, surprised by how quickly the car accelerated. I hadn't really expected to be driving myself and it felt good to be in control of the vehicle. We proceeded up through the pass that ran between the San Gorgonio and San Jacinto Mountains and then headed southeast down towards Indio.

"What's your name?" he asked, and I told him mine. "I'm Bob," he said. He looked like a Bob.

"I was in Los Angeles for a couple days visiting my sister. Now I'm on my way back to Phoenix. It's good to finally get out of the smog, eh?" he said. I noticed that the sky was now a deeper shade of blue.

"Yeah," I agreed, "I grew up back there and it seems to be getting worse every year," I mused, "even after that spike in gas prices that we had last year." There was a gas shortage the year before and gas had spiked over 65 cents a gallon. "Now with everything happening in the Middle East, it's only a matter of time before gas goes over a buck a gallon," I added.

"Vietnam may be behind us, man," he said, "but that Persian Gulf is a powder keg and it's about to explode. They've got them oilfields out there to hold us hostage over, man. And I got to tell you, they don't think like we do. They think if they can blow themselves up and cause devastation and destruction in the name of Allah, they'll go straight to heaven with an endless supply of virgins to fuss over them. Crazy shit like that, man."

I decided to let it pass. "So tell me about 'Nam," I asked.

"I was a helicopter pilot over there," he said, "in search and rescue." For some reason he decided to stop talking at this point and we drove on in silence. I sped up to 70 mph when the traffic thinned out and asked if he thought that was okay. The speed limit was still supposed to be 55 mph on account of the 'energy crisis'.

"Don't worry man, out here them California highway patrol guys got to clock you before they can write you up. I'd keep a lookout for 'em, though, especially them onramps."

I made it a point to frequently check my rearview and side mirrors, but it did feel good to zoom down the freeway in an air-conditioned Caddie. I loved my sports car, but it would have been a lot bumpier and noisier rolling over the sun-cracked high desert asphalt.

"And you wouldn't believe the shit I saw over there, man," Bob continued. He lowered his chin with his eyes squinting as he said this. His hands were clenched tightly into fists and I saw now that there were dark circles under his eyes: obviously he hadn't slept much over the past few days. I decided not to ask about that and waited for him to continue.

"You only saw the censored crap that made its way to American newspapers for mass consumption. *Life* magazine posted some pretty graphic stuff, I know." He paused to look out the window as we passed a cluster of Joshua trees. They aren't trees really but cactuses that look like trees, strange looking things if you've never seen them before. "Some things that happened over there, nobody was allowed to talk about that stuff man," he continued. "Government secrets, they told us. No sir, we weren't supposed to talk about stuff like that."

"I flew injured GIs out of the bush under harm's way, and a lot of them didn't make it, you know?" he continued. I nodded but realized that I really didn't actually know.

"When you look into their eyes and hear their screams, it gets real personal, see? Horror mixed with fear, and then relief as they realize their bodies are being lifted out of the bush away from enemy fire. One time a few bullets pierced the armor underneath my chopper as we were making a quick ascent, passed right through both my legs," he muttered as he looked down to them. He closed his eyes for a few moments, reliving the scene. Then he turned and gave me a piercing look. "That's why I use them handles back there to drive," he said, gesturing with his thumb to the backseat.

Then he settled back and fixed his gaze down the highway. "I had a girlfriend before I left for 'Nam," he said after a few more minutes. "She was dating another guy by the time I returned from the war, some pansy who got conscientious objector status so's he could avoid the draft. I told her how I thought about her every day over there, how it had kept me going, how I had been counting the days to get back to her. But she didn't care about any of that man, just turned away from me." His eyes squinted and he pressed his lips together tightly. "She said I was a 'warmonger', whatever that means, that I had signed up for this, and that she couldn't understand why I had to volunteer and go fight over there in the first place. What should I have expected after leaving her like that?"

I couldn't think of a reply. But for some reason I tried to explain how distant the war felt to me, blissfully unaware of guys like him piloting their choppers in and out of the bush, hovering over rice paddies with bullets zinging up.

"It's hard for me to process what that war must have been like from your perspective," I said. "While you were over there fighting, pretty much all I was thinking about was heading out to the beach, listening to Led Zeppelin on the radio while driving in my car, curling my toes in the sand while waiting for waves on a sunny day, letting my hair grow long, stuff like that. And since this was my senior year of high school I've been pretty busy figuring out which college I should attend and whether or not my folks could afford it."

"My friends and I would drive out to Hollywood, sneak our way into Whiskey a Go-Go so that we could hear the latest bands," I continued, feeling the need to elaborate for some reason. "One time we got to see Van Halen play there, back around when they were just getting started." I paused at this point, trying to think of anything I might have regretted. "But I wish I could have been old enough to go to Woodstock," I said. "I play that album all the time. That's about the only thing I regret about not being older just now, I'm sorry to say. I guess my point is that we saw the war on the evening news, read about it in the local papers, but it wasn't real to us. It makes me feel bad now that I think about it."

"My dad was over there," I went on. "He hasn't talked about it much." I noticed that the freeway had expanded to three lanes as we headed through the town of Indio. "I did find a shoebox full of medals in the guest room closet last summer when I was visiting him," I said. "But I have no idea what they're for. Maybe I'll try to ask him about those medals when I get back to Florida, if I can get him to open up about it that is, probably not though. He would say it's all still 'classified'."

The sun was beyond its zenith now, on its way out to the Pacific Ocean. I was trying to be respectful and open with Bob so he'd let me keep driving his car. I really wanted to get to Phoenix by night fall, having no desire to get stuck out here on the desert at night. Little did I know what would be in store for me when I reached El Paso.

The speedometer on the dash said we were doing about 100 mph now, but Bob didn't seem to mind. I decided to crack the window open and breathed in the desert air. The air smelled fresh, with a hint of cactus blossoms that must have sprouted following last week's rain storm.

Irrigated farmland quickly gave way to the parched desert as we left Indio behind. Barren hills moved slowly by in the distance, grizzled with erosion from flash floods and desert winds. I studied the crusty soil while we drove along, wondering how it managed to support the dry sage brush and ocotillo that were scattered about. Squat barrel cacti rose up here and there, miserly vessels of the scarce rain that fell. And an occasional Joshua tree gave comic relief to the otherwise desperate landscape.

"So like I said, I'm heading out to Florida to see my dad," I said, and then exhaled through pursed lips. "And a girl..." Bob nodded knowingly when I said that.

"I probably would have gone though, to Vietnam I mean, had I been drafted that is," I added for some reason. I thought again about the draft card in my wallet and the lottery number that I had been assigned. The United States had ended its military involvement the previous year, March 29th 1973. Boys came home and the draft stopped. "I guess I was lucky, but I'm still confused about the reasons why we went over there in the first place. It doesn't make sense to me thinking about it, considering the outcome of the war."

"Part of me just wants to forget it altogether," I continued. "Another part wants to know what it was all about. Peace is cool, at least it sounds good when people sing about it. I just can't see true peace and love happening though without a basic respect for human rights. World peace, yeah everyone wants that I guess. But it isn't cool to just look away when people's rights are being taken away from them in other parts of the world. Maybe war is the only option left sometimes." I hoped it would make sense.

"You seem to have an ounce or two of wisdom rattling around up there, Brett," Bob said. "Hang on to it." I was glad he wasn't pissed at me for spewing hippie crap earlier. We both left that behind us and drove on in silence.

"You know Brett, I'm pretty tired," he said. "So if you don't mind I think I might just nod off for a while. Watch the temperature gauge so we don't overheat." It was his way of saying that we should slow down, I realized, so I slowed to a more sensible 70 mph. With that he reclined his seat, let out a sigh and promptly fell asleep. I wondered why in the world this Vietnam vet would trust a longhaired kid like me; still he snored peacefully as I gripped the wheel, heading straight for the eastern horizon. I settled into the rhythm of the road, the hum of the motor, the muffled sound of tires rolling over the hot dry asphalt, and decided to turn off the radio so Bob could sleep.

As we made our way out through the Mojave Desert, I noticed a few abandoned one-room shacks standing in various stages of dereliction, seemingly planted out there in the middle of nowhere. I wondered what kind of person would build such a hovel and live in it for any reasonable period of time, only to leave it abandoned and forgotten. What caused a man to go on this type of hermitage? I noticed that most of the shacks had been built within 100 yards of the freeway (or at one time highway). I figured they must have had a means of transportation into town, only then to return to their self-imposed solitude. They probably even had a bank account they could draw from for weekly supplies. The desert landscape passed us by at 70 mph and I welcomed the changing scenery, studying every cactus that we passed.

Those desert hermits must have gazed at these cacti for hours on end, probably helped settle their inner demons I thought to myself. Again I imagined that the Joshua tree branches were reaching skyward in prayer. The older and bigger ones had lots of branches attesting to a growing list of concerns over the passing years.

This might be as good a time as any to confess that my friends and I weren't always able to find a party on those Saturday nights back in high school. But during the last few months of our senior year, since most of us had finally reached the age of eighteen, there was another option. Mountain Meadows was a rundown golf course clubhouse out by Puddingstone Lake, near the Pomona Speedway. A group of aging hippies rented the clubhouse to host local rock bands on every other Saturday. They also produced psychedelic light shows, and yeah, it was pretty cool. They would even let you in if you had a student ID and said you were over eighteen. And if you happened to have a fake ID that said you were over 21, they would give a wristband that permitted you to buy beer once inside. This wasn't too difficult in those days, making fake IDs I mean. Driver's licenses were much easier to modify, photograph and duplicate. All you needed was a special attachment for a Polaroid camera plus a bit of amateur artistry. I had used that fake ID a few times and gotten away with it, but we usually just smoked pot out in the parking lot.

Once you paid the dollar gate fee to the hippie doorman and made your way inside, it hit you. The pulse of rock music took over your body. Bands onstage experimented and jammed with guitar riffs that fed off the crowd. Drum solos would pound away for over twenty minutes sometimes. Stage fog spilled out to the dance floor, illuminated by racks of colored spotlights that were spinning around and projecting off of everyone and everything, one and the same really. Psychedelic liquid light shows projected onto the ceiling, giant colored amoebas combining and dividing in random patterns. The hippies who ran the place were trying to create a hypnotic atmosphere, but really we just came to party.

Apart from being a cool place to do all that in a semi-legalized manner, Mountain Meadows was also a haven for hot looking chicks. Some of them wore miniskirts and see-through blouses, others wore Cleopatra makeup, and some went for the vamp look with fishnet stockings. All of them were usually buzzed and very approachable, or at least most of them anyway, you just had to play the odds. My friends and I would smuggle in beers and use them like playing cards. "Want a beer?" I would say, and the chick would peel off from her friends and walk with me back though the crowd to a place where we could talk over the music. "So, want to dance?" would usually be met with a smile and a yes.

One time my friend Mike and I smuggled a jug of red wine into the women's bathroom lounge where we passed it around and had the chicks all to ourselves. This turned out to be an inspired tactic that worked pretty well until some of the other guys started barging in. Some of the chicks protested when they realized that their fortress had now been penetrated.

Mike was an excessively handsome guy, the kind of guy you wanted to hang around since all the girls were attracted to his vicinity. He never had to ask a girl to dance; all he needed to do was smile and she would take his hand and lead him out onto the dance floor, time and time again. Verbal communication had never really been Mike's way.

But for me, I generally found that it helped to talk to them first. My dancing was not exactly a full on art form, but I learned that if I maintained eye contact and smiled, a girl would usually respond and match my moves and then I would match hers. That worked out pretty well most of the time. One time a girl caught on to what I was doing and decided to do the Charleston while the band played a cover song by Elton John, so I went along with that. Instead of turning away when the song was over, I walked her back to her pack of girlfriends and introduced myself. Wound up experiencing my first French kiss that night. Mike patted me on the back when I returned to the group. Eye contact can be really helpful.

I slapped my face alert, thinking it was probably a good thing I wouldn't be driving by myself the entire way to Florida, lost inside such meandering thoughts. The sun had started to set by the time we reached the sleepy town of Blythe, California, gateway to Arizona on the Colorado River. Traffic slowed with the speed limit signs and we passed an array of sun bleached industrial buildings, stores and restaurants advertising home cooking. The town was surrounded by farmland fed by the river.

Bob snorted awake and asked me to look for a coffee shop.

"I forgot to ask your last name," I replied, and sure enough just then a coffee shop appeared on the left. I was impressed by his timing. "In case we got pulled over that is," I finished my sentence.

"Robert Burrill," he responded winking wryly as I pulled into the parking lot and found a space. "Sorry, I should have told you where my registration card was before nodding off. Hope you remembered to slow down like I said though." I hadn't, but that was a lesson that I would try to remember next time. "But hey, thanks for driving, my friend" he said as I pulled to a stop. "I really needed the nap."

I pushed his wheelchair into the coffee shop and we took a table by the window. A waitress with a red striped apron walked over with two ice waters and set them down on the table in front of us, handing us our plastic menus. "It was a sudden thing, me leaving for LA," he explained. "My sister just had a stroke and wound up in the hospital."

"Is she okay?" I asked.

"Yeah," he said. "Guess it was what they call a mini-stroke. She's back home now resting. Sure hope she doesn't have another one though."

"Anyway, so now I've got to get back to Phoenix," he said. "I'm in the middle of a job."

"What's that?" I asked.

"Eh, it doesn't matter," he said. Clearly he didn't want to talk about it just then so I let it go.

"Tell me about Phoenix," I asked.

He scratched the back of his head, still coaxing himself to wakefulness. "I started managing construction out there after the war. The VA placed me there, apparently it was the only job they had available for a guy like me, meaning "handicapped". Phoenix has been growing steadily ever since the late 50s. Lots of jobs out there now and the future looks pretty bright I guess, just so long as we keep on getting that water from the Colorado River. That river over there," he pointed, "happens to be one the most litigated bodies of water in the country. Every drop has already been allocated to somewhere, often double booked it seems. It flows down through seven states and every one of them fights about it. Farmers fight about it, towns fight about it; it never stops and probably never will."

"But like I said, Phoenix is doing pretty good these days," he continued. "Hot as hell over the summer months though," he laughed.

We ordered eggs with sausages and biscuits with gravy. When the plate arrived I instantly grabbed my fork and dug in, realizing that I hadn't eaten anything since breakfast. A trucker sat by himself at the counter, alone with his thoughts and staring blankly while flicking cigarette ash into what was left of his cold coffee. A sign on the wall advertised shower rentals for two dollars. I'd store that knowledge away for future reference, thinking I might need to find another truck stop café like this at some point down the road. Bob paid the bill and we went back to the car, buckled in and pulled back into traffic, headed straight for the Colorado River.

Dusk had settled in over the desert when we crossed over the bridge into Arizona. I found a knob on the dash and pulled it out, turning on the headlights. My eyes soon adjusted to the gathering darkness as we headed up a grade and over the ridge. A full moon was rising when we made our way back down to the desert floor, illuminating a field of saguaro cacti off in the distance. Their thorny arms were reaching skyward as if pleading for rain. I felt like I understood them.

"So what are you going to do when we reach Phoenix?" Bob asked. "It'll probably be after 10 pm by the time we get there."

"I've got a friend out there who I'll probably stay with overnight. He used to smoke way too much pot, dropped out of high school our junior year, and I hadn't heard from him until just a couple of months ago when I got his letter from Phoenix. The letter said that he had found Scientology back in LA. They got him off drugs, had him sign into the program, and then sent him off to Phoenix to work there as a counselor. Something about once you join the church you have to go wherever they send you. But he said in the letter that he was really happy and that I should stop by whenever I passed through Phoenix. I guess this is the time."

"I've heard a thing or two about Scientology," Bob muttered in a disapproving voice. "Cult organization if you ask me," he said. "You sure you want to go there?" He eyed me warily.

"It will be okay," I said. "I just want to see my friend. You know where it is?"

"Yeah, I know where it is," Bob said. "I supervised a renovation project for that crazy looking brick building a couple years ago. Not in a very nice part of town."

He was done talking now and we drove on quietly for the next couple hours. Just as I was starting to feel the need to slap myself awake, Bob decided to click on the radio and found an AM country and western station. He settled back in his seat and started humming along with Merle Haggard. I rolled the window down again and enjoyed the cooling desert wind blow against my face. That should keep me awake too; I wasn't a particular fan of country.

After way too many country songs as far as I was concerned, we made our way down the last grade and saw Phoenix in the distance, with the city lights getting brighter as we passed through the suburb of Avondale. When we reached downtown Phoenix Bob instructed me to exit at McDowell Road and follow the sign toward 44th Street, where we made a left and continued north.

We passed through a downtrodden shopping district with boarded up windows and bums sleeping out on the sidewalks under cardboard shelters. I rolled my window back up when I felt the heat again, still radiating off the asphalt. Bob was right; this area had seen better days. He motioned for me to pull over in front of a large red brick complex with palm trees facing the street and a sign out front that read 'The Church of Scientology Phoenix'. The corners of the building were trimmed with chiseled granite blocks that gave it a slightly medieval look.

"Well this is it, kid," Bob announced. He grabbed a sheet of paper from the glove compartment and scribbled his phone number and address on it, handing it to me when he had finished. "Here's how to reach me in case you need to. Otherwise, just send me a postcard from Florida."

"Will do," I said, "and thanks again." I helped him reattach the extension handles to the floor pedals, got his wheelchair from the trunk, and wheeled him around to the driver's side where we got him settled back in. After firing up the engine, Bob shifted the car into drive, pressed down on the accelerator handle, and released the brake handle.

"Vaya con Dios!" he yelled out the window as he drove away.

CHAPTER THREE

I SHOULDERED MY PACK and hiked into the front lobby of the Church of Scientology in Phoenix Arizona. A young woman with long blonde hair and a slender attractive figure came around the counter to greet me and her face was smiling brightly with piercing and engaging eyes. She had on blue bell-bottom jeans, a white T-shirt with beaded Indian necklace, and was wearing silver earrings that dangled from her earlobes. They were etched with images of Indian petroglyphs and seemed to twinkle when she nodded hello. She studied me with a flawless sincerity, unavoidably penetrating the outer layers of my guarded personae, and I couldn't help but smile back at her. Most people don't look at you like that when you first meet them.

"Welcome," she said, taking my hand. "How can I help you?"

I was mesmerized by her beautiful and penetrating eyes. They smiled back at me waiting for an answer. After coming back to my senses I said that I was here to see John Winterbourne, a friend of mine from high school.

"Oh, you mean Johnny! He was my first counselor here and helped me get started on my path to *clear*. You know him?"

"Yeah, he said that I should stop by if I ever passed through Phoenix. So here I am, I guess," I said, shrugging my shoulders and trying to look more positive than I felt.

"Well, let me see if he's still here… He works pretty late most evenings." She gracefully walked down a darkened hallway to find him. After a few minutes she returned with John. He smiled and gave me that same piercing look that I had gotten earlier from the girl, fixing his eyes on me as though he were channeling my energy somehow. There was a practiced serenity about him now too, like I had never seen before. I felt my shoulders tense up for some reason and I wasn't sure what to say.

What little I knew about Scientology came from a book I had read the year before called *Dianetics*, by L. Ron Hubbard. I recalled something about *engrams*, which were supposedly repressed memories of painful experiences that resided in our corporeal subconscious and prevented us from being truly 'able', aware, or at peace. Counselors like John worked with young impressionable kids, many of them barely eighteen, to help them get their lives straight just like he had. The counselors would have their future converts, or potential customers or whatever, hold tin cans that were connected to electrical sensors showing when their answers to certain questions would happen to trigger an *engram*. The book portrayed *engrams* as transcendent aberrations of the mind and body, sort of hidden micro vortexes of negative energy that kept us from functioning at our otherwise full potential. Of course everyone wanted to reach their full potential, whatever that was, hence the allure.

The job of the counselor was to coax these *engrams* to surface so that the mind could erase them, under the guidance of the counselor of course. This was the tricky part and required the counselor to have a considerable level of training, which was apparently why the Church of Scientology required its members to dedicate so much of their time to the Church in order to receive it. They participated in sessions like this on each other too, progressing through various stages of enlightenment or something like that. After going through enough of these counseling sessions, with diligent personal study as directed by the counselor, buying more workbooks and studying them as directed by the counselor, it was theoretically possible for the troubled person to release their *engrams* and eventually reach a state of freedom called *clear*. All well and good I thought, but really all I wanted was a place to stay the night just then and perhaps a bit of lighthearted reminiscing with my friend John, or at least the guy who I remembered was my friend.

"How's it going, John?" I said at last.

"Hey Brett, it is good to see you again," he said. "A bit of a surprise, I must admit, but yes, it is good to see you. I'm doing fine, by the way," he continued. "And I'm glad that you decided to stop in. Anyway, it's really good to see you." Since he had said that it was good to see me three different times, I was inclined to believe him.

"Yeah well I'm just passing through actually, on my way to Florida," I said. "Remember what I told you about my dad, how I had planned to go and work for him back there last summer?"

"Yes, I remember that Brett," he said. His diction now was a bit slower and more precise. There would be no "yeahs" from him. "Do you still have any issues with your dad? We can talk about them..."

"No, I'm okay," I said. I didn't really want to discuss my subconscious confusion about a father I didn't know all that well. "It's just that I met a girl out there when I went to see him, so now I'm headed there again to find out what she means to me, if anything."

John gave me a 'knowing' look, as though he knew my pain or something.

"Tell me about it," he said.

"No-no really, I'm okay," I said at last. "I just thought it would be a good idea for us to spend some time together before I start college next fall." I regretted that last part considering John had dropped out of school following his junior year. He had decided that he needed to "find himself" after a particularly stoned day on the beach. And then just like that, having learned about it from a flyer someone had handed to him on the beach, he drove up to LA and walked right into the Church of Scientology. After six months of study there they sent him out here to Phoenix to be a counselor, so now he was a part of it. I wasn't sure I understood any of this, but I had to admit I was a bit curious about it myself.

The radiant girl standing next to John was absorbed in the conversation that he and I were apparently having. This made me uncomfortable and I decided not to continue. I didn't want her to think I had some sort of baggage here. Maybe I wanted to hit on her later but I could tell by her look that wasn't going to happen.

"I'm not planning to stay here long," I said. "Probably head out first thing tomorrow morning, you know?"

John gave me a reassuring grin, letting me know that he was done with this topic for now, that it was okay to move along. Apparently his concept of time was different than mine was now. He was probably thinking there would be time later to get back to my issues. I wasn't sure I wanted to stay long enough to find out.

"Sure Brett, that is OK." He said. "Listen, I'm about finished here anyway. Let us go back to my place and I will introduce you to my other roommates from the church."

We climbed into his beat up Rambler sedan and drove through a rundown neighborhood with tiny two bedroom houses, some with boarded up windows. Patches of dry grass adorned the front yards and most of them badly needed a coat of paint.

We pulled over to the curb in front of one of these run down bungalows. There was a rotten green plaid sofa on the front porch with a couple guys sitting there staring out into the street. When we entered the front room, I saw three other guys pacing around and looking like they had been waiting for John to come home, evidently in need of some direction. Sure enough, I was instructed to set my backpack by the door and we all piled into the Rambler to get something to eat.

We pulled into the drive-through lane of a take-out Mexican fast food joint and John asked each of us what we wanted. When we drove up to the drive through window, he recited every one of the food items from perfect memory.

"So John, how did you remember everyone's order without writing anything down?" I asked as the food was being prepared.

"It's quite simple really. The mind pretty much does what you tell it to; you just have to learn how to free yourself from distractions, how to focus on what is really important at any particular place and time" he said. "That is what the pathway to *clear* is all about, my friend." The cashier handed the bags of food and drinks through the window and John passed them around correctly to each of us as ordered.

"Brett here will pay," he said, pointing back at me. The others quickly nodded their approval. This caught me off guard but I decided to go along with it, pulling out a twenty dollar bill from my hip pocket that I kept there in case I ever got separated from my backpack, something that possibly could happen if I didn't make nice here. "That's all I've got," I said. John paid and pocketed the change. Most of John's passengers had already finished eating their food by the time we got back to the house.

After kicking around in the living room with John and his other housemates, answering their questions and hearing more than I wanted to know about Scientology, how I should just drop everything and stay with them, it all seemed pointless to debate. So I decided to just thank them and move on the first thing in the morning. Suppressing a yawn from the long day that I had endured, I carted my stuff off into the kitchen where I was able to close the door and roll out my sleeping bag on the tile floor. I zipped in and pulled it up over my head, trying to ignore the conversations that were still taking place out in the living room. I would wake up at the crack of dawn and get out of there before anyone else woke up, assuming they actually did sleep.

My plan didn't work out too well unfortunately. I got wakened around 2 am with the kitchen light on and the sound of one of the housemates eating cereal, clanking the bowl with his spoon and staring down at me while he crunched away. I squinted up at him, not really desiring further discourse.

"Why do you think you need sleep?" he mumbled between crunches. "It is completely unproductive, you know. You're missing the best time of the day, a quiet time for study and meditation." I shut my eyes and attempted to ignore him.

I woke again around 5:30 am with a fitful strain in my neck and a throbbing headache. The kitchen light was still on but thankfully it was quiet now. I cracked open the door and quickly surmised that everyone had already left for the day. Apparently they started whatever their Scientology gig was pretty damned early. I felt entitled to eat some of their cereal since I had bought them dinner the night before. I hadn't changed out of my jeans so I was pretty much ready to go. I brushed my teeth in the kitchen sink, rolled up my sleeping bag, and hiked the several miles back down to the freeway onramp.

I stood there for another couple of hours waiting for my next ride. Maybe I was being punished by some sort of "bad karma" having not managed to stay up all night ruminating with John and his fellow seekers. I started to experience a sinking feeling, or maybe just sleep deprivation or both.

A guy in a beat up Mustang drove past and slammed on the brakes after seeing me. He thrust the shifter into reverse and backed down the ramp to where I was standing. Then he rolled down the passenger window and shouted out over the rumble of the throaty engine.

"Brett! What is up, man?" I was pretty sure that I had seen him before back at school, although I couldn't recall him being at graduation.

"Perry, yeah I remember you!" I said.

He was one of those guys I would often bump into at parties on a Saturday night, but we were both pretty buzzed most of those times. I didn't remember seeing him much around campus, except maybe freshman English. Oh yeah, we had taken a woodshop class together when I was a sophomore. I remembered that he liked that class and came pretty much every day.

"So dude, what brought you all the way out here?" I asked.

"Funny, I was just about to ask you the same thing," he said. I told him that I was hitching to Florida and needed a ride out of town.

"Get in," he laughed. "I'm on my way to Tempe to sign up for classes at Arizona State next fall." I tossed my backpack in the trunk and settled into his torn leather passenger seat. He floored the gas and spun the tires, rocketing the Mustang up the ramp onto the freeway.

"I must have missed you at graduation," I said after the car's speed had leveled off and my body returned to equilibrium.

"Yeah, I heard you stood up in front of the class and gave a cool speech." He smiled wryly. I grimaced, looking out the passenger window at the cacti as we passed them by.

"Yeah, whatever," I replied returning his smile, somewhat relieved that the event was behind me. "So how come you missed graduation?"

"My mom got a job transfer and moved out here after my junior year, but fortunately one of our former neighbors let me stay with them so I could finish school back in California."

"Wow, I didn't know that," I said.

"Yeah," he said. "Then I wound up meeting a girl out here in Phoenix over the summer while I was staying with my mom, and the next thing I knew she was pregnant. We got married last February and I tried to hitch back here to Phoenix every weekend after that so I could be with her and my son. That's probably why you didn't see me around much toward the end of the school year. Anyway, so I did manage to graduate but I didn't think it was worth the money to rent a cap and gown. My heart was here now. So I hitched back to Phoenix for the last time and here I am." His long brown hair bounced like a slinky when he nodded to emphasize a point. He seemed to be pretty happy nowadays.

"Having a son probably saved my ass," he continued. "It got me to stop drinking and doing drugs. Now I'm planning to go to college," he said. That explained why I hadn't seen him around school much.

He was pondering something. "I want to become a guidance counselor so I can help prevent other kids from going in the wrong direction I was headed. Phoenix is a good place for that, you know? Our economy is still recovering from the gas crisis and it's real hard to find a job when you're young just starting out. These kids are going to need direction, man."

"Man, I really hope things go well out here for you Perry," I said, channeling his thinking. "It looks like you've got everything figured out."

"No, not really," he laughed. "I just decided to be joyful, grateful, and to break life down into tiny little doable pieces."

Perry seemed to be a lot more together than my friend John back at the Phoenix Church of Scientology. He had this serenity about him that was more approachable than John's anyway. I thought I might be getting my first clue as to what I had been struggling to express when I wrote my graduation speech few weeks back. But then my shoulders shrugged involuntarily and I let out a breath to shake it off.

"Sorry the ride was so short," he said as he exited the freeway and pulled over to let me out. "Tempe isn't that far from downtown, but you ought to have more luck hitching rides from this side of town. Interstate 10 runs straight down from here to Tucson, so your next ride should be a longer one. But make sure to fill your water bottle at the gas station over there. Out here in the desert this time of year, it can easily reach 120 degrees by late-afternoon."

I crossed over to the gas station on the opposite side and located a drinking fountain next to the bathroom. The water was hot coming from the spout as I filled my water bottle and sweat was already seeping out of my pores by the time I got back to the onramp. It must be 100 degrees already, I thought, and there was no breeze at all. This was turning out to be a bit more of a survival challenge than I had imagined. If I didn't catch another ride soon, maybe I'd go ask the gas station attendant if a bus came by this way. I squatted down next to my pack to take advantage of whatever shade it could provide.

Facing the possibility of another long wait under the hot desert sun, I tried to distract myself by thinking about surfboards. By the early 70s, fiberglass covered polyurethane boards had revolutionized the sport of surfing. These boards were lighter, a lot more maneuverable, and transformed the sport from one of muscle and balance to another dimension of gymnastics and speed. Some of the greatest surf shops in the world had started right there in Huntington Beach.

Tom was a kid I had met in Boy Scouts and both of us were interested in surfing. He and I would spend hours in those shops studying the newest board shapes and fin designs. But they cost upwards of $150 and we simply could not afford them. So we decided to buy urethane blank "seconds" from the back of the shop for ten bucks apiece and take them home to shape and glass ourselves. Unfortunately this turned out to be considerably more difficult than we imagined.

The first step was to cut the blank length-wise and then glue the two halves back together with three strips of fiberglass sandwiched in between, using a special type of polyurethane resin that had been freshly mixed with a catalyst. The resulting "spine" would provide structural support and keep the foam from cracking when the board was ridden. The sandwiched blank could then be "shaped" with various scraping and sanding tools to achieve the final board design. We mostly just tried to copy board designs that we saw in the surf shops, carefully taking measurements when we thought no one was looking. Before the next fiberglass application, or "glassing", we would spray paint the board and add our logo "Cosmic Surfboards" using a stencil that Tom created.

Then we quickly mixed a larger batch of resin and used it to apply several layers of fiberglass to the top and bottom of the board, scraping off the excess resin with a plastic squeegee. After the resin hardened, we trimmed the excess fiberglass from around the edges and then mixed a third batch of resin so that we could glue the final layer of fiberglass strips around the edges of the board, or "rails". At this stage, the board could be sanded smooth for a final application of resin, using less catalyst this time so it would harden to a glossy finish.

We soon learned that mixing these different batches of resin was difficult to get just right and very easy to screw up. If you didn't add the proper amount of catalyst, and without careful mixing, the resin would harden prematurely and unevenly resulting in separations and bubbles between the fiberglass and urethane foam. All you could do then was grind the fiberglass off with a wet sander and start over. Sometimes we'd mess up again during the second application, and then more often than not Tom would take a sledge hammer to the board and bash it to bits. I wasn't real pleased by those demolitions, having pitched in half the money for the blank and materials. But considering we were using Tom's garage and his dad's tools, I wasn't in much of a position to stop him.

The first time we tried to make a board we successfully glued the spine and got ready to shape it. We started at the top, attempting to create a perfect "nose" that would part the wave cleanly. But after an hour of shaping from one side to the next, we wound up with a board that was less than five feet long. We said a few choice cusswords and decided to turn it into a kneeboard. This turned out to be one of our most successful boards and we got a lot of compliments on it from other wave enthusiasts. It was widely copied by amateur shapers and the design debuted in surf shops the following summer.

On our fourth or fifth attempt, I can't remember which but I seem to recall more than a couple hammer demolitions, we finally managed to produce a respectable board about 6'10" in length. It wasn't buoyant enough for me ride but was perfect for Tom who happened to be shorter than me. We decorated it with spray paint to resemble a crab nebula from outer space, using pieces of cardboard and wire mesh to spray around and through, and it looked pretty cool. *Cosmic Surfboards* was never a profitable venture unfortunately but it gave me a lot more respect for professional board shapers.

My friend Tom would be riding that board back at Huntington Beach about now, I was thinking to myself as I squatted there in the Arizona desert heat, wiping the sweat repeatedly from my face and neck. But then again, I had learned a few weeks ago that he had a rich girlfriend now. She had probably already bought him a new one.

A darkly bronzed, dark-haired man with a Marlboro moustache pulled over in a Jeep Wrangler and offered me a ride. The guy was in his mid-thirties and looked a bit like George Harrison from the Beatle's *White Album*. The Jeep was covered in desert dirt and had oversized tires, so I figured he must go off road a lot. I was disappointed to see that it didn't have a top considering my face was already sunburned and beginning to sting, but the freeway breeze would be a welcome relief anyway. I tossed my backpack in the rear of the Jeep and climbed up into the passenger's seat.

"What's your name?" he asked, reaching over with a firm handshake after shifting into fourth gear.

"Brett," I said, "heading to Florida." I was getting used to my standard introduction. "Sorry but I just ran out of water back there. Have you got anything to drink?"

"There's cold beer in the cooler behind the seat. Why don't you reach around and grab us a couple?" It came as music to my ears. I took my first sip and enjoyed a cool foamy swallow, then took another gulp. A satisfying belch followed that tickled my sinuses. I leaned back and enjoyed the wind blowing against my face.

"My name's George," he said. I grinned, not a bit surprised. "Tell you what; I'm headed down to Tucson to check in on one of my restaurants. Why don't I take you there and buy you some lunch. You look like you could use some."

"Yeah, that would be great," I said, realizing that my day had just improved dramatically. The bowl of cereal I had eaten at dawn was a distant memory to me now, and not a very good one at that. I took another sip of beer and told myself to take it slow in consideration of my empty stomach.

Interstate 10 winds down from Tempe into Tucson through some of the most stunningly beautiful desert landscape on the planet. George seemed to notice my fascination and filled me in.

"The Sonora Desert is lush in comparison to other deserts," he said. "That's because it gets a lot more rainfall this time of year. The summer monsoons will be starting up pretty soon, matter of fact. You might have heard we got one already last week."

"Yeah, that one must have made it all the way out to California since we got rain too," I said, deciding not to mention anything about my car, although it brought up a churning memory of that night.

"One of the things I love about this area is the huge variety of plants and animals," he continued. "This is probably the best part of the state to see Saguaro cacti, for example. Look at that forest of them over there," he pointed.

"I was thinking they must be praying for rain when I saw my first one yesterday," I said.

"Yeah, that sounds about right, for a lot of reasons I guess. Mostly for the rain to come down again, which it does pretty hard when those monsoons sweep through, I can tell you. You don't want to get stuck out here under one of those, my friend. Raindrops so fat they'll smack your skull silly if a downpour erupts.

"There are many other types of cactus out here too. Look over there, see that cluster of cholla?"

The cholla cacti looked to me like a clown's pale green balloon toys on steroids, with every twisted knot covered in foreboding white spiny thorns.

"You don't want to brush up against one of those spiny orbs," he said. "They'll break off and the thorns will anchor into your skin. Hurts pretty bad I can tell you. It's how they spread around the desert, the animals bump into them and can carry them for miles.

George pointed out a few other cactus varieties that I tried to log in my mind for future recollection. The beavertail and prickly pear I had seen before in Joshua Tree National Monument, but these looked healthier somehow. Some of them even still had late season blooms, yellow white and red. I found the organ pipe plants particularly fascinating, a cactus variety with narrow spiny arms reaching skyward from a single short trunk. We passed one near the highway and I commented on the white flowers sprouting from the sides of the pipes.

"Bats pollenate those flowers when they come out at night. Believe it or not, those stems will eventually bud out like watermelons. They taste like one too."

Although the noonday heat was approaching 110 degrees, the wind coming around the windshield of the Jeep felt good anyway. At least it kept the hair off my neck and my armpits dry. Yet I could feel the grit from encrusted salt crystals around the corners of my eyes. I held the beer can against my cheek and enjoyed its coolness, deciding to finish it off before it got warm.

"The desert has a way with people," George shouted.

"What?" I shouted back. It was difficult to hear him above the hum of the tires as we rolled along the hot asphalt.

"Makes your mind wander, doesn't it?" he asked. "You were off there somewhere. Daydreaming takes a whole different dimension out here in the desert." He had no idea I was doing that a lot lately.

"Yeah, I guess you're right," I answered, turning my attention to the present tense. I realized that George needed conversation to pass the time. He probably got more than enough solitude driving this stretch of desert.

"How did you get into the restaurant business?" I asked, figuring that since he initiated this chit chat he may as well take the first story.

"When they lowered the drinking age out here in Arizona it opened up a whole new market for the restaurant business, especially in the college towns like Tucson," he said, grinning from his Marlboro moustache. Arizona had only lowered its drinking age to 19, not 18, perhaps as a concession to its larger neighbor to the west. "I started out bartending at a club called Minder Binders back there in Tempe. Tempe and Tucson are both college towns full of co-eds looking for places to party, the perfect demographic for clubs with loud music, cheap beer and bar food. Minder Binders was supposed to convey a party atmosphere with wild art deco memorabilia scattered throughout the place, and with different types of bands and dance floors on three different levels. It encourages kids to move about and mingle like they would at a frat party. And of course they also get hungry. So when I was still bartending, I got the idea to create a new menu of custom burgers that caught on pretty quick. They decided to make me an assistant manager because of that. Now I run three of these clubs throughout Arizona. I'll take you to the one in Tucson, you'll love it."

It sounded to me a lot like Mountain Meadows back in California, with a bar for 21-and-over types on the upper level that didn't get much business, because most of the kids were younger than that and anyway the hippies at the door never seemed to notice the booze that we smuggled in under our shirts, so why pay extra for draft beer in a plastic cup? I told George about that.

"Man, what a waste," George laughed as he jerked his head back and smiled. "Out here, the college kids have nowhere else to go but these clubs, and most of them have plenty of money to spend, their mommies and daddies out east send them cash whenever they ask for it." I was starting to regret my decision to attend college back in California. But they had offered me a full scholarship and I didn't have rich parents, so that was probably the best decision I could have made.

"How about you?" he shouted.

"Huh?" I shouted back.

"College, you look about that age. So are you planning to go to college I mean?" he shouted a bit louder.

"Yeah, back in California," I answered. "I'll start next fall."

"Oh," he said. He had just learned I would be one less customer he could attract to Tucson, but oh well. "The University of Arizona is a great school if you change your mind. But anyway that's cool. What do you think you'll major in?"

"Don't know yet," I said.

"Probably for the best, keep your options open. Hey, reach back there and get us another beer would you?" he asked. I grabbed a couple and popped open my second one of the day.

"You like the Stones?" he asked. I nodded, my hair still flapping in the breeze. "Well okay then. Grab one of them cassette tapes in the glove box. I opened it and a pile of cassettes spilled out onto my lap. I sorted through them and selected *Sticky Fingers*, one of my favorites. I handed it to him and he popped it in a player that was mounted beneath the dash. *Brown Sugar* came on. He turned it up so that we could hear it over the road noise. I took another sip from my beer, now fully enjoying my ride through the desert as it rushed by. The sky out here was a deeper blue than I was used to with all the smog back home. The desert was a pure and mystical place I thought to myself.

A huge rock formation appeared up ahead to our right, rising up from of the desert in staggering jagged peaks. "That there's Picacho Peak so we've got about forty miles left to Tucson," George shouted over the stereo. The forebodingly grey basalt domes made a striking contrast to the deep blue sky and scattered barrel cacti, desert sage and ocotillo appeared to be struggling for water on its downward slope. Apparently the sandy soil didn't hold much moisture but they were still up there eeking out an existence.

The landscape became more barren once we got past that point so I leaned back and started tapping my hand against the armrest to the music.

"Want another beer" George asked.

"No I think I'm good for now, thanks," I said, enjoying the music and the desert wind as it whipped around me. Eventually a broad mountain range emerged off in the distance to our left.

"Now *those* are the Santa Catalina Mountains," he said pointing in their direction. "We're almost to Tucson, and that's the Oro Valley below them." They rose majestically over the valley and I could understand why folks had decided to settle there. I also sensed that it was cooler now, probably still somewhere in the mid-90s but it felt like a relief to me.

"Yep, that's Tucson up ahead," George said as the buildings drew closer. "We've climbed over two thousand feet in altitude, bet you can notice the change huh? Better toss them empty beer cans behind the seat."

We left the freeway and proceeded east along Speedway Boulevard into town, passing the University of Arizona campus to our right, which George also pointed out, and pulled into a parking lot a few blocks beyond that. It was a restaurant/club called Buffalo Bob's and I could hear the bass guitar and drum beats of a Deep Purple song vibrating through the walls as George pulled into his own designated parking space and switched off the ignition. I followed him around to the main entrance. The music was loud when we passed through the doors and the place was packed full of college kids. Summer school was in session, and since it was Friday afternoon the party had already started.

George guided me by the shoulder to an empty stool at the bar on the lower level. "I'll have them make you one of my famous burgers," he said. He motioned to the guy behind the counter over and shouted above the music. "Hey Charlie, get my friend here a 'California Dreaming' burger and a draft Bud." Then he told me to wait there while he went back to the office to check on the server schedules for the weekend.

I had no idea what kind of burger he had ordered for me, but he seemed pretty convinced that it would be the perfect choice. So I sat there at the bar stool, tapping my hand on the counter with the music and gratefully enjoying the ice-cold beer. The drinking age in Arizona was nineteen and I was only eighteen, but I kept quiet and enjoyed it.

It was pleasantly cool inside the place and all the time I had spent in the hot desert sun faded away as I looked around. This club had plenty of eclectic cowboy memorabilia hanging from the walls, with neon lighting and colored floods throughout. And there were dance floors on three different levels, just as George had described. The rock music was pulsating and loud and energizing. I studied two girls standing at a circular table near the lower dance floor and briefly thought about walking over to introduce myself. But I knew I looked a bit ruddy and was probably underdressed, so I decided to stay put.

To my great relief, a burger plate finally appeared and my mind became focused on eating. It had a third pound of hand-formed medium rare beef patty sandwiched between two halves of a freshly baked bun, with melted cheddar cheese and guacamole, and it was nestled in an ocean of fries. A tall toothpick had been spiked into the bun with a tiny plastic surfboard on top. I pulled it out and set it aside, wondering if I should keep it. So dive in, my stomach said. I practically inhaled the burger in a rush to vanquish my hunger. After I had finished off the beer and sat awhile listening to more songs by The Who, Led Zeppelin, and Lynyrd Skynyrd, my full belly felt better and I decided that I was ready to roll. If I stayed much longer it would get too late in the day to catch a decent ride. I didn't want to fork over the cash for a room in town either, having spent twenty bucks the previous evening unwittingly buying dinner for a carload of scientologists.

    I left a dollar tip at the bar and looked around for George. There he was standing over by the front entrance, chatting up some pretty waitress that he happened to have his arm around. I walked over and announced I was leaving. "Vaya con Dios, Brett" he said, shaking my hand. Strange to hear that phrase twice in the past two days, but it must have helped since my karma felt like it was on a more positive level now. I thanked him again, smiled at the waitress who smiled back at me, and I thought "wait maybe I should stay, no I should go." So I turned decisively and reached for the door.

CHAPTER FOUR

I EXITED THE BUILDING to a mind jolting inferno of blinding sunlight. It felt like I was in a blast furnace as I walked around to the back of the lot to retrieve my pack from George's Jeep. I hiked slowly back up Speedway Drive to the interstate, not wanting to break into a full blown sweat before I caught my next ride.

Fortune could ebb and flow like the tide on the beach, and I knew that one positive experience would not necessarily portend another. I stood at the freeway onramp for over two hours, with cars passing by as though I were invisible. After a while I lost the energy to stand and crouched next to my pack while continuing to hold out my thumb. This certainly wasn't working, and the sun's intensity was unforgiving. Sweat was now dripping down my nose onto the pavement.

At last, a guy in his mid-fifties with a white scruffy beard pulled over in his dented grey Studebaker truck. He leaned out the window and looked me up and down, considering whether to take me along as the engine idled roughly.

"You surely do look like you could use a ride," he called out in a gravelly voice. I marveled at his astute observation, feeling a bit sorry for myself. I would need to pull myself out of this malaise pretty damned quick or I might pass out from heat exhaustion. Shaking my body alert I walked up to the battered old truck, marveling that it still ran. "Yeah, I'd really appreciate the ride if you could help me out," I said. "I'm heading east."

"Well don't just stand there boy, hop on in and let's go!" So I did just that. "Now slam that there door to latch it shut." He ground the shifter into first gear and the old truck lurched forward, eventually reaching a steady 55 mph in the slow lane.

"I'm heading on out to Las Cruces today," he announced with a mostly toothless smile. "Glad to get some company for the road, name's Lester." He released his grip on the wobbly steering wheel just long enough to shake my hand. Lester had long salt and pepper hair with a bit of a wild look in his eyes, but the guy had offered to give me a ride and I was grateful. He handed over a desert canteen and I took several greedy gulps. The old truck had no air-conditioning but the arid breeze coming from the open windows felt good to me anyhow.

"Mine's Brett," I said after exhaling and setting the canteen back down on the floor board. "Thanks so much for stopping back there. I was just about to give up for the day."

He didn't seem to care where I was going or where I happened to be from. As I later came to understand, most people who pick up hitchers just want someone to talk to, doesn't matter if you listen or not. I figured I'd get things started by asking him why he was headed to Las Cruces.

"Glad you asked," he said. So I smiled and nodded for him to continue.

"Well see, it's like this. My brother-in-law works out there for the railroad, diesel mechanic. It pays good money too, with benefits. Anyway, he fell from a locomotive a few days ago and broke his leg. Been driving his poor wife crazy sitting at home, barking at her to get him a beer, stuff like that. I promised I'd come back to visit and see if I could get him out of the house for a while. I've got this old ranch outside of Scottsdale and we just sold off most of the herd, probably won't take on any more cattle until fall, so I figured why not? Summer's a bad time for ranching."

"How'd you get into that, ranching I mean?" I was interested to learn how he had fallen into that line of work.

"My folks left Oklahoma with my sister and me back in the forties. Daddy was a mechanic and couldn't get no work, so he decided to move us out to Phoenix. It wasn't much of a town back then, but there was plenty of broke down cars that needed fixing. The desert's not a real welcome place to have a breakdown; you know what I mean? Folks would pay pretty much whatever we asked to get those cars running again so they could drive them on out. Daddy had heard that a mechanic could make good money out in Phoenix, so that's where we went."

"Anyways, he wanted me to work with him after I finished school, but I wasn't having any part of that business, no sir. So I decided to stay out late one night, found a poker game downtown, and I was winning real good. Sometime around 2 am, this old feller comes up to the table and wants to bet the deed to his ranch against all my winnings. I took a shot of whiskey and called him with a pair of sevens. And I won. It was my destiny, I can tell you. I've been running that there ranch ever since."

If fate had anything to do with card playing, this man was living proof that fate and luck could work together sometimes.

"Oh and by the way, that old feller still works for me. Best ranch hand in Arizona. I figure I'm a pretty lucky soul."

"Yeah, I bet you are," I said.

"No you probably shouldn't unless you're feeling real lucky!" He slapped his thigh and laughed. I figured it was as good a stopping point as any.

We drove on as the old Studebaker's frame rattled with every bump in the road on an otherwise peaceful afternoon. An unusual rock formation emerged to the right of the highway, and it looked like two giant craggy fingers rising out of the desert.

"That there's Dos Cabezas," he said. "Pretty quick here we'll be passing the Chiricahua Mountains, some of the most beautiful mountains you'll ever see, this side of Las Cruces, that is." I could make out a range of tall, irregular peaks that looked like they were over 10,000 feet high. They were ancient rock formations unlike any I had ever seen before, almost other worldly, or perhaps more accurately 'pre-historic'.

"Cochise, Geronimo and their bands of Apache Indians lived back in those mountains until the late 1800's," Lester said. I studied them, wondering how anyone could make their living up there in such a desolate place.

"You ought to head up there and go exploring some time. Plenty of trees and grasslands in the upper valleys, great for hiking and camping," he said as if reading my mind.

"Yeah, maybe I'll make it back out this way again, will keep it in mind," I said.

"So where you hoping to get to today anyway?" he asked, apparently interested now in where I was going. I said I wanted to make it to El Paso.

"El Paso, huh?" he asked. I nodded as we crossed over the state line into New Mexico. A bright yellow sign announced that we had entered the *Land of Enchantment*.

"Well, Texas is a damned big state. Mark my words, you'll thank them stars above if and when you ever make it to the other side."

"I figured I'd head back up Highway 180 to New Mexico once I reach El Paso. I've always wanted to see the Carlsbad Caverns." The truth was that a girl I had met at the beach last spring told me that she would be working there. I was hoping I could show up and surprise her.

"Yeah, probably best you stay up that way," he said. "There's a mighty long stretch of Texas between El Paso and Dallas."

A couple of hours passed with Lester calling out landmarks as we drove by. The desolation of the desert had now been replaced by yellowed grassland, with longhorns grazing off in the distance. Eventually we entered the proud little town of Lordsburg, elevation 4250 feet.

"They built that town back in the late 1800's, along the route of the Southern Pacific Railroad," Lester said. "Had a Japanese American internment camp there during World War II." I imagined how tough it must have been for those families to be taken from their homes to live out here.

We drove by a sign announcing that we had crossed the Continental Divide. I wouldn't have known it if not for the sign, since there was nothing obvious around here geologically.

"The Divide runs up toward that mountain range up there," Lester said, pointing to our left. I shrugged my shoulders.

"You ain't got no idea what you're looking at, do you son?" he asked.

"Um, no I guess not," I said. "What should I be looking for exactly?"

He laughed. "Well my geology might be a bit rusty, but I did read a few books on it after I got into the ranching business. The Continental Divide is a reference line designating the flow of river water across the country. Every drop of water that falls back there eventually makes its way out to the Pacific Ocean. And every drop of water that falls up ahead eventually makes its way to the Atlantic."

I looked around and wondered how that could be true. The terrain around here seemed to be pretty flat in both directions, but I reasoned that it must have something more to do with the mountain range north of us. It would probably make more sense if I studied a topographic map and I filed that away for future consideration.

We reached the town of Deming after about another thirty minutes, a slightly bigger town than Lordsburg but not by much with a population of 9039 souls. I was struck by how far apart these small towns were with nothing but wide expanses between them, so unlike the wall-to-wall cities we had back in Southern California. But still, I thought I could see why people lived out here. New Mexico was a spectacularly beautiful place, especially the jagged and eerie rock formations that we seemed to be passing with unpredictable regularity.

"That's Rock Hound State Park up ahead," Lester pointed to our right after we passed through Deming. "Used to hunt for gemstones out that way, found quite a few beauts over the years as a matter of fact," he said.

As he described the various minerals he had collected over the years, I was studying the road ahead and noticed a green stretch of land appear on the horizon.

"The Rio Grande's over that way," Lester pointed. "We're almost to Las Cruces."

We left the interstate and headed for the center of town, pulling into a gas station at the intersection to Highway 85.

"I figgered you'd have a better chance catching your next ride from here in the center of town," he said with the engine idling roughly. He pointed to our right and advised me to catch a ride south down Highway 85 to El Paso. I was grateful for this information since I hadn't had a chance to check my map yet.

"You sure you don't want to stay the night right here in Las Cruces?" he asked as I stepped away from the truck. "Sundown will be coming soon and my sister makes a pretty decent pot roast."

"No, thank you anyway," I answered firmly. "I'd still like to get to El Paso by nightfall."

"Suit yourself!" he said, waving out the window as drove away. Black smoke spilled from the old Studebaker's exhaust pipe as Lester ground through the gears and headed north on Highway 85.

A striking mountain range towering above the prairie to the east of the city made a majestic backdrop, a ruggedly beautiful geological wonder unlike anything I had seen before. Its jagged peaks resembled cathedral organ pipes, and the late afternoon sun was reflecting off of them in a deep shade of orange, almost the color of sweet potatoes. I wasn't a bit surprised to learn years later they were called the Organ Mountains. Gazing up at them emoted a peaceful feeling of sound, almost like music was piping subliminally through them.

A dusty flatbed truck pulled into the parking lot with a gaggle of Mexican farmhands piled on the back. "Hola amigo! Jou need a ride?" the driver called out to me. He had a dark bushy moustache and yellowed teeth. I had taken a few years of high school Spanish so I was ready for this. It had also come in handy when I was surfing down in Baja. "Where Jou headed?" he asked in a lilting voice that reminded me of Cheech Marin.

It looked like they would be heading south on Highway 85. Based on what Lester had told me, Highway 85 would connect with Interstate 10 so that would be the direction to El Paso but I wanted to be sure. "I need to get to El Paso," I said.

The driver smiled and nodded. "Si, we are headed to El Paso! Jou must come with us amigo! Hop on back." The farmhands who had been riding on the flatbed were beckoning for me to climb aboard. I wasn't sure why they had pulled over for me, but they seemed to be amused by the gringo who needed a ride. It was decision time again and I was not quite ready, having barely had a chance to get my bearings. I knew that I might be stuck here for another couple hours if I didn't accept their offer so I lifted up my backpack and accepted a hand from one of the men reaching down to hoist me aboard. The truck accelerated onto Highway 85 and left Las Cruces behind, headed south as I had hoped.

The farmhands were talking rapidly in Spanish as the truck merged back onto Interstate 10. I tried to relax and process in my mind what they were saying as they chatted away. Apparently they were headed back to their families in El Paso. To my relief, we passed a sign announcing that it was only 44 miles ahead. The old truck's suspension had worn out long ago, and the flatbed bounced up and down over every crack and bump in the highway. The wind was whipping around the cab and the farmhands were huddled together against it. I hugged my backpack and kept my head down as we continued to bounce along. So much had happened that day already.

I knew we'd be nearing the Rio Grande after crossing into Texas and could almost make out the river about a mile off to the right of us. Mexico would be over there on the other side, I knew, but it was hard to distinguish one side from the other really. It was just another border on a map.

I had hoped they would pull over to let me off when we reached El Paso. After we passed the downtown area I pounded on the rear window to get the driver's attention. Apparently he couldn't hear me above the Mexican mariachi music that was blasting from the radio. A few of the farmhands decided to help and started pounding along with me. The driver looked back and I could tell by his expression that he was sorry he hadn't remembered to stop. He took the next exit to Highway 180 and pulled the old truck over to let me off.

"Adios, amigo!" he shouted as they drove away. All of the other farmhands were waving back as well.

I finally got to check my map and saw that Highway 180 was indeed the way up to Carlsbad Caverns, New Mexico. I could probably make it there tomorrow morning as I had hoped. But I happened to be standing on the outskirts of El Paso at the time.

I looked back toward the city and paused as the sun was setting over the horizon. There were wisps of pale orange and red in the sky that gradually changed to pink and violet. I followed the contours of the darkening hills and was struck by how perfectly they framed the scene. I remember wishing I had brought a camera along to capture this moment, but I told myself to take a picture in my mind instead. We should all do that from time to time.

Should I try to catch another ride before nightfall? It would be a long hike back into town. I was almost dead tired from standing out in the desert heat between rides all day. But I had made it this far.

Standing there in the gathering dusk, I made the decision to keep going. I would continue hiking down the highway until a ride came along.

After about a mile or so of hiking, when darkness had finally settled in, I began to realize that Highway 180 wasn't exactly a tourist throughway. A lone car would pass every fifteen minutes or so, but none of them stopped or even seemed to notice me. I was walking further away from the highway now, not wanting to risk getting hit by a passing motorist, which probably wasn't helping my cause much.

I tried to convince myself that it would be okay to bed down for the night out here if I needed to. Then I started thinking about rattlesnakes. Probably wouldn't be out at night, would they? Didn't they only come out during the daytime, to warm themselves in the sun? But there might be scorpions. I wondered what other types of desert predators might be waiting to snap at me if I were caught unawares. Maybe I should collect a few sticks of mesquite wood and build a fire? I had a small flashlight in my pack....

A beat-up Datsun sedan screeched suddenly to a halt and a skinny kid stepped out with long black and ratty looking hair. I studied him warily as he approached. He had cigarette dangling from the corner of his mouth and was wearing sunglasses even though it was dark. It made me uncomfortable that I couldn't see his eyes.

"Well it must be my lucky day!" he said after looking me up and down. "I needed a partner tonight and here you are. Get in!"

I knew I had about two seconds to decide. This kid looked like a speed freak and he was clearly in a hurry. I could either bed down beside the highway for the night or get into his car. But the choice wasn't all that simple since he knew now that I was out here. I wasn't sure if I could trust him either way. So I said a silent prayer and made my decision. I had always believed that God would take care of me. Maybe that didn't always cover foolish decisions such as this one, but I shrugged it off and got in anyway.

The Datsun accelerated quickly to ninety and the manic kid next to me reached over to pump my hand. "I'm Jason, nice to have you aboard. You and me buddy are in for a profitable night."

"Uh, what do you mean, exactly?" I asked. I wasn't about to get mixed up with some sort of drug transaction. Jason was flying high on speed; I had seen kids like him before. He was jittery and blurted out words in a pressured, urgent manner.

"Ever heard of a 'repo man'?" He asked.

Now I have to admit, having actually seen the movie *Repo Man* over a decade later that my recollection of this particular experience might have been a bit enhanced *post facto*. But this Jason kid could have inspired the character in that movie. Maybe he freaked out another hitchhiker on a different night and that guy decided to write the screenplay. Art imitates life imitates art.

"Uh, no." I answered. I wasn't sure whether I should ask any more questions.

"Banks hire me to jack cars away from folks who don't make their payments. I used to steal them when I was younger, spent a couple of years in 'juvi' for it too." I knew that juvenile halls were minimum-security correction facilities for underage offenders, so I also knew that I should probably be wary of Jason.

"When I got out," he continued, "I finished high school and found out about this line of work from answering an ad in the newspaper. Banks tell you what kind of car, where to find it, and they actually pay you to steal it back for them. Pays good money too, about five hundred bucks a car! I could live like a king doing just one jack a week."

The beat up little car was doing ninety and cactus blurs whizzed by in the headlights.

"Anyway, I'm heading out to a trailer park to steal one back for the bank right now," he continued. He reached behind the visor and pulled out a small vial with a tiny spoon attached inside the cap. He unscrewed it while steering with his elbows and snorted some of the white powder up his nose.

"Damn, that's good stuff. Want some?" He asked, handing the vial to me.

"No thanks," I said, holding up my hand. This was getting a bit too intense and I had had a long day. We pulled into a trailer park five minutes later. It seemed strange to me to see a trailer park out here on the desert outskirts of El Paso. The land out here must be cheap I figured, desert hermits live in packs sometimes.

"Okay, this is it. You take the wheel and haul ass after me when you see me driving away. It'll be a white Ford Mustang." He pulled a Colt 45 handgun from under the seat and waved it for me to admire. "Just in case..." He sniffled the snot back up his nose so as not to waste any of the speed he had just snorted.

I made a snap decision as soon as he left the car, grabbed my pack and ran back to the highway as fast as I could. I figured if he tried to chase me I'd just run into the desert where he'd hopefully be in too much of a hurry to follow. At this point, the rattlesnakes and scorpions seemed like a reasonable alternative. He saw me get out of the car and shouted an obscenity in my direction, but as I had hoped he didn't come after me. There was still money to be made. He would more likely go back with plan A, drive the Mustang to the car lot to get his money, then catch a ride back to the trailer park in the early morning hours to retrieve his beat up Datsun. This was probably what he had planned to do all along, at least until he had found me hiking along the side of the road. Or maybe he would abandon his Datsun back there for dead. He might have jacked that one too, I didn't care.

So I shouldered my pack and ran down the highway in the opposite direction from town, betting that he would head back the other way toward El Paso, but still glancing back over my shoulder as I ran to make sure that he wasn't screeching up the highway after me. After about a mile I had to stop, panting and completely out of breath. Except for my frantic gulps of desert air, desiccating the back of my throat as it flowed in and out, all was quiet. Yeah, he must be headed back towards El Paso by now I reckoned and a tremendous wave of relief swept over me. It was even darker at this point and I could barely see the road ahead.

I was too full of adrenaline to stop so I continued hiking alongside the highway for about an hour. Several cars passed by during that stretch but none of them even slowed down. I guessed that they couldn't see me, thinking it was about time to get out my flashlight. Then again, I probably would not have stopped for me either at that time of night. The moon began to rise, still almost full with just a sliver of dark curling around its right side. It helped me see where I was walking. And a cool breeze blew gently against my face which revived me somewhat. As the heat radiated out of the desert sand it began to get cooler, eventually causing me to stop and get out my sweatshirt. As I was squatting there beside the highway,

I noticed a faint red light blinking on and off in the distance and chose to make that my destination. As I drew closer, I could see that it was a flashing neon sign and was almost able to make out the letters but not quite. The cinder block building standing next to it looked like it was some sort of nightclub. I wondered why a club like this had been built so far out of town. Eventually the letters on the neon sign told me that it was the 'Red Dog Saloon', still blinking on and off. A twangy country western song was wafting out across the parking lot. There was a lamppost perched over a phone booth at the corner of the lot, so I decided to station myself under that and try to hitch another ride, hoping that I would now be more visible to passing motorists.

Two thoughts entered my head about then. One, a longhaired hippie kid from California would probably not be welcome inside the Red Dog Saloon on a Monday night. But two, it might be possible for me to hitch a ride with one of those cowboys, maybe after he had struck out with the girls. I would have to approach one of them when they came outside. Could I do that? The parking lot was full of dusty pickup trucks, and many of them had gun racks hanging from their back windows. I was starting to feel a bit desperate and vulnerable out there.

I kept staring down the highway into the night, hoping against the odds. A couple more cars and a semi sped by over the next thirty minutes and I tried to wave them down without any luck. I pressed the luminescent button on my watch to find that it was now after 9:30 pm, probably still too early for any self-respecting cowboy to call it a night. Reflecting back on the day, I realized I had been lucky to have made it all the way through Arizona, met some interesting people, and even possibly dodged a gun battle back at that trailer park. Not the kind of day I would have imagined, but I was still okay.

The music stopped playing and I realized that the band had taken a short break. The doors to the saloon opened up and a guy in a white cowboy hat walked out to the parking lot with a girl on his arm. They climbed into a jacked up monster truck and ducked out of sight. Before long the truck was rocking back and forth, and I could hear moans leaving little doubt what was happening inside. Five or six couples came out and did the same thing after that, and several more trucks were rocking away now. Then a third thought came to me. If those cowboys happened to see me out here under the streetlight I would most likely be dead meat for sure. Pervert hoping to catch a peek they would be thinking. This wasn't good.

The only option I had left was to go inside. Maybe I'd just buy myself a beer at the bar and see if anyone would notice. I pulled a couple dollars from of my pack, stashed it in a sage bush next to the phone booth, and walked deliberately up to the entrance, careful not to glance at any of the vehicles that I passed.

All movement just stopped inside the bar when I stood there at the door looking in, and almost every person in the place was looking at me. My first impulse was to run right back to the highway but I was in no mood to possibly get chased down the road again. So I bravely walked up to the bar and found an empty stool. After a long thirty seconds someone put a quarter in the jukebox and everything seemed to return to normal. Hopefully they weren't liquored up enough yet to pick a fight with the skinny longhaired kid who obviously wasn't planning to stick around long anyway.

A fortyish woman with mousy blonde hair was polishing beer glasses behind the bar, with a full bosom, maybe twenty pounds overweight but still quite attractive. As she studied me sitting there on the barstool, her expression suggested both sympathy and amusement. I decided to order a draft Lone Star and rested my hiking boots on the rail. It had definitely been a long day.

There was a dance floor behind the pool table and several couples were doing some sort of line dance with Texas boot stomping thrown in. I studied my weathered features in the mirror behind the bar. Clearly I would not be joining them.

"What brings you out this way honey?" she inquired after I had taken my first sip. I decided to admit the truth and told her that I was hitchhiking to Carlsbad New Mexico, which I estimated was still about sixty miles up the highway.

"Unfortunately I got stuck out there on the highway after dark," I said, not wanting to elaborate. "I haven't been able to catch another ride in hours and there aren't many cars on the road this time of night." I took another measured sip, wanting to make my beer last as long as possible so that I could figure out what to do. She smiled and nodded to herself and I was relieved by my apparent acceptance from the other patrons. The fatigue began to dissipate as I rested my boots on the bar rail. "Do you have any suggestions as to where I might be able to stay the night? I mean, are there any rooms for rent around here, for guests I mean, maybe for people who need to sleep it off, that sort of thing?"

"Honestly honey, I don't think it's such a good idea for you to hang around here much longer," she said, glancing around to make her point. "However... there's a KOA campground about a half mile up the highway, you might want to try that."

So there was a KOA campground just up the road, probably with showers, only a ten minute hike away, and I had been standing out there under the streetlamp for over an hour with no idea that it was there! I wasn't sure whether to feel happy or disappointed that I hadn't just walked on up the road and found it myself. But I concluded that it really didn't matter now. Going into this bar would be another experience I would talk about some day. Finishing off my beer, I felt the tension releasing its grip on my shoulders. I had a renewed conviction that my journey was still on track and that things would turn out alright. Maybe this was a fallacy of my young and adventurous mind, but looking back I still don't think it was.

I thanked her and left a fifty-cent tip on the bar. And I made a point to steer clear of the pickup trucks as I walked back out to the corner. Some of them were still rocking back and forth.

Relieved to find that my pack was still hidden in the bush where I had left it, I hiked up the road to the KOA campground. The office light was off so apparently it was closed for the night. All was dark and quiet in the campground. Not wanting to risk waking anyone, I located a grassy area closer to the highway where I could roll out my sleeping bag and bed down for the night. I had had enough encounters for one day.

After spreading out my ground cloth and arranging my sleeping bag, I reached into a side pocket of my pack and found the dried fruit and nuts to nibble on, sipped some water, and then crept into the sleepy campground to find a bathroom where I could wash my face and brush my teeth. When I returned to my little make shift camp I crawled into my bag and looked up to a riot of stars in the evening sky. I reached back for my bag of pot and felt around for a joint I had pre-rolled. I took a puff and exhaled the blue smoke up into the starry sky. These stars were intense, much brighter than I was used to in the valley where I grew up, on account of the light pollution. The industrial age… progress… hmm.

I studied the creamy cluster of stars stretched across the sky and imagined them extending outward to the edge of the Milky Way. I continued to gaze up while my breathing relaxed, imagining various connect-the-dot shapes and figures in the heavens. This must be how the ancient Greeks saw the sky, when they named the constellations that I had learned about in scouts. There was mighty Orion, strong, sturdy and imposing, with his sword ever ready for battle. There was the Big Dipper and the Little Dipper, Ursa Major and Ursa Minor, the bears, facing off against each other. I felt myself sinking into the ground.

As I lay there, I reflected on my previous summer in Florida lying next to Michelle on the shag carpet in her living room, with a cool humid breeze blowing down to us from the paddle fan overhead. A light rain was splattering through the porch screen outside. It was a Saturday afternoon and her family happened to be out somewhere for the day. My sister was supposedly catching a matinee with a boy she had met, and my dad and stepmother were at home reading the newspaper. Everything felt right and peaceful, and I was savoring each moment with this unique and exciting girl-woman who I scarcely understood. We both enjoyed David Bowie and listening to *Space Oddity*. She propped her head with one arm and gave me a faraway smile. I leaned over and gently kissed her.

"I think I felt a spark when our lips touched just then," she said.

The summer rain was making dramatic background sounds, especially with the lightening. We counted the seconds between flash and rumble, trying to estimate the distance. Suddenly there was a loud thunderclap that made Michelle scream, and she laughed when it was over. Looking into her eyes, I felt warmth in my chest, a slight dizziness in my head, heaviness and lightness all together. I could feel myself breathing in and out. Maybe I was falling in love, I didn't know for sure.

"Remember how we were talking on the beach last summer about the Saturn V rockets?" I asked, thinking about the song on the stereo.

"Oh yes," she replied with enthusiasm.

Later in my dream, I imagined myself in the capsule looking down at the earth. I was in orbit, floating.

CHAPTER FIVE

A SEMI-TRUCK ROARED BY and a gust of displaced air blasted me awake. My watch said it was only 5:45 am, but I could already see in the gathering daylight that the place I had laid down was only a short distance from the highway. I looked back to the still sleepy campground and considered what to do. It was nestled within a grove of mature oak trees, possibly planted there to shade an old ranch house that had long since been torn down. The straw dry blades of grass crunched loudly underneath my ground cloth as I shimmied out of my bag.

Seeing no signs of life at the moment, I got out a towel with some toiletries and walked quietly into the camping area, taking care to minimize the crunching sounds coming from my boots as I walked up the gravel path. I was heading for that full service KOA bathroom where I would try to shower quickly without waking anyone. It was such a relief to wash the grit out of my pores that had accumulated over the past two days, and I felt much more awake when I pulled my jeans back on. I found a clean T-shirt in the bottom of my pack and put that on as well.

I was ravenously hungry but decided I should start hitching straight away so I wouldn't have to pay the camp attendant when he woke up to make his rounds. I rationalized that I hadn't slept in a real campground anyway, and wanted to save the five dollars for breakfast at a diner somewhere down the highway. Returning to the location where I had bedded down the previous night, I rolled up my sleeping bag and tied it to my pack with bungee cords, then trudged back to the highway and crossed over to the other side where I set my boots firmly in the desert sand and stuck out my thumb once more for the third day of my journey.

A beige Ford Taurus pulled over after just a few minutes of standing there. It sat there idling for an uncomfortable moment until the driver finally decided to roll down the passenger window. I walked up to find a young man about a couple years older than me with short cropped red hair, round cheeks and freckles. Cool air billowed out from the car's air conditioner and I knew the heat of the day would be coming soon. "Need a ride?" he shouted in a southern drawl that I couldn't quite place.

"Yeah, I'm hoping to make it to Carlsbad New Mexico today if I can," I said cheerfully, happy to encounter a safe looking ride after the harrowing experience I had had with repo-boy the night before.

"Well hop on in!" he said enthusiastically with an accent that was neither southern nor Texan but somewhere in between. As I hoisted my pack, he got out of the car and walked around to open the trunk, motioning for me to put it there. I was hesitant to do that until I saw that the back seat was loaded with clothes. Also there were two watermelons on the floorboards, plus several cardboard bakery shop containers. I settled into the passenger seat and the driver waited until I had fastened my seatbelt before accelerating back onto the highway.

"I'm heading home to Oklahoma to stay with my folks for the summer. Just got done with my sophomore year back at UT El Paso," he said with a proud smile and a nod. "My grandma lives back there near the campus, which was pretty convenient whenever I had dirty clothes that needed washing you know? I just left her place early this morning. She's the one that gave me them watermelons back there, grows 'em herself in the backyard and man I gotta tell ya, they're the best tasting melons there is."

As we accelerated to sixty-five I stared absently at long cactus shadows being cast by the rising sun on the desert landscape. This was a new day, so different from the one before, and I was making good progress on my journey.

"Oh, and she also bought me them lemon meringue pies back there. You hungry?" he asked. "I could eat 'em any time of the day. Why don't ya reach around and grab us one of them boxes!"

My stomach rumbled and there was no way I could refuse this invitation. I reached back and felt for one of the boxes, carefully lifting it over onto the front seat between us.

"I got me some napkins in the glove compartment if you don't mind grabbing some of them too. You might even find a plastic knife in there as well. I sort of make it a habit to hang on to plastic cutlery; you never know when you might need it." We were soon shoving the thick and gooey wedges of lemon meringue pie into our mouths and it was delicious, probably the best I'd ever tasted or at least it seemed so at the time, with graham cracker crust too. The desert sped past as we munched and swallowed. Feeling soothed by the air conditioner with the glucose high already kicking in, I settled back in my seat and enjoyed the ride.

"Name's Tim," he said. He licked his fingers and reached over to shake my hand, pumping it enthusiastically.

"Mine's Brett", I replied, "from Southern California. I couldn't quite place your accent earlier, by the way. Guess I've never met anyone from Oklahoma before."

"You're the one with the accent surfer dude, not me!" he laughed, apparently trying to sound like he was from out my way. My sun bleached hair had once again given me away, but he probably thought everyone from California was a 'surfer dude'.

"Oklahoma was a great place to grow up," he went on, "my brothers and me...."

I was having a difficult time focusing on what he was saying but I tried to listen as he prattled on, occasionally remembering to nod my head for him to continue.

"Our houses aren't built right up next to each other like you folks do out west, there's plenty of open space between them for sure. And we don't got no fences neither, in the backyards I mean. Kids run around and play out there from house to house. And when two or more families happen to barbequing out there on a Saturday night, most times we'll just pool what we've got so's we can eat out there together under them twinkling Okie stars...."

Inevitably my mind wandered back to a different memory from my previous summer in Florida.

It was about 6:30 in the morning on a Saturday. Michelle and I had driven her car down to the western edge of the causeway just north of a bridge that connected Daytona Beach with the mainland. The sun had already baked the morning dew away and its rays were reflecting brightly on the causeway. On the Atlantic side, the sandy beaches would soon be crowded with carloads of sun bathers and their boom-boxes. But the water was calm on the causeway and everything was quiet, except for the occasional flock of pelicans swooping down over the water, looking for their breakfast beneath the surface.

We had bought a shrink wrapped package of chicken backs the day before for crab bait. The price had been marked down because they were past their expiration date. Right now, in my mind anyway, those grey chicken backs were tied to a string that I had knotted around them with oyster shells to weight them down. I had tossed them out into the water to lure blue crabs over to a fish net that I was holding close to shore from a long aluminum pole.

Michelle taught me to catch crabs that summer and it went something like this. Wait after you see the first few tugs on the string until the hungry crab has gotten a firm hold on the bait. You can usually tell that by holding onto the string. Then, slowly reel the bug toward shore in the vicinity of the awaiting net. When you get it there, slowly and carefully pull the fish net underneath the crab and yank it quickly out of the water. Sometimes there could be two crabs in there.

We slowly and carefully reeled those critters in, oblivious to their impending doom, and tossed them into a cheap Styrofoam cooler that we had purchased at a Seven-Eleven on the way out that morning. We had also bought a bag of crushed ice that we used to slow down their crab metabolism, made them sleepy so that they could be stacked in the cooler without tearing each other apart. I decided to let Michelle do the crab fishing while I focused on netting and cooler patrol, making sure that none of the scratching critters would claw their way back out.

We happened to be drinking Bloody Marys at the time and the whole experience got funnier as the morning progressed. Michelle was jumping up and down giddily every time an unsuspecting crab happened to be scooped into the net. She would make a victory shout and quickly chuck the chicken bait out again to lure another victim.

We also managed to lure a few stone crabs into our net, but the law only allowed us to keep one of the claws assuming they had two to begin with. Michelle explained to me that crabs regenerate a claw if they lose one in a fight, but they cannot defend themselves if they are missing both claws. Tossing a stone crab with no claws back into the water would be its death sentence.

Our cooler was pretty full around mid-morning and the heat and humidity were starting to take a bite out of this enthusiasm for crab catching, so we decided to head for home.

Michelle instructed me to drive to Jake's apartment complex off Highway 436 in Casselberry. He had finished high school the year before and was tending bar at a seafood restaurant that she had just interviewed for in downtown Orlando. He had left mom, pop and younger sister behind once he had saved enough tip money for a deposit on the apartment that he lived in now. I presumed that he had probably dated Michelle but they never talked about it. Yet the three of us had become fast friends over the course of the summer. We knocked on his door and Jake opened it with a new girlfriend standing behind him. She happened to be holding a joint between her slender fingers and the stereo was playing at mid-volume, a very electronic and ethereal song from *Roxy Music*.

After making an assessment of the two of us standing there, holding our cooler full of skittering critters (the ice had already begun to melt), Jake's eyes finally told us that we would be invited in. He drew his mouth into a smile to acknowledge that fact, then he touched his left shoulder and swept his arm down in a bow, beckoning us inside.

The mini-blinds were twisted almost shut but a lava lamp in the living room gave off just enough light for us to navigate into the kitchen. There was also a Chinese paper lamp over the dining nook.

I lifted the cooler up onto the kitchen counter and Jake got two large steam pots out of the cupboard, filling them with tap water and adding bay seasoning. He set them on the stove and turned up the heat.

The kindest way to cook crabs is to drop them head first into the boiling water. This would be an instant death, the most humane way. Their shells quickly turned pink, and after seven minutes exactly (according to Jake's rule of crab cookery) we would fish them from the pot and placed them on newspapers that Jake had spread over the kitchen table.

We sat there plucking crabmeat out of the shells and passed a joint around while listening to the stereo. Another record had been released automatically onto the turntable, this time David Bowie's first album, the one with *Space Oddity*.

Here's one of the things about marijuana. Fresh crabmeat tastes like the best most exquisite food you've ever had in your whole entire life. And so we nibbled while we plucked the meat from the shells, yet still our bowls got progressively fuller despite our insistent munchies. We laughed at each other, tossing the empty shells into a large bowl in the center of the table, and we kept on cracking until every available shred of crabmeat had been plucked from the shells.

We had been so preoccupied with what we were doing that we failed to notice our tiny finger cuts. Good thing that Jake had Band-Aids in his bathroom cabinet.

"So hey, you still listening?" my Okie driver asked. "Um, yeah, please keep going," I said. Now I was back in Tim's car heading down Highway 180 toward Carlsbad New Mexico, but I wasn't sure how long he had been talking. I hoped he hadn't noticed that I had spaced out just then, but then again maybe he had. Fortunately he seemed quite happy to prattle on regardless.

"Okay so like I was saying, this past year was the first time I've lived outside of Oklahoma and I got to tell you, I can't wait to get back home for the summer. See my mom and dad, and maybe tease my younger brother, you know?"

"Yeah," I said.

We drove over a dry salt flat that ran for ten miles or so while Tim droned on about Oklahoma. He had lots of uninteresting stuff to share about his family, his neighbors and friends back there. I felt bad that I couldn't pay closer attention but rationalized to myself that I hadn't gotten enough sleep.

We eventually made our way up a grade into the Guadalupe Mountains. Tim had apparently decided to stop talking at this point while he focused on the winding uphill road, and I was enjoying the scenery.

We crossed over the ridge beneath Guadalupe Peak, which towered majestically to the north of us, and continued down into New Mexico for my second time in as many days. 'Okie' pulled over about twenty minutes later when we arrived at Whites City. A sign had been planted there announcing that this was the gateway to Carlsbad Caverns National Park.

"Well here we are," he grinned. "You sure you want to get let off out here?" It was still early morning but the heat had probably already climbed over 100 degrees outside. It didn't feel like such a good idea to get out of a perfectly good air conditioned vehicle for such a brief stop. But then I pictured Susan in my mind, the tanned blonde girl from the beach who I had met earlier that spring. She had walked right up to me and asked for a surfing lesson, explaining that she was out there on vacation with her family.

It had been a fun afternoon teaching Susan how to surf, and she had given me her address at the end. We would write letters back and forth a few times after that. That was how I knew that she would be working at Carlsbad Caverns this summer. She had written that she worked there Tuesdays through Saturdays. Today was a Tuesday so I was pretty sure that she'd be there.

I thanked Tim and stepped out onto the parched sand to get my pack out of the trunk.

While waving goodbye as he drove away, I hiked over to the sign demarking the entrance to the national park. I must have hiked a couple miles by the time I reached the information kiosk but there she was, my Susan from the beach, standing behind the counter in her cute park ranger uniform. Her eyes widened and her lips parted in attractive astonishment when she saw me.

"Brett! What are you doing here?" I was startled and pleased that she had remembered my name.

"I told you I'd look you up if I ever came through New Mexico, and here I am!" I was glad that I had showered that morning and happened to be wearing a relatively clean T-shirt, Led Zeppelin World Tour, from 1972. "Actually, I'm hitching across the country. My last ride took me up Highway 180, and when I saw Carlsbad Caverns on the map, I just felt that I had to stop and see you…see the Caverns, I mean."

"Well, oh my goodness, I'm so glad you decided to stop and say hello! I wasn't sure I'd ever see you again. Guess it's time for me to pay you back for those surfing lessons now huh? Maybe I can take you down into the Caverns as a guest of an employee, me that is." This was perfect, since I wanted to preserve my cash for other contingencies down the road.

"Susan, I'd be honored to have you as my tour guide," I smiled, fingering my hair back behind my ears. She flipped her hair over her shoulders and smiled back with perfect white teeth. I felt an attraction brewing that I knew should be repressed, so I broke eye contact and looked away, hoping she wouldn't notice.

She unclipped a radio transmitter from her belt and held it to her lips. "Calling Glen, over?" she said. "Hi Glen, it's Susan here. Listen, I have a friend here who just showed up unexpectedly and wants to see the caverns. Would you mind if I go on break to give him a quick tour?" She listened for a half-minute and her brows knitted. "No, he's just a friend, for heaven's sake! He's the one who taught me how to surf when I was on vacation in California last spring, remember?" Another twenty seconds, and then finally "Okay, I promise. Thanks." I was looking forward to going down into the caves, grateful to get out of the heat.

After a couple of minutes, a ruggedly handsome guy about six foot four, with bulging shoulders and biceps and a crew cut, another football player type, walked up and gave me an unpleasant sideways glance, then reluctantly relieved Susan of her kiosk duty so she could show me the caverns. I decided not to say much, just set my backpack behind the counter and followed Susan down the winding pathway into the Natural Entrance, admiring her athletic legs until it became too dark to see them clearly. I tried to stay close behind her as darkness deepened. We passed through the Devil's Den for a self-guided tour of the Big Room below.

My pupils slowly adjusted to the dimly lit path as we made our way into the Big Room, it was a remarkable geological sight unlike anything I had ever seen before. I hadn't expected such a dazzling display of color and light. Ultraviolet flood lamps had been strategically placed to illuminate the cavern in a kaleidoscope of fluorescent colors. My mind wandered back to a geology class I had taken in high school. I knew the elemental compositions of minerals and how geodes were formed. But it was still hard to fully grasp this dazzling geological wonder before me. Susan must have sensed my bewilderment since she was waiting patiently for my mind to adjust. I glanced sideways and saw that she was smiling.

"All of the rock formations down here have a name, and some of them sound pretty silly I might add," she said. Thousands of tiny stalactites about the diameter of soda straws extended down from the ceiling. I found myself drawn to Susan's legs, now visible again. She made a waving gesture with her arm. "This is Doll's Theater," she said.

I gazed in a 180 degree arc and tried to imagine dolls dancing among the illuminated mini-pillars. Celestial bodies above and gemstones beneath the earth, all could be named, I mused.

We walked further and made our way to the Big Room Photo Gallery (aptly named), and spun around to take in the expansive

Temple of the Sun, a morass of rock formations of various colors protruding upwards and downwards. More floodlights had been strategically placed to illuminate these geological marvels, a spectacular display. We stopped at the Crystal Spring Dome, a giant stalagmite rising up from the floor, about 15 feet tall and over 10 feet in diameter. "It's still growing, believe it or not," Susan whispered. I stood there watching it for a moment and could almost believe that. The massive formation appeared to be motionless yet was seemingly alive. There was a railing around it, probably to keep away visitors who got an urge to touch it.

We walked over to the Bottomless Pit and I leaned against the rail, feeling as though I were being sucked down into it. "That's a bit of a problem for the rangers," Susan said, reading my expression. "They have to rappel down there once a year to fish out all the trash that people toss in. The tourists think it's a fun experiment to listen for how long it takes for their trash to reach the bottom."

"Stupid," I agreed.

Then we entered the Hall of Giants, with even larger stalagmites standing as a foreboding sentry blocking our way. Susan pointed out the Lion's Tail, a huge stalactite extending from the ceiling with a plume of rock at the bottom. It actually did resemble the tail of an immense lion that had gotten stuck in the mud, hundreds of thousands of years ago.

She glanced at her watch and saw that it was time to return from her break, shrugging her shoulders that it was time to go. We hoofed back up the steep walkway into blinding sunlight, and it took some effort for my eyes to readjust once we had emerged. The heat of the day would soon return with a vengeance, baking into my clothes. We hiked back to the information kiosk where Glen was waiting with an impatient expression. He stepped back from the counter and Susan resumed her duties, giving him a firm nod that it was time for him to go back to wherever else it was that he was supposed to be.

When he finally left, Susan flipped her hair over her shoulder and smiled again, but this time not with her eyes as though she were holding something back. She knew I was just passing through and was probably embarrassed by Glen's behavior. It was time for me to go.

"Thanks for making time for me, Susan," it felt good to use her name. "It was amazing down there and I really enjoyed it."

"Yeah, most people say that when they come back by here," she said.

"Let me know the next time you plan on visiting California and I'll try to return the favor," I said. "I'd be more than happy to let you borrow my surfboard again." She nodded and smiled, this time with her eyes along with the rest of her face. I grabbed my backpack, hoisted it up onto my shoulders, and hiked back to the highway.

Now I understood why they called New Mexico the "land of enchantment". It was surprisingly beautiful in its vastness but wildlife could also be found, almost everywhere on closer inspection. Having just emerged from the bowels of the earth, my senses had become more keen as my eyes darted around, settling on a bird making a saguaro cactus its home, a cholla in bloom and small claret cup flowers peeking out of the sandy soil.

After twenty minutes or so of this extrospection, I was startled by a beat up old pickup truck which had pulled over abruptly. Three Hispanic farm workers were sitting up there together in the cab with their brown faces peering out beneath dirty straw cowboy hats while the truck idled.

This reminded me of the previous ride that had gotten me out of Las Cruces. But instead of farmhands on back, the flatbed had wood rails and was hauling about a half load of hay. I figured they must be making their rounds to the local ranches.

The man nearest the passenger side leaned out the window and called over to me, "adonde vaya usted?" My Spanish kicked back in.

"Yo quiero vayar desde Carlsbad, si ustedes se pueden," I answered, thinking in Spanish not English, which somehow felt appropriate out here on the high desert.

"Jump on the back," he said with a mouthful of crooked teeth, revealing a better command of the English language than I had expected, or maybe he preferred not to listen to my butchered Spanish. I hoisted my pack onto the truck bed and climbed aboard. It was a good feeling to have my T-shirt flapping in the wind again as we accelerated onto the highway. I could tell the truck's suspension was shot, much like the other farmhand truck I had ridden on before. After about five miles of this we entered downtown Carlsbad and *mis compadres* pulled over to let me off.

I grabbed my pack and stepped down onto the hot pavement, turning around to thank them as I steadied myself. "Gracias" I said, touching my fingertips together with a slight bow. All three of them waved back at me as the truck sped off, turning left at the next block.

I decided I'd walk to the corner diner and left my pack leaning against the wall outside, tucking my T-shirt into my jeans before walking in. The place had no air conditioning, with only a fan whirring noisily from the ceiling and a chain was rattling as it spun around. Two men dressed as auto mechanics were playing pool. Other than that, it was pretty empty. I walked over and sat at a bar stool near the end of the counter. I wanted to eat a decent meal. Having digested the lemon pie I had consumed earlier, I was crashing now from the sugar high.

A balding middle-aged guy who had a dirty apron tied around his ample belly came out from the hot kitchen to take my order. His oily black hair looked like it hadn't been washed in days and his face was flushed from working over a hot grill. Beads of sweat dripped down his cheeks as he studied me from behind the counter. I quickly selected something from the menu, ordering a double cheeseburger with fries and a large cola. The soda came first and I drained it two or three gulps, begging for another.

"Pretty thirsty there, huh?" the proprietor-cook shouted out from the kitchen. I listened to the patties sizzle, they would soon be devoured.

"Yeah I guess," I replied tentatively, not feeling the energy to engage in much further conversation. I could hardly wait for my food.

"So you're just passing through, I hope?" he asked, eyeing me from the other end of the counter. The sizzling had stopped and my burger was being assembled.

"Yeah, why?"

"Well there ain't much work hereabouts, and we don't take too kindly to hobos around these parts I'm none too sorry to say."

"Well sir, I can assure you that I'm not a hobo, so you don't need to worry about that. Just passing through… and by the way thank you for making my lunch," I didn't want to provoke him before he served me my food.

"That'll be a buck twenty plus another thirty cents for that extra coke you got there," he said, not willing to release his grip on the plate until I had paid up. He let go once I pulled two dollars from my back pocket and set them on the counter. Then he snatched up the bills and headed back into the kitchen. There would be no change coming back. I shrugged inwardly and continued to swallow my food into a grateful stomach. When the plate was empty I walked back outside, shouldered my pack and hiked down Highway 285 until I was outside of town. I stood there beside the road facing south and stuck out my thumb, hoping to hail my final ride out of New Mexico. Several more trucks whizzed by without stopping.

I was just getting ready to hike back into town when a dark red metallic Super Sport Camaro pulled over. A man in his late-twenties leaned out the window and squinted when his eyes had made contact with mine. He had a shaved head and looked like a bantamweight wrestler. "Get in and let's get you off the highway, kid. Don't you know that it's illegal to hitchhike in New Mexico?" I wasn't sure whether that was true and frankly this guy was kind of scary, so I weighed my options and realized that there weren't any. Downtown Carlsbad didn't seem to be a particularly good place to catch a ride anyway, and they did not take kindly to "hobos". So now I was being told that it was illegal to hitchhike here in New Mexico just as I was about to leave the state! I knew that I needed to get back down to Texas and that made up my mind.

"Hey thanks, but I didn't know I was breaking any laws back there" I said, trying to look sincere as I approached the car.

"Well come on then" he said, his face relaxing as he made his final assessment of me. Time to catch another one of those ocean waves I decided. He motioned for me to put my pack on the back seat and I climbed in and fastened my seatbelt. Baldy wasn't wearing his.

"I'm on my way down to Corpus Christi today. Where are you headed? "

"I was planning to head east through Dallas," I said, estimating the minimal distance I would need to travel with this guy before our intended routes parted.

"Suit yourself; I'll drop you off in Pecos. You can catch a ride from there east on Interstate 20." I was relieved to have that settled between us.

He put on a pair of aviator sunglasses and fixed his gaze down the highway with both hands gripping the wheel. I settled back into my seat and tried to relax, seeing that we were now doing about 90 mph.

My side trip to the Carlsbad Caverns had consumed the better part of the morning and I still wanted to make it to Dallas before it got dark. The clock on the dashboard said it was 2:12 pm, but my watch read an hour earlier. I realized I was in the Central Time Zone now and wound it ahead, thinking I might have still a decent chance of making Dallas by nightfall, considering we were nearing the summer solstice. Dallas would be a major milestone for the third day of my journey.

"Thanks again for picking me up back there, I really appreciate it." It's always important to thank the drivers.

"Kid, I used to hitchhike down through here myself so don't you worry about it, it's cool. I also had hair like yours back then believe it or not. But then I went to 'Nam and well you know, things kind of changed for me after that. I felt different when I got back to the U.S., so I decided to go ahead and look different too, hence my new haircut here!" he laughed, patting his scalp. I realized that I had misjudged this guy and my shoulders began to unknot.

"Too bad you're not going down to Corpus Christi; I could surely use the company. It's a long drive."

"Where were you coming from?" I asked.

"Well, I had an assignment in Roswell for a few days, can't really talk about that though." I noticed the government tags near the lower corner of his driver's side windshield. They were U.S. Air Force and apparently he was some sort of officer. I knew this because my father was a retired Air Force major and his car had similar tags. Those tags had gotten him a crisp salute when we drove through the gate at Patrick Air Force Base last summer, near Coco Beach. He and my stepmother liked to take advantage of the military discounts at the commissary whenever they happened to be out that way. We had eaten at the officer's club afterwards.

"I'm a test pilot for the Air Force now, still in the service," he continued. This was not a great surprise to me after studying his demeanor.

I studied the winding Pecos River off to our left and watched it empty into a reservoir as we crossed back into Texas. The landscape flattened considerably after that and I could see now what had motivated him to bring me along. There wasn't much to look at really, just low lying grasses and desert shrubs scattered about.

"Those funny looking woody plants out there are called Mesquite," Alan pointed. "Indians used to gather the dead wood from those plants to make their fires. Burns real good. You should try it if you ever get stuck out here."

"What's your name?" I asked, hoping that he didn't mean it.

"You can call me Bill," he replied giving a slight nod while continuing to stare straight ahead.

"Mine's Brett, from Southern California."

"Yeah, I pretty much figured that. You look like one of them rock and roll types, am I right?" He actually turned his head to look in my direction this time when he asked the question.

"I like to catch as many bands as I can," I offered, seeing that I was still wearing my Led Zeppelin T-shirt.

"Well check it out." He reached over to the glove compartment and pulled out an 8-track tape, The Who *Live at Leeds* album. He plugged it in and turned up the volume. "This music reminds me how I feel when I'm doing flight tests. I wish I could tell you about the types of aircraft I get to fly, but that's all classified." As I considered that, with the speedometer now pushing 100 miles per hour, I focused on a drum solo that Keith Moon was playing. Keith was a genius who would later flame out from over indulgences, but his spirit lived on through this thrashing rendition that was becoming indelibly etched inside my head. Baldy Bill tapped his hands on the wheel as the Camaro sped down the highway. It filled time between the passing mile markers.

CHAPTER SIX

WE GOT TO PECOS SOONER than I was expecting but that shouldn't have been much of a surprise considering how fast Baldy Bill had been driving. He pulled over at the other side of town and pointed to the entrance ramp for Interstate 20. "Take care there Brett, you can catch a ride from there and it'll take you east all the way to Dallas," he said. "And I hope you have an amazing journey my friend." It had been a short friendship to be sure, but his physical presence is still etched in my mind. I grabbed my pack and stepped out of the car, waving thanks as I stepped away. Baldy Bill nodded.

Then he hit the gas and the Camaro sped back down Highway 285 in the direction of Corpus Christi. I stood at the onramp with my thumb held out, shifting my mental gears once again. There was still a sizable distance of Texas to get through today if I wanted to make it to Dallas by nightfall, but having made it this far I was pretty sure I could do it.

Two men in a Ford 350 pickup truck with double back tires turned at the onramp and suddenly screeched to a halt. For a second there, I was afraid that they would jump down out of the truck and run after me. The younger one in the passenger seat stuck his arm out of the window and motioned for me to jump on back, so I jogged up to find two Texas cowboys perched up there in the cab, and both wore Stetsons. I was pretty sure they were father and son since they looked to me like twins that had been born thirty years apart. Neither of them turned a head back when I climbed up into a greasy truck bed that was loaded with farm tools and heavy chains. Stetson Senior gunned the diesel engine and the truck accelerated onto Interstate 20, headed east toward Dallas. A couple hunting rifles were hanging from a rack mounted on the rear window. I was back in Texas.

With the wind buffeting wildly, I crouched down and grabbed the side rail. I was trying not to bump into any of the dirty farm equipment, or fall back on the greasy truck bed. Soiled jeans would make it almost impossible for me to catch another ride unless I wanted to keep on riding in the back of other people's trucks. The wind whipped my hair as I balanced my knees over my boots while the truck swayed as though I were surfing a wave.

Just as we were getting underway I looked over to the access road running alongside the freeway and saw another truck speed up trying to match ours. Two other cowboys were waving madly out the window to get our attention. Stetson Junior noticed them first and tapped Stetson Senior's shoulder, and he veered abruptly and slowed when he realized who they were. This made it difficult for me to keep my balance and I finally lost my grip on the rail, falling forward and staining both knees on the greasy truck bed. They were shouting back and forth but I couldn't hear what was being said with all the wind noise back there. Stetson Senior decided to pull our truck over to the side so he could hear better and skidded to a halt in the dirt, which caused me to fall back and get grease stains on my butt as well. We had only travelled about a half of a mile, but I was ready to get out.

"We're sorry about all the dirtiness back there," Stetson Junior shouted back as I stepped down. "Those boys over there are friends of ours, so we're going to pull off at the next exit and meet up with them if that's alright with you." It wasn't really a question. "Y'all can catch another ride right from here if you like." Then Stetson Junior touched his finger tips to the brim of his hat and nodded out to me once I had stepped down onto the grass. Stetson Senior floored the truck and it sped down to the next exit, made a power turn back down the access road and sped over to the other truck that was waiting for them.

I made a feeble effort to swat the dirt out of my jeans but the grease stains would not brush off. I'd have to change them if I wanted to ride again in a passenger seat, I thought to myself. So after the trucks had driven away, I crossed over the access road and crouched behind a bush to change into my second pair, carefully watching the freeway to make sure no trucks with gun racks were approaching. I wrapped the greasy ones in my ground cloth and stowed them in the bottom of my pack, hoping I could find a place to wash them out at some point down the road.

I was feeling somewhat more presentable now, so I crossed back over and stood alongside the interstate to hold out my thumb, moving it forward when a car passed by and back again to repeat the process. I decided to hike down a ways until I reached a patch of irrigated farmland. Fields of alfalfa sprouted in neat and endless rows to the right of the highway. I could see they were irrigated from long sprinkler pipes supported on steel wagon type wheels. Apparently they were powered along by water trucks. One of these sprinkler lines happened to be hooked up to one at the moment, with dozens of water jets spraying in circular arcs as it rolled slowly down the rows.

After an hour and a half of standing there I still hadn't made any progress. Thunderclouds were coalescing on the eastern horizon, and they looked like they would soon be heading straight toward me. I took a swig from my water bottle and poured some into my bandana, using it to wipe a surface layer of dust off my face and my neck. Perhaps I should try to look more relaxed, I thought. I crossed one boot in front of the other and confidently held out my thumb, steadying myself with the other hand grasping the rail of my backpack.

At last a green Pontiac Firebird pulled to the side of the road about twenty yards ahead. I grabbed my pack and ran up to find another balding man in his late twenties, but this one had blond sidewalls and a neatly trimmed goatee. He pressed an electronic button that lowered the window. "Need a ride?" he called out.

"Yeah," I sighed, "I'd sure like to get off the side of this highway. I've been feeling kind of exposed out here." I bit my lower lip, frustrated with myself for appearing so needy. He gave me a knowing grin as he surveyed me.

"Well, welcome to Texas and hop on in!" he announced with enthusiasm. He had on a white short-sleeved Oxford shirt with bright red silk tie that barely made it down the slope of his protruding belly. I looked him in the eye and he seemed sincere enough, so I lifted my pack onto the back seat and climbed on in. I was still fastening my seatbelt when he hit the gas and jolted the Pontiac forward with extreme acceleration. Somehow it seemed like every driver out here liked to floor their engines, like it was their Texas-born right and heritage. Anyway, I was glad to be moving down the highway again.

"Man I love this car, just bought it a few weeks ago," he said. "So… I'm headed to Dallas to meet up with my wife for dinner and a movie. You're welcome to ride along if you can keep up with me." I wasn't quite sure what he meant, but I was hoping he wouldn't be as talkative as that kid who gave me a ride outside El Paso. According to my last glance at the map, Dallas would still be a couple of hundred miles or so.

"You're driving all the way to Dallas, just for a movie?" It was the obvious question he had apparently been expecting.

"Hell yes! We Texans don't think anything of driving four hundred miles for a nice dinner. Look around! There's prairie scrub out here as far as the eye can see, nothing to do out here but floor it mister and get on down the road, you know what I mean?"

"Yeah, I surely can see that," I said, glad to be off the side of the road and back underway.

"My wife drove out to Dallas on business a couple of days ago. Can't let her wait for it, you know what I mean? Don't want her to start getting any other ideas out there with me not around," he winked. The speedometer read close to 100 mph, but with the air conditioner on and the windows up, the ride was still pleasant and smooth.

"Hey, you want a beer? I've got some sitting on ice in the cooler back there. Matter of fact, reach back and get me one too while you're at it." I was starting to get used to this, unfortunately. I lifted the lid and pulled out a couple of cold Heinekens in green bottles.

"Here, I've got me a bottle opener under the visor." When he pulled it down I could see a hash pipe strapped in place with a wide rubber band. "Oh yeah, and we can probably fire that baby up in a little while. Do you like Hendrix?" With one hand still on the wheel, he fumbled under his seat and found the cassette, expertly inserting it into the deck without glancing down. *All Along the Watchtower* came on and suddenly I had an urge to party, which was probably against my better judgment at the time. But I wouldn't have to wave down another ride the rest of the day so long as I "kept up" with this guy. I figured I'd be in Dallas before nightfall, where I'd try to find a cheap motel, wash my pants in the sink, and maybe even sleep in a real bed of sorts. "Good choice," I nodded at the cassette player after he popped the cap and handed me my beer. I glanced at his white dress shirt and beige double-knit slacks, thinking that I might possibly have another Vietnam War veteran sitting here next to me, considering his age and confidently assertive demeanor. But even though this one had apparently decided to enter the white collar workforce and start wearing a tie, he was obviously trying to recapture the youth he had given up over there.

"My name's Alan. By the looks of you, I'm guessing you're from California."

"Yeah mine's Brett. Funny how people keep getting that right."

"Nah, you just sound like one of them surfer dudes. I guess I should know, since I spent a whole damn summer out there in Venice Beach back in '64."

"Well I suppose you look a bit different now than you did back then," I couldn't resist saying that since the beer had loosened me up.

"Ha-fuckin'-ha!" he said in a way that sounded like he wasn't all that tweaked by it. "Yeah, maybe that's true. Okay so now I sell life insurance, but I probably make more money in a single day than I did over the entire summer back then. Keeps me on the road a lot, but the way I see it, that's no reason not to party. I've got me a

Blaupunkt AM/FM cassette stereo here man, the best electronics that money can buy." He turned the volume up another notch and a bluesy guitar riff came on. *Hey Joe...* it was another signature Hendrix song. The day had taken me through a considerable number of visual and emotional gyrations, but it felt good to have my tired lower back supported by a plush leather bucket seat after having stood back there by the roadside for hours. I enjoyed the music and took another pull from my beer.

"So Alan, what's your story? I mean, what made you decide to move out here to Texas?" I ventured, somewhat interested in having a real conversation on this leg of the trip, especially considering we'd be riding along together for another couple hours. If I could keep us moving he'd probably get me to Dallas with plenty of daylight to spare.

"Well like I said, I spent a whole summer out there in Venice Beach, right before I got drafted to go to 'Nam." I had been right about that. He paused, thinking about it for a minute. "I met Jim Morrison there, you know, the lead singer for The Doors? He would sit along the canal, scribbling some notes to himself. So I walked up to him one day and asked what he was writing about. Maybe Jim recognized me when he saw me, or maybe not. A lot of us hung out on the beach together that summer, surfing during the day and dropping acid at night, just sitting around bonfires and watching the sparks travel up into the evening sky. Anyway, he starts shouting out these questions about life, you know, one right after another. I tried to answer but he didn't seem to hear me, like he had his eyes fixed on some distant horizon and I was in the way. But those questions kept on coming anyway, louder and louder, and they sounded to me like accusations that didn't make any sense. I just stood up and walked away, man. I guess he was in too deep for me." He seemed a bit saddened by this, sitting there in his oxford shirt and silk tie.

"It was a sunny day," Alan said while continuing to stare straight ahead, in the general direction that we were headed, fortunately, with his hands firmly gripping the wheel. "I just went on down to the beach and watched the sun set."

"When I got back from 'Nam," he said, switching mental gears, "I started thinking about Abilene, the place where I grew up. I needed to get over all the craziness from Vietnam, you know? I wanted to get back to a place that made more sense. So that, my friend, is why I decided to move back to Texas."

We finished off our beers and Alan pulled down his visor to get the hash pipe, reaching underneath the dashboard to retrieve a small baggie. He opened it while steering with his knees, grabbing a pinch of the light brown hashish and pressing it into the bowl of the pipe. He lit it with a disposable lighter, took a toke and handed it to me, returning his hands to the wheel to my relief. I deliberated for a couple seconds and decided to take a toke myself. The car was headed straight down the highway with almost no traffic at all. I exhaled and decided to take one more, convincing myself that this would be okay.

Alan plugged in another cassette tape and Hendrix wailed out *Foxey Lady* on the guitar. I became absorbed with the music and time seemed to melt away. I resolved to buy the album when I got back home.

"Want another hit?"

"No, I'm good."

"Suit yourself," he said, taking one more toke and then rolling down the window to tap out the ash.

I was enjoying the cool air coming from the dashboard vent and adjusted it so that the air would hit me straight in the face, basking in its coolness.

"So Abilene," he continued. "I went back there to stay with my parents for a while until I could find myself a job. They made me cut my hair and promise to go to church on Sunday as a condition of living with them again. Then this one day after church services, I saw my future wife Nancy outside on the patio serving lemonade. It was a hot day too, man, kind of like this one. All at once I understood the reason why I must have come back to Abilene, and it was Nancy. We had grown up together, see? She had written several letters to me when I was over in 'Nam. Maybe she was just trying to support the local troops, make sure I was okay, but it got me thinking about her day after day. I guess she was in the back of my mind the whole time I was over there. But man, when I set eyes on her again that day back in Abilene, a whole new direction of thought took over my brain; I got to tell you what."

Alan slowed to sixty-five when we reached Odessa and maintained that speed until we had passed through Midland.

"Got to watch out for the smokies around here," he said.

"Um, what?"

"You know, the highway sheriffs. They wear these Smokey the Bear type hats."

He proceeded to tell me that Odessa had been founded in the late 1800's as a water stop for the cattle drives. It was also a cattle shipping point since the watering hole happened to be near the railroad track. Midland was founded around the same time and served as the midway station for the railroad since it was half way between Fort Worth and El Paso, according to Alan. El Paso seemed like a long time ago to me now.

I looked over to a high school football stadium. The stands were huge, about forty or so rows high. My high school back in California had much lower aluminum bleachers. "Folks out here surely do love their football," Alan said as he noticed what I was looking at.

We drove on for a while without saying much after that, which was okay with me. I had no reason to rush him along since we still had plenty of time to pass. The tape ended and he fumbled under his seat for another one which he inserted into the deck, this time the *Harvest* album by Neil Young. I owned it on vinyl and had played it many times. This was another good music selection I thought to myself.

"So does anything kind of fall into place like that for you, back there in California I mean?" he asked like he really wanted to know.

"I don't know," I said, looking ahead to the vast horizon, "I guess I'm still trying to make sense of most things."

"OK then, give me one example of something that does make sense to you and why," he challenged me, "and grab us another couple beers while you're at it!" he added to keep things lively. I grabbed a couple more cold ones and he popped off the tops. We both took long pulls and I rolled the frothy brew around over my tongue, focusing on the beer's crisp hops and malty sweetness.

"Ever been to Tijuana?" I asked.

"Nope, never have, although I've crossed over the border from El Paso to Juarez a couple times. Didn't think too much of it myself," he said.

"Well, there's this river basin outside Tijuana, just across the border, with lots of poor people living in cardboard shacks. They call it *Cartolandia*. And there's this bridge that the city built over it so that tourists won't have to pass through it, but you can see it as you look down."

"You have to walk past dozens of brown skinned Oaxaca Indian women as you walk on over that bridge, holding out their cups and rattling the coins, begging you to drop in some change as you pass by. Their children beg right along next to them, little girls roaming among the tourists and smiling, holding out their cups and smiling brightly when you drop in a dime. Man, those little kid's faces are always brimming with hope since they know that change will buy them something to eat. But the older women, those faces are sad and worn. For the kids it's a game, but their mothers are downtrodden and desperate, just trying to get through another day."

"Although none of this seems fair, it does make sense to me on a different sort of level. When I toss my change into their cups, and look into their tired but grateful eyes, I can see that I'm a human being just like they are, only a lot luckier."

"Now the fact that I happen to be one of the lucky ones doesn't make a whole lot of sense, doesn't seem fair somehow, but the knowing that I am grateful certainly does," I continued and then stopped. I had lost my train of thought and concluded that I was probably done anyway. Why had I gone back to this memory?

Maybe it was because I had been feeling particularly lucky just then, and grateful as well.

"Good answer," Alan said, accepting my story since he was probably stoned also. He took another pull on his beer and set the bottle down between his legs while focusing on the road ahead. He had done this before. We passed a trailer truck with 16-foot Bass fishing boats stacked on back, each of them in white shrink wrap plastic. The driver gave a brief toot from his horn as we passed. He had citizens band antennas rising up from both sides of the cab.

Droplets of rain began splattering against the windshield as we drove beneath a darkening layer of cumulous clouds that were threatening rain. Then it became noticeably darker and flashes of light illuminated the horizon, followed a few seconds later by deep bellowing rumbles. Alan switched on the windshield wipers as the droplets turned to rain. The flip-flapping of the blades was rhythmic and soothing. With a heavy downpour now pelting the roof of the car, I was glad that I wasn't standing out there drenched in rain and invisible to passing cars. Alan's radial tires continued to grip the rain soaked pavement as we sped along at over 80 mph. He had slowed down some because of the downpour, but not by much, and the wiper blades continued flapping on their highest setting.

A flash-bulb of lightening cracked in front of us just when Neil Young's last song on the tape ended. A hiss and a click followed and the player dutifully shut itself off. Alan reached beneath the seat and found another tape, *Creedence Clearwater Revival*. I wondered whether he was simply picking them at random, but concluded that he must have prearranged their order when *Born on the Bayou* came on the stereo. The choice could have not been more perfect as John Fogerty's bluesy guitar riff accompanied the pounding rain.

I glanced at my watch and saw that it was half past four. We had just passed through the city of Abilene and I was relieved that Alan hadn't decided to stop there for some reason, only to leave me standing by the freeway in the pouring rain. But he'd promised to take me to Dallas and I was starting to believe him, apparently a man of his word. Yet our passage through Abilene had jogged his memory and he resumed his narrative. "Nancy was the prettiest woman I had ever seen, still is. She wouldn't go out on a date with me until I had a job, so I went back to City College and got this job with the insurance company. How about that for a smart girl, huh?"

"Anyway, so now she's my wife, and quite frankly she's *still* the prettiest thing I've ever seen."

Alan seemed content inside his own skin, even though his job required long distance driving between towns in central Texas, drives that could stretch on for hundreds of miles, while listening to rock music to make the time pass in his air-conditioned Pontiac. He knew who he was and where he was headed on the Texas plains, someone who wound up as an insurance salesman, an extremely poor dresser, but happy nonetheless.

"I'm headed to Florida to visit my father and see about a girl I met there last summer," I decided to take the conversation in a new direction, considering what Alan had just shared with me. "I probably think about her the way you thought about Nancy when you were in 'Nam, a girl who's stuck in your head while you're somewhere else, beckoning you to go back there to find out about her. I guess it's why I started out on this journey three days ago."

The wildly flapping windshield wipers were barely able to strip away the pelting rain. John Fogerty's haunting guitar riffs matched their frequency perfectly when he launched into *Green River*, and somehow it didn't seem like much of a coincidence just then. "Anyway, I can't seem to get her out of my head."

"Yeah, kid, I do know what you mean," Alan glanced over to me with a knowing smile. I wondered whether the girls out in California would think his beige polyester pants were sexy. I had never been through Texas before and tried to make out the features of the passing landscape, but visibility was poor through the sheets of rain, no better than fifty yards ahead in any direction. The speedometer now read 85 mph with the tires were struggling for purchase on the drenched pavement. They made a loud whining noise. I wasn't ready to talk about Michelle though, my mind wasn't clear enough, so I decided to change the subject. I shook my head and tried to think about Dallas.

"I'm really grateful that you picked me up back there when you did," I said. "I had no idea it could rain like this."

"Everything happens big out here in Texas, that's part of its charm." He smiled. "Sometimes we get hailstones the size of baseballs coming down out here. You've got to watch out when that happens, drivers will tend to stop right under an overpass when those hailstorms erupt, not wanting their precious cars to get dented, know what I mean? And it can get pretty scary when other cars plow into them from behind, just multi-car collisions waiting to happen. I saw a nasty wreck like that a couple weeks ago outside of Fort Worth. Hailstorms," he nodded.

As he said this, he straightened his driving posture and gripped the wheel firmly, with shoulders erect and eyes keenly focused on the road ahead while the wiper blades continued flapping wildly against the rain drenched windshield. The man was solidly engaged in his effort, although his head kept on bobbing to the music, a real driving machine. He was confidently piloting this road rocket, having probably driven stoned many times before, with its 454 cubic inch engine roaring mightily as the sports car pierced through the drenching rain. I had little idea what would happen next, but somehow everything seemed under control as we drove on. So I decided to settle back and enjoy the buzz, however temporary that might turn out to be.

"Hey Alan, thanks again," I shouted to him over the music.

"Yeah, I bet you're glad I came along now huh?" he teased, his eyes crinkling but remaining focused on the road. "You're welcome. Now grab us another couple of beers back there," he demanded with a mock attempt at levity, visibility was still pretty poor. "We've got about another hour to kill until we make it to Dallas."

Sipping on my third beer of the day, I enjoyed the feeling of being on my own, on this adventure with no urgent deadlines to think about. During my past four years of high school, I had been constantly thinking about what had to be done that week, the next hour, even the next five minutes. Time had always seemed to matter, but right now it really didn't, and that felt like freedom to me.

Thankfully the rain stopped and the clouds soon parted, and as they did several pillars of sunlight beamed down onto the wet farmland. A vibrant double rainbow emerged in front of us. The sun was now headed out to the Pacific Ocean, a fireball that would soon be quenched.

I rolled down the window and breathed in the humid air. Its moisture condensed rapidly on my air conditioned skin, which was pleasing at first, but soon it began to feel like a Turkish sauna. It glued my hair to the sides of my face and I couldn't shake it free, so I rolled the window back up.

"Now that'll teach ya!" Alan laughed.

This helped me to understand why folks out here were so fond of their air-conditioned cars and houses and shopping malls. A hundred years ago, Texas homesteaders must have sweated out their days while scratching out a living here in the dry prairie soil, waiting for evening so they could sit out on their porches and rock to the breezes.

"Now ain't that a beautiful sight?" Alan said, nodding at the double rainbow ahead of us. I realized that the cassette tape had stopped, how long ago?

"Yeah," I answered, taking in the vividness of the colors displayed there before me, "yeah, it really is."

We passed a road sign informing us that Fort Worth was forty-nine miles ahead. I realized that we had made it through a respectable stretch of Texas which had probably taken weeks to pass through by covered wagon. I felt more alert now and was excited with anticipation, wondering now what Dallas would be like.

"You know Dallas is a pretty big city," Alan ventured. "Got any idea where you might like me to drop you off?"

"Just inside the city limits I guess, so I can say that I made it, however I'd rather stay close to the interstate so that I can get back onto the highway and gone first thing tomorrow morning," I said.

"I'll need to find a cheap place to stay, just hopefully someplace where I won't get shot or anything."

"Well I know just the place." Time seemed to be moving faster as we merged onto Interstate 30 and made our way through Fort Worth. When we reached the Dallas city limits I shook myself back to sobriety, having no idea what to expect when I stepped outside. I knew Dallas by name only, not as a place, but the yellow line I had traced on my map ran through it, and so now here I was. Alan took the Commerce Street exit down an underpass that ran beneath a railroad bridge and made our way onto Main Street. He pulled over as soon as we got there and shut off the engine.

"This here's Dealy Plaza. You should be able to find a number of cheap hotels around here, all within walking distance. Thanks for riding along with me, Brett. You did a great job keeping up with me good buddy, and it helped to pass the time. We partied the miles away, now didn't we?" He laughed. "Take care of yourself Brett; it's been a pleasure having you along for the ride."

I was still coming off the buzz from all the beer and hashish and realized that it was time to step back into the real world for the next stage of my cross-country adventure.

"Thanks for taking me along for the ride, for your hospitality along the way, and for getting me all the way out here to Dallas. That was a good thing, man. And I enjoyed talking with you." I was feeling a lot more confident than I had felt at the beginning of my trip, and laughing inwardly at how scared I had been. I had arrived in the big city of Dallas, the half-way point of my journey, and I was caught up in the feeling of adventure. I stepped onto the sidewalk and shouldered my pack.

"Me too," he called out to me. Then he pressed a lever on his armrest and raised the passenger door window, cranked up the stereo knob on his dashboard, gunned the engine and shifted away.

I leaned into my shoulder straps and hiked down Main Street through the middle of a triangular grass field. There was another grassy area running down the hill from my upper left, and next to it stood several tall buildings. One of them looked a bit familiar. It was a red brick building, seven stories high with lots of windows and it was directly across the street from the plaza. When my gaze returned to the triangular plaza, I saw that a small American flag had been planted in the ground directly across the street from this building. I walked over to it and found an engraved brass land marker on the ground. Studying it, a sudden sadness came over me as a memory from my early childhood years returned.

I was seven years old on November 22nd, 1963, a day when I happened to be walking home from school with a handmade card for my mother's birthday. I had carefully cut the red heart from construction paper and pasted it on the card. Then I printed "Happy Birthday Mom, Love Brett" on the inside with a ballpoint pen, because I wanted what I had written to be "permanent". I opened the front door and saw that the curtains were drawn, and that it was dark inside the house.

I walked slowly into the living room and saw my mom sitting there cross-legged on the carpet in front of the television set, and she was crying. It wasn't usually on this time of day so I was curious to find out what she was watching. Walter Cronkite was speaking in a serious tone of voice. I recognized him from the evening news which I secretly watched from the hallway when my parents thought I was asleep. He was saying something about President Kennedy.

"Mommy, what's wrong?" I asked, holding the card behind my back and hoping that she would be surprised, but becoming more concerned and even a little bit scared when I saw that her crying wouldn't stop, even though I was there now.

"Honey, the President of the United States has been shot. I'm sorry sweetie, but mommy is very sad. We don't know yet if he will be okay." I held the card out in front of me and she read it quickly. Then she hugged me tightly but kept on crying. I knew something bad was happening and felt a sudden sadness, but I couldn't understand why. The President was our leader; he had told us that we were going to the Moon, so how could he not be okay? I was often doodling pictures of multi-stage rocket ships in class.

I bent my head down and studied the bronze land marker. This was the location where President Kennedy had been shot, it said. Then I looked back to the brick building on the other side of the street and realized where I was. It had been the Texas School Book Depository. Lee Harvey Oswald had fired his rifle from the sixth floor of that building. As I jaywalked across Elm Street toward it, most likely right through the place where Kennedy's head had been struck, I recalled the scene that had been re-broadcast so many times on television after that fateful day. All of a sudden I realized that I was standing in the middle of the road and a car was approaching. I would probably get hit if I didn't get out of the street. The driver was just about ready to press his horn when I made eye contact and jogged over to the other sidewalk. Walking up to the brick building, I replayed in my mind what had happened there. There was another brass marker, this one was bolted to the wall and I read it slowly, remembering.

"Formerly the Texas School Depository Building. This site was originally owned by John Neely Bryan, the founder of Dallas. During the 1880s, French native Maxime Guillot operated a wagon shop here. In 1894 the land was purchased by Phil L. Mitchell, president and director of the Rock Island Plow Company of Illinois. An office building for the firm's Texas division was completed here four years later... In 1937 the Carraway Byrd Corporation purchased the property. Later, under the direction of D. H. Byrd, the building was leased to a variety of businesses, including the Texas School Book Depository.

On November 22, 1963, the building gained national notoriety when Lee Harvey Oswald allegedly shot and killed president John F. Kennedy from a sixth floor window as the presidential motorcade passed this site."

I paused on that word "allegedly", shaking my head as I considered the implication that this case had never been solved, even though the Warren Commission had ultimately concluded that Oswald had killed the President and that he had acted alone. We had discussed this topic in my high school civics class, and although

I hadn't paid much attention at the time, standing before this placard brought the details back into vivid focus.

The sun had set now and it was deathly quiet with a gentle breeze caressing my face. I could almost hear the motorcade as I thought about the scene from the telecast, and I imagined the crowds of people who must have filled this square, the black and white images from the day when Kennedy got shot were coming back to life inside my head. As I replayed the scene in my mind, I shuddered at the memory of our president's head slumping down in the 1961 Lincoln Continental convertible with Jackie bending over him as it sped away from the scene. Then I looked up to the sixth floor of the building in real time, to the place where the shot had "allegedly" been fired. It was vacant now, with remnants of fire damage apparent as I looked inside, yet it would bear this plaque as a badge of infamy for future generations. I felt a strong sense of unfairness that whatever happened that day had never been fully resolved.

I decided to move along, shouldering my pack again and made my way back to Main Street. Then I headed several blocks east until I found a rundown hotel, which was about twenty feet wide and seven stories high, sandwiched between a row of dirty granite edifices that probably had been respectable at one time but were now all in decline. Overcoming indecision, I went up the front entrance steps and entered a battered oaken hallway. There were scuffs and scratches on the floor and walls, testifying to an endless procession of short timers who now included me. A short round man with pale gray skin was sitting behind a Plexiglas window. He had cheaply dyed black hair and looked like he hadn't spent a day outside in his life. He nodded curtly and called out to me through the slot beneath the window. "So I bet you need a room for the night," he said with an auspicious grin.

"Yeah, I just got in to town. How much?"

"Five bucks for the night, plus fifty cents for a towel and soap if you want to take a shower down the hall. There's a sink in the room." That sounded like a luxury to me just then.

"I'll only be staying the one night," I said firmly, counting out five crumpled bills from my back pocket and pushing them through the slot. I told him I had my own towel and soap.

"Suit yourself." He snatched the bills as I thrust them through the slot and studied them before placing them in the register. With a displeased look on his face, he handed me a key that was hooked to a purple plastic medallion, room number 24, on the second floor. Then he returned to his newspaper. I would get nothing more from him, so I decided not to ask further questions.

Clambering up the stairs, I located door number 24 and entered a narrow and dusty room. It contained a lumpy single bed, a coat rack with several bent hangers, and a small desk beneath a window that faced the street. My first action was to take advantage of the sink, filling it with warm water and scrubbing my soiled jeans with a bar of soap. After rinsing and wringing them out a few times, I decided that they looked presentable enough and hung them on a hanger to dry, arranging my towel on the floor below to collect the drips. Then I walked back downstairs, attempting to ignore the man behind the counter who likewise ignored me, and strolled down the street to a sandwich shop where I consumed a Rueben sandwich, fries and a coke for a buck fifty.

Exiting the sandwich shop, I noticed a used bookstore on the corner and decided to go inside. I browsed down the over stacked shelves until I found an annual from 1963. I pulled it out and noticed that it was badly worn. A lot of curious browsers must have handled it over the years, probably searching for the same information I was looking for now. Flipping through pages to the chapter covering the Kennedy assassination, I studied photos and diagrams and other details from that infamous day. A mug shot of Lee Harvey Oswald was staring back at me from the page. He seemed to be pleading with me somehow, as if something wasn't right, but I couldn't help him now since he was already dead. I shut the book and put it back on the shelf. The woman behind the counter was an untidy blond in her mid-thirties. She was not very attractive and did not seem interested in helping me on this quiet

Tuesday night. She nodded with a joyless smile as I thanked her on my way out.

A wave of fatigue crashed over me as the food began to settle in my stomach. It had been a long day. My feet felt like lead bricks as I trudged down the sidewalk. I hadn't slept very well on the open ground the night before; so lumpy bed or not, I headed back to the flophouse hotel. Once inside the room I washed my face in the sink and brushed my teeth, then stripped to my boxers and settled between the scratchy sheets. I pulled a rough wool blanket up to my chin and fell fast asleep.

It was July 11th, 1969, and I was attending Boy Scout Jamboree in a tent city outside of Farragut Idaho overlooking Lake Pond Orielle. It was early evening, a busy day of scouting activities was now behind us, and a full moon was rising. This would be a special night I knew. The camp organizers had mounted dozens of television sets on poles around the campground with gas powered generators so that our fifty thousand scouts from across America could watch the Apollo moon landing live. I stood there among about five hundred other scouts in the early evening, a swarm of boy humanity, we were all standing on tiptoe to see the television set mounted on the pole above us. "The Eagle" landing module had just touched down on the surface of the moon twenty minutes before and we were holding our breath, waiting for the first human being in history to set foot on the moon. I looked up to the real moon overhead and could scarcely comprehend what was happening on the television set perched above me.

We had all cheered loudly when the landing module had finally settled onto the moon's surface. But it seemed to take forever for Central Control in Houston to confirm that the lunar module was stably planted on the surface and wouldn't sink beneath the lunar dust. I wanted to see if what I had learned in science class was true, that a man could bound about with ease under the moon's one-sixth gravitational pull, way up there on the actual moon I was looking at now.

Then Neil Armstrong descended down the ladder, ever so slowly. I think we all kept holding our breath, an exceptionally quiet moment for a bunch of rowdy boy scouts. One step, then another, it felt like time itself had slowed to one-sixth its normal speed. My calves were beginning to spasm, having spent so much time on tip-toe trying to see above the other scouts. Astronaut Armstrong stepped down on the lunar surface and planted a foot firmly, and then both feet. A human being was actually standing on the lunar surface!

"That's one small step for man…one giant leap for mankind."

And then, just as I had imagined, the moment came. Neal Armstrong was up there bouncing about, the first man in history to walk on the actual surface of the moon. It was like my science class predicted, the one-sixth gravitational pull, and despite how tired I was from standing down there on the heavy earth, it gave me goose bumps. President Kennedy had challenged us to safely land a man on the moon within the decade, during his inaugural address back in 1961. But he never got to see it happen. I was thinking about his speech while Neal Armstrong was up there on the lunar surface, bounding around like a kid playing hopscotch.

CHAPTER SEVEN

I AWOKE TO A THROBBING HEADACHE, unsure where I was at first or how I had gotten there. It was particularly hot in this tiny room with a bright sunlight beaming through the window. I had forgotten to lower the blind the night before. While I slowly regained consciousness, I looked around and saw that my jeans were still hanging on the coat stand, recalling that I had washed them the night before. I reached over and touched them, relieved to find that they were dry now. However the room felt stuffy and I was desperately thirsty.

So I stumbled out of bed and made a few tentative steps over to the sink. I turned on the tap and was startled by the pleasantly cold water flowing through my fingers. I lowered my head beneath the faucet and enjoyed the chilling relief as the water drenched my hair and splashed down into the sink. Then I cupped a hand to my lips and took in gulps as fast as I could swallow, quenching my thirst and feeling somewhat better. I reached over and unzipped the outside pouch of my pack, removed my first aid kit and found the much needed aspirin, popped a couple in my mouth, and returned to the faucet for another quick swallow. The towel that I had placed underneath my pants was also dry so I blotted my face and hair with it, wishing I had paid the fifty cents for another clean towel.

I combed my hair and parted it down the middle, and then I pulled the freshly washed jeans back on. They felt stiff around the knees when I bent down to put my socks on and tie my boots. I would wear the faded blue work shirt again today, the one I had worn on the first day of my journey, wishing that I had washed it too the night before. But now it was time to go out and find some breakfast.

When I tromped down the stairs I could see that the night attendant had been replaced by an anorexic woman in her late fifties. She had bleached blond hair, darkly tanned and wrinkled skin, with bright blue eye shadow and cherry red lipstick smeared across her thin lips. She looked up expectantly when I passed by. "There's a diner down on the corner sugar," she said it in a gravelly voice that attested to many years of heavy smoking.

"Yeah thanks, I ate there last night," I answered as politely as I could despite my still throbbing headache, and strode through the door into the blinding sunlight outside. By the time I reached the diner, my shirt was already sticky with sweat.

A tiny bell jingled on the back of the door as I entered the diner. A row of men were sitting there at the counter. They turned around to inspect me briefly, but quickly lost interest and returned to their fried eggs and coffee, so I figured that my presence here was okay with them. The diner had more customers on this Wednesday morning than the night before, and I wondered whether any of them worked at the former Texas Book Depository. I sat on an open stool at the end of the counter and grabbed a menu.

The woman I had seen at the bookstore the night before was working behind the counter. She studied me for an uncomfortable moment and decided to speak.

"My friend Byron runs that hotel back there you've been staying at," she said. "He told me you came in last night with a backpack, figured you must be hitching. You should know that it's illegal to hitchhike anywhere in the Dallas city limits. When you're ready to go, you ought to think about walking up to the Greyhound station and getting yourself a bus ticket out of town. It's about four blocks up the road from here, and one block over on the left."

"Thanks," I said, realizing that I should take her advice. "Thanks very much. I really appreciate it."

"You're welcome, honey" she smiled.

My grumpy stomach told me to get the breakfast special, so I ordered two eggs over easy with a stack of pancakes, and with two slices of bacon on the side. I also asked for a cup of coffee and poured cream and sugar into it when it arrived, since I had not then been a regular coffee drinker. I enjoyed its warmth as I sipped it through sun-chapped lips, and it settled my stomach some. Somehow the simple act of sipping coffee revived me and I began to look forward to the coming day.

My breakfast plate arrived with a small ceramic cup of warmed maple syrup on the side that I poured over the pancakes, holding it there until the last few drops came out. I grabbed a knife and fork and tucked into my food, but then I remembered that I was in a public place and attempted to eat it more slowly. It made my stomach feel even better and I vowed to eat more balanced meals in the coming days. I also promised myself that I'd try to go for a run that evening. Hangovers could be a wellspring of resolution it seemed.

"Well now you look like you just might live," the waitress behind the counter commented in my direction as she was stacking freshly washed plates onto a shelf behind the counter.

"Yeah, I think I just might," I said with just one swallow left to go. With that done, I took a final swig of coffee and finished off my meal with a glass of ice water. As the coolness hit my stomach I realized that my headache was gone; the aspirin must have finally kicked in. More fully revived and with a full stomach now, I stood up and walked over to the register to pay my bill, a dollar forty, and returned to the counter to leave a fifty cent tip for the waitress. She probably needed it more than I did anyway, and I was grateful for her advice about the bus, however I made sure to keep a dime in my pocket in case I needed to make an emergency phone call somewhere.

My gait became steadier as I loped back to the hotel and took the stairs two at a time back up to my room, where I gathered my belongings and cinched them inside my pack. Hoisting it onto my shoulders once more, I grabbed the key from my nightstand, took one last look around to make sure I hadn't left anything, and shut the door. I wondered where I might be sleeping that evening. But it was time to go.

I shoved the key back under the Plexiglas window slot and the woman looked up from the desk to wish me a good day. I saw past her caked mascara and took in the sadness in her eyes. She probably wished she was going on a trip like mine, or so I thought. My day would be another blank slate to be filled in with adventures, with no job holding me down and nothing preventing me from leaving just now. Who wouldn't envy that, I asked myself?

"Take care," I said, taking a business card from the tray and sticking it in my pocket. "Maybe I'll send you a postcard from Florida."

"That would be nice," she smiled, her face brightening. Having done my good deed for the day, I strode back out into the sunlight.

I walked up the four blocks and over two as instructed by the diner waitress and located the Greyhound station. Buses were pulling out from a garage beneath the building, spewing black diesel exhaust as they motored down the boulevard toward the freeway. The terminal's aluminum frame entry doors had large wooden handles and it required a hefty pull to open one of them, I had to put my whole body into it. The door whacked my pack as the pneumatic hinge pulled it shut behind me, nudging me into the main lobby. It was noisy inside with a cacophony of conversations going on all at once. People were standing around in random groups, or resting on rows of wooden benches with luggage stacked around them on the floor, creating a challenging obstacle course for me to navigate. Cigarette smoke rose up from every direction to the oak beamed ceiling, and there wasn't much contrast between the beams and the sooty plaster roof they supported. The terra cotta floor showed considerable wear down the aisles from decades of foot traffic, and it was badly yellowed around the edges from multiple layers of wax that could no longer be scraped away.

I weaved my way through the crowded terminal to a ticket line of expectant travelers, slowly queuing forward in various stages of boredom. I shrugged my shoulders out of the straps of my pack and lowered it down next to me, grasping the rail and hopping it along beside me as I queued toward the ticket window. I realized that I had no idea where I was going, so I unfolded my roadmap and studied the detail surrounding the Dallas metropolitan area, continuing to shuffle on as folks behind me grew impatient. Terrell Texas would be the first city beyond the beltway cluster that funneled back to Interstate 20 headed east.

I paid two dollars and fifty cents for a bus ticket to Terrell, knowing that the money for this fare could have gotten me a pretty decent lunch somewhere along the way, but I figured that it would be much better spent that way than to risk getting arrested for hitchhiking. I sure hoped no hitching laws would be enforced beyond the Dallas metropolitan area. At least I would be less conspicuous out on the open road than trying to bum a ride here in town, competing with panhandlers and the like.

I slipped the bus ticket into my hip pocket and weaved back through the crowd to the waiting area, where I eventually found a seat at the end of a crowded bench near the middle of the lobby. I leaned my pack against the armrest and stretched out my legs, feeling the muscle fatigue dissipate. It was 9:30 in the morning and the bus was scheduled to depart in forty five minutes. I hated losing so much time but there was nothing that I could do, so I fidgeted with the zippers of my pack, making sure again that I hadn't left anything back at the hotel. Thus satisfied, I stretched my legs again and surrendered to boredom just like everybody else.

A man walked up to a row of empty phone booths along the sidewall of the waiting area, pulled a phone handle to his ear and started talking, but he hadn't put any coins into the pay slot which seemed a bit odd. He had long brown hair, faded Levis, a white T-shirt, fringed leather jacket, and a floppy suede leather hat that he pulled down over his eyebrows. It was the kind of hat you could buy from street vendors across the border, I remembered from my road trips down to Tijuana. His head was nodding a bit too often, and I was pretty sure that he was having a fake conversation with himself. But after a few minutes he returned the receiver to its cradle and walked away, so I forgot about him until he returned and repeated the process several more times. Our eyes met and he turned and walked toward me, nodding and smiling like I was his long lost friend. He reached out and shook my hand, leaning forward to whisper into my ear. I was too startled to resist his approach since he was pretty convincing.

"Dude, you want to buy some drugs? I've got Acapulco Gold, mescaline, acid, and speed, whatever you want."

Realization sank in. The guy was a pusher, and the phone thing was just his way to avoid getting tossed for loitering. He wasn't traveling anywhere. And buying something from this guy did not seem like a good idea.

"No, man, I'm fine right now."

"OK, suit yourself, but if you change your mind stand over by the phone booth and we'll talk."

He looked back to the booths and walked in the direction of a teenaged kid in bell-bottoms with a striped shirt and vest, long black hair parted down the middle, round sunglasses perched on his nose, a Beatles type. The kid had pimples all over his face but seemed quite happy after Mister Drug Pusher got there and whispered in his ear. They shook hands, exchanged a few words, and then left the terminal together. I resolved to put the whole scenario out of my mind and went back into my boredom.

Glancing at my watch I could see that I still had twenty minutes left to wait. As if on cue, he returned with a sealed bag of cookies and Beatles kid walking beside him. After looking around, he offered the bag to Beatles kid who took a cookie out and munched it. Then he handed the bag of cookies over to the kid, turned on his heel and went back to a phone booth for another fake conversation. The kid walked back into the crowd, nibbling on another cookie. I figured it must be how the drug transfer happened. Putting actual cookies on top and sealing the bag was an innovative touch. I wondered how long Mister Drug Pusher had been running this gig.

It was time to go to the gate and wait for my bus. My feet sank in my boots as I shouldered my pack and trudged down the gangway to stall eleven. I stood at the curb in an underground garage with forty other passengers who were apparently waiting for the same bus.

An attractive brunette girl about my age happened to be standing near the back of the queue. She looked pretty cute in her blue bell-bottom jeans and pale yellow halter-top, so naturally I gravitated toward her. I nodded when she smiled back at me, her oval green eyes connecting with mine as I breathed them in. Glancing down shyly, I noticed her purple painted toenails in cork soled sandals. When I looked back into her eyes, my face apparently made a dopey looking grin that I tried to get back under control, not sure what to do or say next exactly. Fortunately she gave me another smile which allowed me to exhale, warmth was now returning to my fingertips.

"I'm going to Baton Rouge to visit my sister. How far are you headed?" she asked in a seductive southern accent.

I briefly thought about asking her to hold my place in line while I ran back to the lobby to upgrade my ticket; however this would have taken my journey off in a completely different direction than I was intending. I felt conflicted enough as it was, on a three thousand mile road journey to Florida to see about a girl who didn't even know I was coming.

"I'm only headed as far as Terrell," I said decisively. "I'll be hitchhiking from there." I was relieved to have found my voice. Relax your shoulders Brett, my mom always said.

"That must be exciting for you," she said, studying my face.

"Well it's been interesting so far, I must admit," I laughed.

The bus driver climbed aboard and settled into the driver's seat, shutting the door and leaving it closed while he studied his clipboard. When our bus departure was announced over the loudspeaker, he opened the door and carefully inspected each person's ticket as they boarded the bus. I handed my pack to the porter as I approached the steps and forced myself to let it go so that he could stack it with the other baggage in the cargo bay. Then I followed the girl I had just met up the stairs and onto the bus.

"Mind if I take this seat next to you?" I asked, probably somewhat sheepishly.

"No, that would be nice, I mean yes please," she said. "Besides, then I'll probably have the seat to myself after we leave Terrell. Just kidding," she laughed. "Have a seat, surfer boy. You are from Southern California, am I right?"

"How did you know?"

"Boys don't wear their hair long like that out here, except for maybe the druggies. You don't look like a druggie to me, now are you?" she laughed again. I liked the way she laughed.

"No of course not and thanks, I guess." She located a window seat and I took the aisle, settling in beside her.

The driver pulled the handle to close the door and eased the bus out of the tunnel into downtown traffic. We passed the used bookstore and downtrodden hotel where I had stayed the night before. It felt a bit strange to see them again so soon after I had said my mental goodbye. After a few more turns, we drove up the bypass onramp and headed east along the beltway. I studied downtown Dallas as it passed on our left and was glad that Alan hadn't let me out in that part of the city the previous evening, it looked like an expensive concrete jungle.

"So tell me about California," she said after the bus had reached cruising speed.

"Tell me your name first," I ventured.

"Cynthia. But you can call me Cindy if you like."

"OK, 'Cynthia but you can call me Cindy'. It's a pleasure to meet you. My name's Brett." I extended my hand and gently shook hers, temporarily lost again in her green eyes. Actually they were a mixture of colors, with speckles of blue, yellow, and brown, but the first and overall impression I got was green.

"Likewise," she shook back. "So?"

"So what?"

"California, dummy! What's it like?"

"Well, I guess it all depends on where you live. California is a pretty big state."

"I know that, silly. I got to travel to Sacramento two summers ago with 4-H. We even had a day in San Francisco and I got to ride a cable car. But I've never been to Southern California before, always wanted to go. I'm thinking about applying to San Diego State after I finish high school, always wanted to live out west."

"I just graduated. Got a scholarship to go to a college back in Southern California, but lately I've been having second thoughts about that. See, my father lives out in Florida and I'm going there to see him now." She looked at me quizzically but must have decided that it wasn't any of her business.

"My mother and father got divorced when I was about four and my sister was two," I continued. "She moved us out to California to start a new life."

"That must have been very brave of her." Cindy seemed genuinely interested, nodding and willing me to continue.

"Yeah, my mom first visited California during her college days, and one of her closest girlfriends had moved out there after they graduated. So I guess after the divorce, my mom decided to move out there and stay with her friend until she could get back on her feet, make a better life for herself and my sister and me.

"The California population has grown considerably since the early sixties. There have been lots of changes over the years with all the folks moving out west for the promise of a 'better life'. My mom got remarried and moved to the Pomona Valley, which was really a great place to grow up when I was a kid, with lemon groves and vineyards and we could ride all over the place on our bikes. But now the cities have expanded and construction has gone out of control. I'm pretty sure every city will keep building until there's no open space left in the valley. Anyway, my mom had two more children after marrying my stepdad, my half-brother and half-sister. They really completed our family and I'm happy with the way things worked out," I continued. "So that's where I live now. But yeah, like I said, I'm going back to Florida to see my real father."

"So you don't live near the beach?" she asked.

"No, actually we live about fifty miles inland. But that doesn't keep me from getting out there as often as I can. I like to head out with some surfing friends of mine, and we've been doing it almost every weekend since I was fourteen. We used to ride our ten-speed bikes down there with sleeping bags strapped to the racks and spend the night at Bolsa Chica State Beach, then body surf and ride back home the next day, but that was before we got our driver's licenses."

"And your parents let you do that?"

"Yeah, I guess," I shrugged. "I promised my mom I'd call her when we got to the beach and so now I always carry change in my pocket for the pay phones. I'd call her from Newport Beach when I got there to let her know I was okay."

Estimating how much time we had until we reached Terrell, I decided to give her a Cliff notes version of Southern California.

"Anyway like I said I love to head out to the coast. You can smell the ocean from about five miles inland, like the coastline is beckoning. I never get tired of it. We usually travel down Beach Boulevard to Pacific Coast Highway and head up the coast where the waves are bigger and there are fewer tourists.

"Just north of Newport is an estuary that's fed by the Santa Ana River whenever we get rainfall, which is not all that often. You reach Huntington State Beach after a few miles, although we like to continue on up to Huntington City Beach, pretty much our surfing mecca. They've got over a dozen surf shops within a city block of the pier. We used to buy foam blanks from Jack's and Greek surf shops and take them home to shape our own boards. North of that is Huntington Cliffs, another great spot for surfing where waves can get pretty gnarly sometimes. Big, I mean." The memories were fun to recant, although I didn't have time to explain them all in detail, so I decided to pick a couple and continue.

"If you're a kid like us without much money, it's best to continue north to Bolsa Chica State Beach where you can camp out overnight. You can burrow a foxhole in the sand and lay your sleeping bag down in it. Sometimes we'd collect trashcans from up and down the beach to line the perimeter of the burrow, to block the wind you know? There's nothing quite like falling asleep to the sound of the crashing surf, and waking up to it again in the early morning fog. It can be bit disorienting when you first wake up, but in an enlightening sort of way I guess.

"We'd often go to Howard's for breakfast, a place down on Coast Highway just north of Newport Beach. Ever tried chorizo con huevos?" I asked, knowing the answer would be no but eager to explain.

"Yes, as a matter of fact," Cindy laughed. "We've got Tex Mex out here you know!"

"Well I guess I didn't know that. But anyway, the surfers liked it because it's pretty cheap and gives you the energy you need to surf all morning. The spiciness of the chorizo kind of shocks you awake, which is a good thing when you've been sleeping on the beach all night. It also masks the bitter taste of the crappy coffee they serve there.

"Then we usually go to Jack's sandwich shop on Huntington Pier for lunch. You can buy a basket of tortilla strips with chili and cheese for only fifty cents with all the free hot sauce you want. That pretty much keeps you going for the rest of the afternoon."

Our bus merged back with Interstate 20 at Mesquite and was now headed east. I figured we had about twenty minutes left until the bus stopped to let me off.

"We don't have much more time, so let me tell you what it's like in the surf if that's okay."

"Yes, I'd like that," she said, still interested I was pleased to see.

"One time the surf was really huge. We didn't have our boards, since we had ridden our bicycles down there that weekend. If we couldn't catch a ride, we'd cycle down to camp and bodysurf, like I said. On this particular morning it was overcast and windy when we woke up from a fitful sleep, since the wind had been blowing all night. The trashcans we had dragged around the perimeter of our foxhole to block the wind had simply amplified the howling noise. It was pretty clear that a storm was coming and we thought about riding back home, which would have defeated all the effort we had made to get there. But then we looked out to the water and saw these huge sets of storm waves coming in to shore, as large as any we had ever seen before. The waves were cresting around ten feet or so, but the water was choppy and their shape was poor. So we decided to pack up and ride our bikes down to a place called the Wedge on Balboa Peninsula. It's just a little ways south of Newport, north of a rock jetty that forms the mouth of Newport Harbor.

"The Wedge is usually a good place to bodysurf since the waves build in size when they encounter the jetty and then bend northward to run almost parallel to the beach. The amplified wave makes a roller coaster like elbow turn which can be a wild ride even under mildest of conditions.

"The waves on this particular day, when we got to the jetty, must have been over fifteen feet high. We watched them from shore and tried to psych ourselves up to go in, let go of our fear. With surf like that, fear is your enemy. If you give in to it, you're going to get hurt, that's pretty much guaranteed. Anyway, my friend Dean decided to head out so I followed him in, kicking frantically with my flippers to get out past where the waves were breaking.

"So then you sit out there and wait for a mountain of water to rise up. When you do see one coming toward you, you've only got a second or two to decide what to do. And you've only got two options. One, swim like crazy and try to catch it. Or two, bail out and dive under before it starts to curl. If you time it wrong you'll get trashed either way. I finally decided to catch one against my better judgment, but it was too late. It curled brutally over me and I got spilled a dozen feet down into its guts. The crushing whitewater kept me under for what felt like forever, violently wrestling my body back and forth in the churning surf. The last thing you want to do at a time like that is struggle, since it uses up your oxygen. You've got to relax your limbs and take the beating, waiting for the white water to pop you back to the surface. So my lungs were burning for air by the time I made the surface, and I only had time for one quick gulp of air before another huge wave came at me, spilling me back into the churning water. This happened at least a third time, I sort of lost count.

"Okay, so by now my fear had progressed to panic. Let me tell you: with waves coming at you like that, you simply *cannot* give in to fear." I wondered whether I was crossing the line between credible and embellished bravado, however as I retold this story I could feel my fear returning and I thought Cindy could tell. Her green eyes were darting about to examine my face and eyes.

"Go ahead, apparently you made it. What happened next?"

"I swam like an animal on pure instinct to get twenty yards farther out beyond the break, because I could see an even bigger set approaching. By now Dean was nowhere to be seen.

"Then this gonzo wave comes up and it's starting to crest. I just looked up and decided to paddle down onto it, not wanting to get crushed again. I stroked my arms madly, water polo style, and kicked my flippers as hard as I could, sliding chest first down the crest into the heart of the wave. I thrust out my right arm and arched my chest to get control, steering my body to the right of the break as I slid down. It turned out to be an incredible ride but I sensed that something was wrong, that I was headed the wrong way, south not north. Every nerve ending was firing as I slid down the wave at a violent speed. It was all I could do to steer clear of the crushing white water.

"Then it got real calm all of a sudden. I was treading water and trying to figure out where I was. And you know what? That wave had tossed me into Newport Harbor, over a rock jetty that usually rises six or seven feet above the water."

I stopped for a few seconds, reflecting on this. "That was a pretty insane thing to do in hindsight, but I guess the thing that amazed me most was how my higher thought processes had given way to instinct. I wouldn't have made it otherwise."

I delivered the punch line after another pause. "Dean climbed over the jetty and helped me out of the water, laughing his ass off. He had bailed out immediately and swam back to shore. I didn't think it was funny at the time, but I guess I understand now that he was just relieved. Guys can communicate in bizarre ways, you know?"

"Yes I see," Cindy said, as my eyes refocused back into hers. She had been a pretty good listener and I appreciated the opportunity to retell this story. The adventure that I was reliving restored my confidence and made me more enthusiastic about my present journey, in a strange sort of way.

We were now passing through another expanse of farmland that ran on in every direction. I realized that I had been monopolizing the conversation.

"So tell me something about you and where you live," I collected myself, trying to convey the genuine interest that I was feeling for this attractive and attentive young woman.

"Well I grew up in Plano, a small town north of Dallas. Not much to say about it, really. High school football is really big out here on Friday night. The whole town lives for football, like you would not believe. I'm a cheerleader and I'm hoping to make squad leader next year," she said somewhat demurely.

"So let's see... well, all the boys drive pickup trucks and wear cowboy hats, even though most of them don't cowboy." She paused for a moment.

"I guess you could say we take to rodeo like you take to surfing." She nodded to herself, seemingly encouraged by this awareness.

"Do you 'rodeo'?" I asked, sensing that the answer must be yes. How else could she have listened so attentively to my bodysurfing experience?

"Well, yes actually!" She smiled with straight white teeth, a beautiful sight and I was hooked, eager to hear the rest of the story.

"So?" I said after another pause.

"I own a horse that I work out with every chance I get, we like to go barrel racing together." She gathered herself and I willed her to continue.

"It takes a lot of practice until it becomes instinctive I guess, sort of like you were saying. You lean way over with your horse into the barrels, the tighter the turn the quicker you can get around them, and then you both accelerate over to the next barrel and on back again in a figure eight pattern, fast as you can. You can start out either from the left or the right, depending on how you grip the reins, but then you have to come around again the other way. You get scored for time and form for completing a double eight. The first lap is a whole lot easier than the second lap, I can tell you! It's really hard to keep the turns both tight and quick at the same time.

"Anyway, I love to compete. It's like you trot out into the arena, aware of all the people watching, and then you just get completely focused. You can feel it in your horse too. When you're both ready, you accelerate together into the barrels and it all begins. The wind whips around your ears, with the muscles of the horse tensing and thrusting against your knees, the shifting of balance and acceleration. I love it, I really do."

"Yeah well, OK. I think I see what you're saying, the rush of adrenaline. Makes sense now how you could listen to me. It's pretty cool, huh?"

"Yeah, it's pretty cool," she laughed, emphasizing the word 'cool' with her best attempt at a Southern California accent.

"Well I'm very happy to have made your acquaintance," I said in what thought was a genteel Texas accent.

We both laughed at that. And it truly made my day.

The Terrell city limits came into view and I began to prepare myself emotionally for another long day of hitching. This bus ride had been enjoyable, but now I needed to focus on the unpredictable task ahead. I was feeling more confident though, quite unlike my first day of hitchhiking which seemed long ago.

The bus left the freeway and weaved its way into town, pulling into a small terminal where several people were standing around and waiting for the bus.

"Well I guess this is where I get off. I really enjoyed talking with you, Cindy. Thanks very much, you really made my day."

"Me too," she smiled back. "I hope that you do decide to move back to Florida, if that's what you want." She was pretty perceptive.

"Oh, I'm pretty sure that wherever I wind up, there I'll be," I laughed back, trying to sound more confident than I felt, the reality of having to get off this bus was sinking in.

I climbed down the steps and waited outside for the porter to retrieve my backpack from the storage compartment. He handed it to me and I slid my arm into the shoulder strap, swinging it around onto my back. I was grateful to have it again as I cinched my hip belt to distribute the weight. After a brief trip to the restroom behind the terminal, where I splashed cold water onto my face to revive myself, I hiked back to the freeway onramp.

The bus pulled back onto the freeway after a few minutes and I waved, unable to see through the tinted glass. I watched until it was no longer visible, then stood and waited for my next ride.

CHAPTER EIGHT

A GOOD TWENTY MINUTES HAD PASSED without a single vehicle approaching the onramp, and it was now close to 11 am. The sweat was seeping from my pores as I stood there under the hot Texas sun, and the work shirt I had put on that morning back in Dallas was already wet and sticky against my skin. I shifted my weight from side to side, trying to relieve my fatigue and began humming a rock tune to amuse myself, *Communication Breakdown* by Led Zeppelin. This lifted my spirits somewhat, however after another difficult period of standing there and waiting, I got the picture that this wasn't working. But there were definitely cars whizzing by on the freeway, and I was beginning to feel a bit desperate. So I decided to hike up the onramp and try my luck from alongside the freeway. At least the passing cars would see me, although I knew now that it was against the law for me to hitch from there.

Cars and trucks blew past and one occasionally honked menacingly, making a high to low pitch sound as it drove by. I had learned in physics class that it was due to the Doppler Effect, something about sound waves compressing and then expanding when moving objects ran past a stationary listener. The hot air displaced by the passing vehicles would almost knock me off my feet, but then it would get quiet again until the next car passed. Cars seemed to come by in clusters for some reason, and there were long stretches with no cars at all. Around me was nothing but farmland. I looked out and watched a lone tractor lumbering down seemingly endless furrows.

A trailer-truck slowed and pulled over to a stop about 50 yards ahead of where I was standing. It was loaded with speedboats wrapped in white plastic. The driver leaned out the passenger window and waved back for me to approach. I had seen this truck before, I realized with a feeling of déjà vu and premonition. Something didn't feel right, but again I had no reasonable alternative, so I shouldered my pack and hiked on up to it.

"Climb on up, boy, and you'd better make it quick before some damn patrolman comes by and gives me a ticket." He looked to be about fifty with thinning gray hair combed over the top of his large head, about two days stubble on his face and neck, and one cheek was puffed out from a thick wad of chewing tobacco that he was chawing rhythmically like a cow, but with greater urgency. He wasn't about to wait much longer for me to decide.

Up to now my luck had seemed to hold up pretty well so I decided to give this ride a go. The passenger door opened out and I climbed up and hoisted my pack around to the back of the cab, then settled into the seat and tried to relax. The driver pulled the truck back onto the freeway and shifted multiple times until it had reached speed. Neither of us spoke for the next several minutes which was perfectly fine with me.

Glancing about the cab, I saw a number of crumpled paper bags from fast food restaurants discarded on the floorboards around our feet, along with paper coffee cups and other such detritus. The driver looked out of shape with a sagging neck and a huge belly protruding over his belt. He continued to chew and rolled down the window occasionally to spit out the tobacco juice. I was thankful that he hadn't done it on the floorboards.

We rolled along for about thirty miles and it didn't seem like the driver was interested in talking so I stared out the passenger window. Farmland out here in eastern Texas seemed to run on forever and I was finding it difficult to sit still, shifting around and fidgeting with nervous anticipation. There was no car stereo in the dash and we still had over 100 miles to go until we reached the Louisiana State Line. I was hoping the landscape would get more interesting once we got that far.

A voice squawked from a citizen's band radio underneath the dashboard: *"breaker-breaker, this is Cowhand. Bubba, you got your ears on?"*

The driver reached down and pulled the handset up to his mouth, thumbing the switch on the side to engage the mike. "Yeah Cowhand, I'm here. What's your twenty? Over…"

"I look to be about marker 287, just watched a smoky pass by that I figured you should know about. I saw him and slowed too soon for him to clock me, but he looks hungry. He's probably about five minutes behind you, so keep your eyes open."

"That's a big ten-four, good buddy. Thank you kindly, over."

"Ease on back and I'll let you know when the road is clear, over."

"You bet. Thanks for the heads up Cowhand, Bubba out."

"What's your name, boy?" he asked finally, glancing over to acknowledge my presence.

"Huh? Oh, sorry, my name's Brett," I shook myself alert and answered. "I'm hitching from Southern California, headed for Florida," I continued, deciding to save him the obvious follow up questions.

"That a fact?" he said in mock surprise, another glance sideways for a more careful look this time. He surveyed me for several seconds, and then returned his attention to the highway. "You one of them surfer boys?" he asked with a grin that was more of a grimace. I knew I had nothing to hide, but somehow he made me feel like I needed to be careful with my answer.

"Yeah I surf back there whenever I can. But I guess that doesn't matter too much around here, that right?"

"I guess that's about right." We drove on for a while and I was more than content to let the minutes pass.

The citizen's band radio squawked a few more times, and he reached down to adjust the knob, making it a bit louder so that we could hear it over the reverberant diesel engine. I had heard about truckers and their CBs, driving down the highways of America while chattering away with their silly call signs. And here it was happening right next to me; our cab connected to other cabs up and down the highway, folks chatting away about mile markers and smokies and such.

Clouds were darkening the horizon up ahead as the truck made its way to the eastern edge of Texas. The driver kept track of other truckers who happened to be headed our way over the CB, asking whether they had seen any 'smokies' along the route, and blathering about various highway oddities that would be of no particular interest to me. Apparently this was a common pastime for truckers on the open highway. I rolled the passenger window down about a half turn and felt the damp breeze blow against my face. It was not a cool sensation but revived me nonetheless. The air was saturated with humidity and the clouds continued to muscle together conspiratorially; I was starting to catch on to their ways. Droplets began to splatter the windshield, and just as I was rolling the window back up, the first barrage of rain finally hit us. It must be that time of day, I realized. The driver turned on his windshield wipers and he gave it no mind, continuing to chatter away on his CB.

He finished speaking into the mike, ending with "that's a big ten four Papa Bear, out for now," and returned it to its cradle on the dashboard. With that done, he turned his head over to me and made a longer assessment, eventually nodding his approval. He seemed to appreciate that I hadn't interrupted him before, as if that had even occurred to me.

"You hungry?" he shouted above the rain, now pounding down onto the roof of the truck cab like a snare drum. I rotated my wrist and the waterproof watch said that it was past 2 PM. I needed a decent meal to boost my attention span which was starting to wane. This man had offered to feed me, and there was no way I could say "no" at that point.

"Yeah, I guess you could say that," I answered, pursing my lips in anticipation.

He smiled back. "Well alright then! There's a truck stop about five minutes up the highway. How about a nice plate of catfish, best they have around these parts?"

"Yeah, OK," I smiled in attempted encouragement. With the windshield wipers slapping back and forth on their fastest setting, we eventually pulled off the exit ramp and drove slowly into the large parking lot next to a row of other trucks, finally coming to a stop. He left the diesel engine running.

"We won't be too long. Come on, let's run."

We dashed for the entrance and stopped just inside, stamping off the rain and gravel from our shoes on the industrial grade floor mat. A woman behind the counter waved us over to a booth by the front window and we sat opposite each other, grabbing plastic coated menus from the wire rack on the table that also held condiments and napkins.

"Name's Charles, but you can call me Bubba, that's my handle and most people call me that when I'm on the road." Funny how I hadn't noticed this while he was chatting to the outside world over his CB radio. I just figured they all called each other 'Bubba' out here in Texas, at least when they didn't know who they were talking with.

"I'm on my way from Southern California to Florida, like I said." He hadn't given his name at first when I had given him mine. I figured I'd let him ask the questions from here on and waited for him to offer up information about himself.

"Well, it looks like you're headed in the right direction!" he laughed.

"Thanks," I said, probably somewhat sheepishly as I sat there clasping my hands in front of me and waiting for the next question.

"You ever travelled through the south before?" he asked next.

"I spent last summer out in Florida working for my father, building custom houses." He hadn't asked about that part yet and I realized that I was getting ahead of myself, but figured that my work in construction might make a good impression.

"No, boy, I meant the real south. Have you ever been through Louisiana?"

"Well no," I answered, wondering what he was getting at.

The waitress came up and asked what we wanted to drink. "I'd like a coffee for me," Bubba said. "And what would you like there Brett? A coke?"

"Yeah, that'd be fine, thanks." I was really looking forward to a tall coke with ice.

"And we'll have a couple of them plates of your nice catfish," he smiled back to the waitress.

"You got it," she said, writing down our order and turning on her heel to return to the kitchen. 'Bubba' rested his elbows on the table in front of him and propped his chubby cheeks on his knuckles as he surveyed me. "Would you call yourself a prejudiced person?" he asked next.

"Oh heck no, why?" I wondered what I'd said to create that impression; unsure whether I should feel defensive about it.

"Yeah, that's pretty much what they all say out west. You folks got no idea how them niggers live out here in the south."

I was lost for words and thought about bolting out the door to hail another ride. But my backpack was still in Bubba's cab, and it was still pelting down rain outside. No suitable response came to mind, so I simply nodded and tried to act like it didn't bother me.

"Tell me, boy, you look like you just finished high school. Out on a big adventure now, huh?"

I still couldn't think of any words to say. I felt my shoulders knotting up and tried to shrug them loose, relaxing my forearms on the table.

"Yeah, I thought so. Well, alright then." He shrugged his shoulders and smiled, signaling that it was all okay. I shrugged my shoulders in reply and tried to smile, turning my thoughts to the meal that I wanted to come soon. As if on cue, the waitress returned with our drinks and set two steaming plates of fried catfish on the table, with peas, biscuits and gravy on the side. It wasn't the most nutritious meal I had ever seen but it did smell delicious. I grabbed my knife and fork and tried a few bites. Comfort food was entering my belly and it settled me down some. The tense moment faded away as we sat there eating our food. Bubba finished his plate before I did and had two more cups of coffee while I kept on eating, until every morsel had been scraped off my plate. I had also downed two more cokes by this time.

The bill came to $4.50 plus tip. I offered to pay my share but Bubba waved me off, pulled six dollars from his wallet and placed them under a salt shaker. Then he stood up, obviously ready to get back on the road. The rain had abated and the clouds were dispersing when we walked outside. The sun peeked out and shined a beam in the direction of the Louisiana state line. We hopped up into the cab and Bubba released the air brakes, shifted the rig into gear and eased it back onto the highway, gathering speed with every shift. There wasn't any chatter on the CB and we both drove on in silence, digesting our food.

Soon the state line came into view and as we crossed over into Louisiana I realized that I had made it out of Texas. The tire noise got louder as we rolled along the poorly maintained asphalt. Apparently the State of Louisiana had a leaner budget than Texas.

"So Brett, I've just got one more question and then maybe I'll let the subject pass, alright?"

"I guess that would be okay," I said.

"Did they have many of them niggers back at your high school? I hear schools out west are pretty well integrated these days." He had a distasteful look on his face when he said this.

"You mean black kids?" I answered deliberately. "Yeah, we had maybe a couple dozen at my school. Some were on my track team and they happened to be my friends."

"I bet they were fast though, right? You know all them young niggers are fast." He stared off ahead, nodding to himself. "Yeah that's a fact. But pretty soon they get fat and slow, because they're too damn lazy and don't want to do no work that's what.

"So tell me something, Brett, do any of them nigger families live nearby you?" It was technically another question.

"Not too many of them, actually. There is one black family living a couple of blocks north of me, though. Their oldest son Earl played on our football team. His father is a preacher in the town next to ours, but he didn't want his son to grow up over there because they had too many gangs, so he moved his family into my neighborhood so that Earl could go to my high school."

"Yeah, I'll bet he did. Wanted to get his boy a white education I'll bet, yes sir."

"Bubba, you know, I'm not real comfortable with this subject. Would it be okay if we talked about something else?"

We drove on for a couple of minutes while I waited for his reply. Bubba flexed his fingers around the steering wheel, gripping it and nodding with determination. "Tell you what," he said. "Why don't we take a little detour south of Interstate 20 and I'll show you how them niggers live." This was not a question either. "We'll take Highway 71 south from Shreveport and follow Route 4 through some of them towns where segregation lives on, my friend. Then we'll head back up to I-20 at Monroe and I'll still be able to get you to Vicksburg Mississippi by supper time. That'll be my last stop for the day and then you'll be on your own."

"I'd really rather stay on I-20 if that's okay with you," I said in an even voice, attempting to sound contrite and positive.

"Hell no! I bought you your lunch so now you're going to ride with me through some of the poorest nigger towns in the south, and that's that. It's time for some Dixie education, boy. Ain't that what you said you came out this way for?"

"Uh, not exactly," I said. "Look, I don't mean any disrespect, but could you please pull over and let me off?"

Bubba's answer was to stomp down on the gas pedal and accelerate the tractor-trailer up to 75 mph. We rolled through Shreveport and then cut down Highway 71 before I could protest. After about twenty miles, we turned onto Route 4 and headed east through a series of towns called Ringgold, Castor, Lucky and Friendship. There wasn't much in them to describe really, just a few small buildings lining the highway to verify what the city limit signs had told us was correct. Sometimes I could see a few houses down side roads near the "center of town". They appeared to be well cared for and all the lawns had been freshly mowed. These towns all looked pretty quiet. I guessed this was the way people liked it.

Just as I was getting used to the monotony, Bubba turned off at a gravel road that would take us to a place where the "niggers" lived, according to Bubba. He slowly navigated the rig down a dirt road that ran along the creek. There were tiny clapboard shacks in desperate need of paint with porches sagging this way and that. Barefoot black children ran along beside us, curious why a trailer truck carrying brand new speed boats was driving past their way.

"Look at all them kids, got no shoes, dirty clothes that probably haven't been washed in weeks."

I rolled down the window and waved out to them. The kids smiled up at me and I smiled back. There were old cars parked randomly in the front yards, or correctly weed-strewn fields. Some of them happened to be Cadillacs that were well past their prime. Most were up on concrete blocks without tires, their hoods opened skyward. There was also a lot of junk outside these shacks as well, even old kitchen appliances that looked like they would never be fixed.

"Shit stops working, they just haul it outside to rust, don't care," Bubba sad, setting his jaw in disgust.

Clotheslines were draped hither and yon with badly worn clothing hanging out there to dry in the humid afternoon heat. I must have shrugged my shoulders because Bubba was nodding and smiling. He probably thought I was starting to get it.

"Now you see what I mean. That's how them niggers live here in the south," he nodded definitively. "Look at all that junk and trash scattered everywhere, not a garden or watered lawn in sight. Now you know why we don't allow them niggers into our nice white neighborhoods. It's because they live like animals," he said while making a downward motion with his thumb.

I was feeling a bit rattled if not downright uncomfortable, but thankfully Bubba crossed over the railroad tracks at an asphalt-covered road that he said would join up again with Route 4, which it did. We were back on the road to my relief.

I was hoping Bubba's lessons in economical segregation were done now, but that would not to be the case. My "education" would unfortunately continue as we made our way through several more of these small towns.

It got increasingly difficult for me to sit there and listen to his ranting on and on. I couldn't comprehend this intolerance that he exemplified and even seemed proud of. There wasn't any justifiable reason to condemn these people as far as I was concerned, but I was careful not to comment on that, which caused me great internal stress. They just happened to have the misfortune of being poor, that's all. Jobs weren't plentiful down here in the south for people of color. They fished in the creeks so they wouldn't starve. I sat there and took it, not at all proud of myself for keeping my mouth shut but more preoccupied with my own safety.

When we got to Jonesboro we turned north onto Highway 167 and made our way back to Interstate 20 via Ruston, about 35 miles west of Monroe. Apparently Bubba had decided that he'd made his point. He was probably also thinking about getting home for dinner. Our little side trips through Louisiana had consumed a good two hours of road time according to my watch, which now read a little past 5 pm. We were now rolling back down Interstate 20 and maintaining a steady 70 mph.

As we made our way through the remainder of Louisiana, Bubba settled into his ritual and got back on the CB, almost as like he had forgotten I was still there with him. With a sense of relief I nodded off.

When Louisiana ran out of road the rig bounced over a rough patch of highway and I woke abruptly. We were crossing over the Mississippi River. Shortly after that Bubba pulled off at a road sign for the Vicksburg City Limits. He seemed to be about as done with me as I was with him when he pulled over. I would soon be free again.

"Well I hope you enjoyed your southern education, boy," he said.

"Uh, it was interesting, to be sure. I guess you gave me a lot to think about." I nodded, attempting to appear enlightened as though he had done me a favor.

"Yeah, well I hope so," he said. I reached for the passenger door but he motioned with an outstretched palm for me to hold on a second. "I showed you all them things back there in Louisiana because I wanted you to understand something, boy. Respectable white folks got to take a stand, you understand what I'm saying to you?" I didn't.

He narrowed his eyes, deciding whether or not he should continue. Finally he asked "ever hear of the Ku Klux Klan, boy?"

"Uh, yes, I think so," I said, quite anxious to get out of the cab.

"Well I'm the Grand Wizard of the Vicksburg Mississippi chapter. But don't you never tell that to nobody, you hear?"

"I wouldn't dream of it mister, you can count on me for that," I replied in a hesitant voice but meaning every word of it.

His face softened just a little. "Anyway, I thought you might as well know who bought you that lunch back there. So now you can go and have a good day out there," he said, motioning that it was now okay for me to go. I grabbed my backpack from behind the seat and climbed down from the cab, setting my feet on solid ground again and feeling grateful for my new found freedom.

"Y'all take care now," he said as I stepped away from the truck clutching my pack.

"Thanks, you too," I shouted up to the cab. Bubba tooted the horn after shifting into second gear. I was glad to see him go.

I caught a short ride to Jackson where the driver let me off at a fork in the road with a sign pointing down to Highway 49. I stood there at the junction and studied my map. It would take me southeast through Mississippi down toward Hattiesburg, which was where I figured I'd spend the night. I wondered whether I could make it that far before it got dark, not wanting to repeat the foolhardy chance I had taken outside of El Paso.

A jacked up yellow muscle car pulled over. It looked like it had been driven pretty hard, with an Alabama license plate and a Dixie flag decal that was stuck on the rear window. A longhaired kid about my age glared out at me as I approached, apparently deciding whether or not I would be a worthy passenger. I wondered why he had stopped to begin with. The car was littered with trash, half-eaten hamburgers, wrappers, and crushed beer cans. And there were lots of unopened bags of chips, Ho-Hos and Twinkies piled up on the back seat that looked like they'd been snatched from a convenience store. He had a reckless kind of look that gave me pause, and I decided I wasn't going to accept a ride from another crazy person at this late hour in the day. Plus, the Alabama license plate suggested that he wasn't really headed my way anyhow. He probably just wanted my money if I had any.

"Where are you headed?" I asked, doubting whether the excitable rebel kid was really headed down Highway 49 as he seemed to imply.

"Where YOU headed?" he asked back mockingly, letting me know that I needed to go first.

"I'm heading down to Hattiesburg, got an uncle down there I want to visit," I lied, thinking that even if he was going my way, I had no desire to go any further with him than that.

"OK, well alright then. As it turns out I'm heading your way too. Maybe I can give you can ride. You got any money for gas?" It was clear now that he was trying to scam me.

"So about how far is it to Hattiesburg?" I asked to see if he knew.

"Oh, about a hundred fifty miles, give or take," he said, trying to appear convincing. "Yeah you head down through Hazlehurst and Brookhaven and it's the next town after that, you know."

I thought about it for a minute, glancing about while stupidly hoping that another car might stop and give me a second option. Hattiesburg was only 70 miles away according to my map. And Hazlehurst and Brookhaven were down Highway 51, not Highway 49. I was glad I had studied the map before, realizing with a fair certainty that this kid was reciting something from memory about a trip he might have taken once down to New Orleans. He wasn't heading down to Hattiesburg, but he obviously did want to take my money and rebel boy here wasn't safe. I decided to take a pass.

"Sorry, man," I said. "I've changed my mind, it's getting late, you know? So, I think I'll just hike on back into Jackson and find a place to spend the night."

"Suit yourself," he said. Then he rolled the window up, gunned the engine and laid some rubber, screeching away in the direction of Alabama just as I had expected, not at all down Highway 49 like he said.

I decided to hike a ways down Highway 49 before I stuck my thumb back out, wanting to make sure the next car that pulled over would actually be heading my way. This became a new rule for the rest of the trip, never hitch at a fork in the road.

After a couple miles of this I felt calmer and more focused. The sun was low on the horizon now and I could feel the heat dissipating out of the asphalt. Pretty soon a cool breeze would return. Cars sped by every once in a while but I didn't mind hiking along the highway just then, enjoying my freedom.

Then a black Cadillac Seville slowed down and pulled over. When I walked up the passenger window lowered electronically.

"Y'all need a ride, honey?" a black woman called out to me in a strong southern accent. Other women had called me honey but this one seemed like she meant it. She wore a burgundy evening dress and the black man sitting behind the wheel was wearing a charcoal gray suit with a blue satin tie. I recalled the dilapidated Cadillac cars I'd seen up on blocks, out in front of those shanties back in Louisiana, but then shrugged it off and decided to get in. This would be my last ride of the day I decided, sensing that my luck would probably run out sooner or later.

"Yes I'd appreciate it, if you wouldn't mind," I smiled back.

"Well hop in back, sugar", she said. I opened the rear passenger door, hefted my backpack over to the opposite side of the leather seat and climbed in after it, securing the seatbelt.

"We're heading down to Hattiesburg," she said after we motored back onto the highway. "You think that'd be alright with you? Y'all got no business being out here on the open road here after it gets dark." I had finally found some luck.

"Hmmm," the mister nodded with a deliberate driving posture, apparently not much of a talker.

"Sure, I was planning to spend the night there anyway," I said.

As we drove on without talking, I collected my thoughts together from the day's events. It had been an eclectic day to be sure. I looked out the window and watched the sun flashing between the pine trees until it eventually set below them.

Frankly I was grateful for the quiet, and the air-conditioned Caddie lifted my spirit. I breathed in and out and thought about Bubba back there in Vicksburg, probably home by now barking at his wife over the dinner table. He was wrong about these people I knew. You really can't judge a book by its cover. I had heard that many times. It applied especially to people of color down here in the South.

The Cadillac pulled over smoothly to the side of the road right after we had passed the Hattiesburg City Limits sign. The woman turned around and studied me again.

"Here we are, sugar. Now my husband and I are going to have us some dinner and spend the night down here at my sister's place. You should be able to find yourself a motel or something downtown. Just keep on walking on down that a way." There was no invitation to join them and I didn't mind.

I opened the passenger door, grabbed my backpack and stepped out onto spongy clay that had gotten a sprinkling of rain earlier that day. My hiking boots sunk in as I hefted the pack onto my shoulders. "Thanks, thank you very much," I said, giving them an earnest wave. "You've both been very kind and I really appreciate it." I hoped that I wasn't overdoing it since they simply nodded in return, but I really was grateful for this kind turn of events which took me down to Hattiesburg just as I had planned. My skin was cooler now from having ridden in their air-conditioned Cadillac, and their peaceful demeanor had apparently rubbed off on me. Those two had really brightened my mood, I realized. I gently shut the door and they drove away slowly, making a right turn about a mile down the road after they had reached the center of town. I hoped they would enjoy their dinner.

I thought about finding a motel and considered how much money I could spare, estimating the amount of cash I had left stashed inside my pack. I had spent about thirty-five dollars so far from the two hundred I had started with. Not too bad for three days and close to two thousand miles of travel. Only a few hundred yards separated me from the first cluster of buildings, small businesses and shops. There was a Waffle House restaurant, a tall rectangular building to the right of the highway, but it was closed for the evening. And there was a gas station directly opposite the restaurant, standing on a huge lot of pine trees. It looked like an oasis to me at the time. The sunset to my right was a brilliant array of colors diffracting through nimbus clouds that were dog piled on top of each other above the horizon. Crickets responded to the cooler air and began their evening courtship. So did a large number of cicadas perched up in the trees.

Glancing up and down the highway, I couldn't see any traffic so I jogged over to the other side to ask the gas station attendant for directions. He must have seen me coming and met me by the gas pumps as I approached. An embroidered label over his shirt pocket said his name was 'Jim' and he was happy to serve me.

"Folks around here don't take too kindly to hippies such as yourself, no offense. Y'all just passing through, I hope?" I fingered my hair nervously while considering what to say to that. I was in the south now but I was no longer afraid, having survived much worse than this man seemed capable of. I was feeling connected to my new surroundings for some reason, like I was beginning to belong here somehow.

"Nice sunset isn't it?" was my final answer. Jim's eyes relaxed and there was a hint of a smile.

In an effort to appear more presentable I pulled my hair back over my ears so it would be out of my face. "Most kids wear their hair like this where I live," I said. "I'm no hippie mister, just passing through on my way to Florida," I tried to look sincere. "But I could really use a place to stay the night." I extended my hand and gave him a shake with a tentative smile. He gripped it and shook slowly, making sure that I maintained eye contact which I did. Thus satisfied, he let go and stood back.

"Well even so, I really don't think that Sally down there at the hotel would be inclined to take you in 'bout now." He thought for a minute. "Tell me about yourself, where you from?"

"Southern California."

"Thought so," he seemed to have expected that. "Boys out here wear their hair cut short like a man, no offense, except maybe them kids who don't got no jobs. Can't afford to cut it I guess, but they's mostly rabble rousers and troublemakers that bunch, always blasting music way too loud out of them beat up old pickup trucks when they pass by this here gas station, like they don't care." Having completed his rant, he shoved his hands into his pockets and leaned against a fuel pump. Apparently he was still sizing me up. "Out here, if you want to get a job you get a haircut. It's just that simple."

"Well, I worked at a movie theatre back in California until I finished high school a couple weeks ago. That's how I managed to save up the money for this trip," I said, wanting him to know that I was no freeloader. I thought about the time I had spent working at the theatre, standing there at the ticket counter tearing ticket stubs for hours on end, with stiff legs and sore feet. It was kind of a fun experience most of the time, or at least it seemed that way in hindsight. I made some good friendships with other kids who worked there, and got to have free popcorn and soda any time I wanted, with plenty of time to finish my homework at the front desk during the 'late man' shift after the snack bar closed. "We took turns ushering and watched those movies so many times that we could easily identify almost every one of them from a single line of dialogue, a game that we played at parties after work. I must have watched *The Sound of Music* over forty times, often twice nightly."

"That's one of my favorite movies," Jim smiled. He was warming up to me.

Dusk was settling in and wisps of a cooling breeze flew by as we stood there next to the gas pumps. He was fiddling with the keys inside his pocket, getting ready to lock down for the night.

"You seem like an okay kid, I guess," he said at last. "Tell you what, why don't you just bed down out back for the night. There's nothing but forest behind the station so nobody will bother you. And I'll leave the bathroom door unlocked so's you can wash up later."

"Yeah that would be really kind," I said without hesitation, happy that I would save what a motel room would probably cost around here, about seven bucks I figured. I could use that money to buy a full breakfast at the Waffle House the next morning. It felt like this was supposed to happen, probably why I got let off up the road back there.

Jim walked over to the office and returned with a handful of padlocks that he used to lock up the pumps. He whistled a southern blues tune while he worked. Then he returned to the office and switched off the power, causing the street sign out front to flicker off. I could hear his keys jangle as he locked the office door. When he returned, I saw that he was cradling a canvas pouch like a football. The stars were coming out and the moon was rising; now beginning to wane but still plenty bright.

"I've got to take this here bag to the night deposit box at the bank down the street; he gestured down to the pouch. "But I left the door to the men's restroom unlocked for you like I said. I'd appreciate it though if you'd lock it after you're done."

"Yeah, thanks." It was all I could think of to say.

We stood there on the oil stained concrete, breathing in and out with our feet firmly planted on the earth while crickets chirped and cicadas whined in the evening air. A barrier between us had evaporated and a peaceful silence now surrounded us.

"Well, it's about time I got on home to the wife and sat down to dinner," Jim said. "You got anything to eat in that pack of yours?"

"Yeah, I've got a bit of food that should tide me over until morning, and I'll probably use the money I'll save on that motel room to buy some breakfast over at the Waffle House tomorrow," I pointed with a smile that he probably couldn't see.

"Well good then. Okay, I guess you'll be all right." He stood there in another silent state for a minute or so before speaking again. I waited.

"There's something I'd like to know if you don't mind," he said, breaking the peaceful silence that surrounded us. "I'm guessing you missed Viet Nam."

"Yeah, I still got the draft card in my wallet though. It has a pretty low lottery number on it… but fortunately the war ended before my number came up."

He laughed at that. "Lucky thing for you the war did end, my friend. Guess you probably would have been drafted for sure if it hadn't."

"Yeah, I know. I wasn't quite sure what I would have done." I said, having decided to confide in him. "My father was a fighter pilot in Korea and Viet Nam. I guess I didn't get much time to know him growing up. And his father, my grandfather, flew for the Air Corps in World War I, and his older brother, my uncle, flew for the Air Force in World War II. So I guess we've been a family of fighter pilots, up until me anyway." I was getting used to telling this story, having encountered a number of Vietnam War vets on this trip.

"He persuaded a general and a congressman to write recommendations for me at the Air Force Academy," I continued. "But since I'm nearsighted and color blind, I knew there was no way they'd let me fly. So I decided that there wouldn't be much point to going there." I waited for it to sink in, mainly for my own benefit. My father would have been proud of me had I applied to the academy like he wanted, but I knew it was not for me. The war had not been popular from the perspective of my generation. "Most kids my age thought it was a colossal waste, but I guess I'll have to wait until I'm older to see if we were right," I said at last. It was strange how this trip across the country had caused me confront these feelings.

"Anyway I did manage to miss the draft so now I'm standing here talking to you while hitching a ride to Florida, with a nice scholarship at a college back in California next fall. It's just how things worked out for me I guess."

I paused to give me time to reflect some more. "But I guess if I had been drafted, I probably would have gone off to 'Nam." Somehow I felt like adding that comment again. "It just didn't happen."

"Yeah, well then..." Jim looked at me now with a hint of camaraderie... if that were possible.

"I got drafted to Korea, but the doctor said I was 4-F, bum knee injury from high school football. Wound up serving my time stateside at Quantico, mostly desk jobs." Again there was a pause while that thought settled in.

"My son went off to 'Nam though. He was a corpsman and had to attend to a lot of badly injured kids over there, many of them didn't make it," he said. "I didn't hear much from him when he was over there, just a few of hastily written notes to let me know he was okay. That was about it.

"When he got back home, I could tell that his spirit was troubled. He'd spend all day in his room listening to a big expensive stereo system that he had bought over in Japan before shipping home to the States. When his former high school buddies came by he didn't want to talk to them, just stayed up in his room. Came down for breakfast and dinner and said very little to me and the wife. I guess it was pretty tough on all of us. He finally left about ten months ago to go work at a salmon processing plant up in Alaska. Haven't heard anything from him since."

We stood there and let the moment pass. Jim drew a breath and let out an almost inaudible sigh.

"Good thing you didn't go," he said at last.

"Yeah, I guess so," letting the silence that followed speak for itself.

"Well like I said, it's time for me to get on home to the wife for dinner." As he said this, he started walking over to the tow truck parked next to the office, signaling the end of our discussion.

"Hey thanks so much for letting me stay here tonight," I shouted over to him.

"Don't mention it," he shouted back. Then he climbed up into the cab, gently shut the door, fired up the engine, and wheeled the tow truck out of the parking lot, accelerating down the road in the direction of town.

CHAPTER NINE

I STOOD THERE GRASPING THE ALUMINUM RAIL OF MY PACK with the other hand resting against a fuel pump. It felt cool against my palm. The faded blue work shirt that had been sticking to my skin all day was no longer damp with sweat, and now it was cool and dry, flapping gently in the evening breeze. Bill's tow truck slowly faded from view as he motored down the road into dusk. A high pitched rumble resumed as male cicadas instinctively sought their mates. I wished them luck.

It had been a motion picture day of changing perspectives, places and people, conversations that had stretched my mind as I listened and responded in ways that I hoped would encourage the drivers to keep me along for the ride. I understood that I was just someone to talk to while the miles passed along. I inhaled again and let it out. It was time to think about getting some sleep.

Shouldering my pack, I hiked behind the gas station to a grassy clearing bordered by a dense forest of scotch pine. Locating a suitably flat area to bed down for the night, the blades of grass were now wet with dew beneath my feet, I took off my pack and leaned it against a tree, unhitched the straps that held my plastic ground cloth which I laid out on top of the wet grass, then my foam pad and sleeping bag. Reaching into the top of my pack, I removed a sweatshirt and rolled it up to use as a pillow. Satisfied, I rummaged around inside my pack to retrieve a toilet kit and towel. With the towel draped over my shoulder, I walked back to the side of the station and felt for the door to the men's restroom, the one that Jim had promised to leave unlocked for me. Finding the latch and turning it, the metal door opened inward with a rusty squeak. I felt around for the light switch and squinted until my pupils had adjusted to the light coming from a flickering neon tube overhead. Then I washed up and locked the door like I had promised Jim that I would. It wouldn't be until two days later when I noticed that my towel was missing. I had left it hanging over the toilet stall.

I could hardly make out my rolled out sleeping bag when I walked back across the clearing, hoping it was still there. The wet grass soaked through the knees of my jeans as I rummaged around in my pack to find the plastic baggie, deciding to light another pre-rolled joint to help me unwind. I draped my jeans over my pack, hoping they would be dry by morning, then shimmied into my bag and gazed up once again into the evening sky. After a few hits I stubbed out the joint and replaced it in the baggie when it had cooled. Now the day was finally over.

I inhaled deeply and slowly rocked my shoulders back and forth to get the wet ground to conform to my body. This was a lot more comfortable than the hard kitchen floor I had slept on back in Phoenix. My body relaxed and surrendered to gravity. The cicadas gradually ceased their high frequency chattering as the temperature cooled. Tomorrow would be another day for them, as it would for me.

While studying another dazzling display of stars, as I had done at the KOA campground outside El Paso, I reckoned back to a field trip I had gone on with my junior high science class. It was to a planetarium where we were supposed to learn about galaxies. A short, balding and bespectacled man used a black globe to project the "stars" on a dome ceiling above us. The globe had thousands of tiny pipe lenses poking out from the surface, some were wider and projected larger beams, appearing as closer stars, and some were very tiny for projecting far away orbs. I had pondered the potential reality that other solar systems like ours might be out there, somewhere out in space. But because of the urban background light and smog that usually permeated the Southern California skies, I had seldom had the opportunity to see stars like this. Out here under the Mississippi sky, they dazzled above me once again. I took another breath and let it out slowly.

I studied a faint cluster of stars and imagined them coming from a distant galaxy. I thought about planets orbiting and spinning out there beyond the edge of human knowledge, soaking up the rays from their respective suns, fueling pools of biotic chemistries that were evolving, replicating, and improving in complexity. So much of God's creation was still unknown to us, yet I knew it was all God's creation nonetheless. I closed my eyes.

An imaginary episode from Star Trek ensued as I faded into REM sleep. Captain Kirk was beamed onto one of those planets that hid behind that smudge of a galaxy I had seen earlier up in the sky. It was a desert landscape with distinctive cactus trees much like the ones I had seen in a Joshua Tree National Monument. As Kirk crouched and rotated around, his phaser extended to ward off danger, we both spied human like beings scrambling behind the rocks, peering out at Kirk and warbling amongst themselves in a sing-song like language that sounded like a mixture of Arabic and Chinese. When I thought about them some more, I realized that they were all female, and surprisingly beautiful in subliminal ways. Kirk must have noticed this too because he lowered his phaser and approached them. Somehow Kirk got all the extraterrestrial chicks...

When I awoke, my bag was covered in thick morning dew. The sun had only recently creased the horizon, and I could hear a car rolling down the highway every few seconds. The citizens of Hattiesburg were now waking up and heading to work. I wanted to get going before Jim came back to open the station, and wasn't really feeling up to talking to anyone just then anyway, so I rolled up my bag and quickly changed into my clothes, unfortunately still moist with dew. Pulling out my water bottle from the side pouch, I splashed a bit of it on my face and took a big swig. Then, willing myself to get on with my day, I cinched up my pack and hiked back to the road.

I was relieved to see that the Waffle House was still there on the other side of the highway, no longer a figment of my imagination but a real place now, and it was open for breakfast. As I crossed the road I was drawn to the smell of bacon. Upon reaching the entrance door, I leaned my backpack against the front picture window so I could watch it from inside the restaurant, opened the door and found a stool at the counter. Within seconds a steaming cup of coffee slid in front of me, apparently I would be welcome sitting there amongst the other patrons at the counter. I added some cream and sugar and took a tentative sip, but it burned my lips so I waited for it to cool. I flipped open a plastic menu and saw that the special of the day was a plate of waffles, two eggs any way (I chose over easy again), with two slices of bacon and two links of sausage. I was ravenously hungry and could hardly wait for the plate to arrive in front of me. I realized that I hadn't eaten much since the afternoon before.

The food was delicious and I enjoyed it with grateful swallows. Unwilling to spend an extra quarter on orange juice, I washed it all down with ice water until my coffee had cooled enough to drink. I wondered whether the indigenous tribes in South America who had invented this caffeinated beverage would believe how popular their drink had become.

"Y'all want some more coffee, sugar?" The waitress caught my attention from behind the counter. She wore a tired smile on a face that looked like it had seen better days and this was probably not going to be one of them.

"Uh, oh hello ma'am," I said, trying to sound polite. "I guess I was pretty hungry." Looking around, I saw that I didn't exactly blend in amongst the southern boys straddling their stools at the counter, wearing their John Deere caps and munching on hominy grits with biscuits and gravy. She must have noticed this because her eyes glanced sideways, back at me, and then narrowed sagely as she nodded.

"Yes, sugar, I guess you were. I saw your pack outside. Where you headed?" The nametag on her uniform said "Lorna". I smiled at her and she smiled back, with a little more energy this time which made me feel better.

"Well Lorna, if you don't mind my calling you that…"

"That's my name sugar," she said. My name wasn't sugar but I decided to let it go.

"Well, believe it or not I've been hitching rides from Southern California; I started out a few days ago. My plan is to make it to Florida to see a about a girl I met out there last summer."

"I see..." she said with more sympathetic eyes. Young love quests were universal I reckoned. She nodded.

"Well?"

"Well what?"

"You want some more coffee or not?" she said with a chuckle, and this time her smile was genuine.

"No, no, that's alright. I think it's time for me to get going anyway, it could be a long day, you know?" I pulled a couple of dollars from my back pocket and laid them on the counter, estimating the bill to be about a dollar sixty with the coffee. Lorna could keep the change. She was okay.

"Thanks very much for breakfast," I said. "It was delicious."

"So I saw," she laughed.

I nodded and laughed too, standing up slowly and patting my full belly. "Well Lorna, I apologize for being so quick with my food. If I ever drive back through here I'll stop by for another bite."

"We'll probably manage to get more food by then," she teased. "You have a good day now, sugar. And watch who you accept them rides from, you hear? Some of the folks out here aren't none too kind to fellers who wear their hair long like that."

"I surely will," I said, thinking back to the repo man who had been jacked up on speed back in Texas, the crazy Grand Wizard of the Ku Klux Klan who I had regrettably accepted a ride from through Louisiana, and the larcenous teen from Alabama who I had wisely refused to ride with yesterday. I wondered whether the Alabama kid had knocked off another convenience store by now. The other two guys, I didn't even want to think about what they were up to.

I felt another familiar blast of heat and humidity as I stepped outside to get my pack. It was going to be a hot and sultry day, probably with another rain storm by late afternoon. I shouldered my pack and hiked through town, wanting to get back to the open highway before hitching my next ride. This gave me a chance to stretch my legs and digest the food which was churning away in my happy stomach. The sun beat down while I made my way through the center of town. Most of these buildings were clad in red brick and white washed clapboards and looked like they had been built around the 1930s. After passing a small drug store, barber shop, clothing store, and a multi-story hardware store at the corner, I reached the town's only traffic light. There was the town square on the opposite corner with old men sitting at a picnic table paying checkers; it was shaded by a large oak tree that told me that they would probably be there for a while.

A granite obelisk rose up in the center of the square. The traffic light was still red so I waited as several old sedans and a 1930's era Ford pickup truck rumbled through in opposite directions. When the light turned green, I strode across the intersection and glanced again at the obelisk. I could see now that it was a World War II monument with a bronze plaque at the bottom listing the boys from Hattiesburg who had been killed in that war. It was too soon to erect a monument for the Vietnam War, and I wondered whether anyone ever would. Folks around the country were still trying to forget about it.

Continuing on, I passed the downtown movie theatre, a Woolworth's, a few other small shops, and then another coffee shop at the opposite end of town. After passing the last of these modest downtown buildings, I followed the road out of town. After another ten minutes of hiking, I decided that it was safe again to stick out my thumb.

I stood there, casually rocking back and forth on the balls of my feet while trying not to appear desperate or edgy. Drivers can read that like a dog picks up on fear. It's important to stay alert and yet you've got to appear relaxed and ready. Someone could be getting bored with driving alone, and they might just see you at that instant and decide to pull over. You wanted to be that guy.

As if almost on cue, a man in a faded powder blue Ford Fairlane pulled over and motioned for me to get in. It looked like a 1963 or '64 model by the fins on the rear. A buddy of mine from high school had bought one of those, jacked it up with racing tires, and got mufflers from Hooker Headers to make it sound tough. I remembered him peeling rubber out of the high school parking lot after school let out; it seemed like a long time ago. But this particular Fairlane was strictly stock and it smelled like it needed an oil change.

"Where you headed?" the man called out. I stepped up and studied him through the rolled down passenger window. He wore a cheap tan business suit with a black polka dot tie that was loose at the collar, and appeared to be in his late thirties. His hair was greased back, probably an Elvis fan I decided. 'Elvis' had the kind of smile that could be highly effective for a man selling women's shoes.

I wasn't sure whether my character judgment was valid down here in the south, thinking back on my last two rides from the previous day. But he did seem harmless enough after studying him some more. I decided to trust him, knowing the next guy might be a Dixie loving redneck.

"I'm just heading down to the Gulf Coast today," I ventured, thinking I could probably manage to listen to this guy for about that far.

"Well now ain't that just the thing. I happen to be driving on down to Gulfport myself!"

The passenger door finally yielded after a few tugs with a loud squeak. 'Elvis' motioned for me to put my pack in back and said "Hop on in!" The vinyl bench seat was badly worn and springs were protruding in various places, which required me to shift around until I could find a tolerable place to sit. 'Elvis' waited patiently, but as soon as I had settled in, he focused his eyes keenly ahead and tromped his foot down on the accelerator, rocketing the old Fairlane up to seventy mph and leaving Hattiesburg far behind.

This time I chose to speak first when we had gotten underway, hoping I might be able to control the conversation somewhat. "I'm actually hitching to Florida to see about a girl, but I've never been down along the gulf coast, so I figured I'd head down that way today."

"Going to see one of them Florida cuties, huh? Yeah buddy I can sure understand that! Got a few girlfriends myself, matter of fact. I just got laid back there in Jackson and now I'm headed down to Gulfport to see my ex-wife. We're still on a bit more than speaking terms, if you know what I mean?

"But whoo-ee, what a wild sex ride that girl back there was, I can tell you what. I met her couple of months ago when I was traveling through Jackson on business, a waitress behind the counter of one of them diners that I just happened to waltz in to. Thought she was real pretty so I flirted with her some, and the next thing I know she tells me her shift is just up and would I like to take a spin in the hay at her place? Well of course I did, again and again as it happened. Dianne, she said her name was, what a woman! I've never met another lady with that kind of energy and imagination."

"So now I stop by Jackson about a couple times a month, and every time I've found myself in the horizontal Olympics with lovely Dianne, hardly ever get any sleep when I'm there with her, you know? It's all lovemaking and very little conversation, just the way I like it. Anyway, last night she started asking me why don't I just move on up to Jackson to live with her? I tried to explain that I need to travel around with my job and all. Couldn't really settle down like that just then. She would have none of that, no sir. Said if I didn't say I'd love her forever she'd toss me out on my keester and I wouldn't get any that night or ever again. Well of course I decided to say whatever she wanted to hear after that. Our lovemaking last night was particularly energetic and really 'hit the spot', you know? But then once she dozed off I pulled my clothes back on and snuck on out of there. That's why I'm up and at 'em so early in the morning, by the way."

"Well, I'm glad you decided to give me a ride," I said, not knowing what else to say. I had been determined to control the conversation but found that impossible with 'Elvis' here, he had a mouth that just wouldn't stop running.

"Yeah, it's good to be on the road again, and you're welcome. I didn't have time to take a shower this morning though, just buttoned up yesterday's shirt and tie, slicked back my hair, and got on out of there, you know? Sorry if I smell some. That breeze feels good though. Hey, you want to stop and get a beer? We can get it to go."

"Um, sure I guess." A cold beer seemed like just the thing to help me deal with 'Elvis' if I was to keep riding with him. Plus I figured he would probably stink more as the morning dragged on, even with the windows rolled down. Body odor was something that I carefully avoided myself, knowing that it could get me booted from a ride at any moment, which is why I tried to take advantage of every shower and restroom sink that I could find along the way. It was no fun being let out on the open highway in the middle of nowhere. Yes, a cold beer would make this ride seem more bearable, even though it was still a bit early in the morning. My formerly regimental rules about 'where and when' had blurred somewhat as I made my way across the country.

We pulled over at a cinder block bar that was surrounded by a sandy parking lot with palmettos scattered about. Several beat up old cars were already parked out there. 'Elvis' parked in between a dented Volkswagen bus and a rusted old panel truck, then shut off the engine and strutted inside. Sixty seconds later he bounded out the door with a couple of fourteen ounce cans of Old Milwaukee beer, each in its own paper bag. He handed one to me through the passenger window. The bag was already wet with condensation from the humid air.

"Keep your can in that paper bag so the smokies don't see it. It'll stay cold longer that way too," he said. With that, 'Elvis' rounded around to the driver's side and slammed the squeaky door shut as he climbed back in. He fired up the old Fairlane with a sputter and a rumble and we were ready to roll. The wheels spun in the sand a few times as we made our way back onto the highway and gathered speed. I took a sip and he did likewise, grinning.

"Now that's a good way to start the morning, don't you think?"

"I don't make a habit of it this early in the day, but yeah, it's not bad at all to be honest." The cool sudsy gulps enlivened me and I enjoyed the tickling sensation when carbonated burps rose back out my nose. I still had a slight headache from the night before, but it was easing by the second I found with relief and satisfaction. I was going to enjoy this ride, I decided. The windows were still down and it felt good to feel my hair buffeting in the wind. Something about the humid southern air, when it blows on your face it feels like a soft caress. I thought of the lyric from a Seals and Crofts song, "Summer Breeze…makes me feel fine," and took another gulp of beer. I figured I'd take the half full perspective about the beer even though the can was already more than half empty.

"So tell me about this girl of yours from Florida," 'Elvis' was obviously interested in whatever juicy details I had to offer. Unfortunately I had none at that point.

"There's not much to tell yet I guess. I'm not even all that sure that she's still my girl, if she ever was before, although she's been writing me letters over the past nine months while I was back in California finishing up my senior year of high school. I met her last summer while working for my father who lives in Florida. We went on five or six dates and then I had to fly home."

"So you had five or six dates with this girl and 'nothing much to tell', huh? Hell, I'd have dumped her after the second date if she wouldn't put out. Well, I guess now you're going out there again to get the rest of it, huh?"

"I'm not sure it's really like that, but I don't know, maybe," I said, not really knowing what I wanted. I imagined my hair all slicked back doing the 'horizontal Olympics' with Michelle. I remembered her playing ping pong with me on the back porch, slamming winners over the net in a bikini, how her thighs and shoulders flexed when she did that. She'd shout a "ha!" of triumph every time she scored a point. I didn't generally like to lose, but with Michelle I didn't mind at all.

"Yeah, I know," he said in a mocking tone, grinning at me with a sideways glance as he took a gulp, then tilted his head to finish the last of the swallow and tossed the empty can over his shoulder onto the back seat. "But just you wait. It's going to make you crazy someday, just like me!" he slapped his thigh and laughed.

"Anyway, I've got this ex-wife down there in Gulfport and now it's her turn for some of my attention. She's not the kind to keep me up all night, just so you know, but quite honestly I could use the sleep anyway."

"So how do you meet all these women?" I asked, genuinely interested.

"Oh, it's quite simple really. You've just got to be a good listener and make them feel like they're the most interesting woman you've ever met, just like that," he said, snapping his fingers. It did sound simple coming from him. I pondered this for a while, noticing that my beer was gone so I tossed it in back with the other empties.

The speedometer in front of 'Elvis' now read 80 mph, which seemed a bit too fast for this winding two lane highway as far as I was concerned. I felt my stomach flutter with every rise and dip. Thankfully he stopped talking and decided to focus on the road as this was happening.

Elvis barreled down Old Highway 49 like a man on a mission, which I guessed he probably was. We passed by an old auto repair garage with a lot of hubcaps nailed up on the walls outside. They brightly reflected the sun's rays as we sped by.

He didn't seem to think that the little Dixie town of McLaurin was worth slowing down for. It came and went before I could absorb it, and when it was gone I decided that the local patrolman must still be having his breakfast.

We entered the town of Brooklyn and drove past a red brick police station with dirty squad cars parked out in front. Elvis had fortunately been savvy enough to slow down for that. We passed through Main Street and I glanced in both directions, trying to figure out why it was called that. There weren't very many buildings to notice. We crossed over the creek and the town was soon a forgotten memory.

Next came Wiggins with enough buildings to actually look like a business district near the center of town. People strolled slowly down the sidewalks like they had all day, which was probably the case.

There weren't any shopping malls or urban areas down in this part of Mississippi. But the buildings in town were well maintained and all of the common areas had been carefully groomed. People lived in a structured balance with everything in its proper place. Change must happen slowly around here.

As we continued onward we passed through dense stretches of Scotch pine forest that darkened the sky and ran on for miles. The sun made strobe light flashes through the tree tops as we drove through them. I shut my eyes and enjoyed the rapidly blinking flashes and shadows as they played off my eyelids.

When we left the forest I squinted until my eyes could readjust to the bright sunlight. It seemed like there was a lot more glare out here in the South, probably because of the humidity. Just as I was thinking about the Gulf Coast and open water, a sign appeared announcing that Gulfport was 5 miles ahead. We crossed under Interstate 10 and made our way down toward U.S. 90 headed east, which I knew ran along the edge of the Gulf according to my map.

We were approaching a vast expanse of blue open water. When we finally reached U.S. 90 Elvis pulled into a motel parking lot and shut off the engine. "She'll be waiting there for me in Room Number 6," he said nodding in that direction. "You're welcome to come inside and join us if you like," he laughed. For a second I thought he might be serious, but then felt relief once I realized that he was just teasing me. I opened the passenger door and reached around to grab my backpack, then stepped out into the humid sunlight. Elvis leaned over and studied me with his arm resting on the seat back.

"Well, you make sure you have a good time out there in Florida, you hear? Especially with that girl you seem hell bent on seeing again," he said. That sounded like pretty good advice as I thought about it. I was ready to catch another ride.

"Hey, I never got your name," I said as I slid my arms through the shoulder straps and shifted the pack into a comfortable position against my spine.

"Nope, you never did," he said. And then he got out of the car and walked over to Room Number 6. He rapped on the door and smiled back at me with a wave. That was my cue that I was dismissed, so I hiked back to the signpost. U.S. 90 East was the way to Florida, the way I was going. I unzipped the outer pouch of my pack and studied my map just to be sure.

I would be using the backside of my map from now on, the part which covered the Eastern United States. This was a significant milestone I thought to myself. I hoped that U.S. 90 would be a good road to hitch rides from. I decided to hike for a while, feeling the need to be alone with my thoughts.

CHAPTER TEN

THERE WAS A WHITE SANDY BEACH about a half mile up the road to my right, and the deep azure water of the Gulf of Mexico extended out to the horizon. The sun glinted off the water in millions of tiny fractals. I cinched up my hip belt to distribute the weight and settled in for a nice hike. It felt good to be accountable only to myself again.

This old pack had been my good friend. I bought it with my own money during my second year of Boy Scouts, hard earned from mowing lawns over an entire summer. It was my companion on lots of hiking and camping trips with my troop. I had especially enjoyed our week long adventures through the southern Sierras. Those treks taught me to pack only what I needed, and to be confident and reliant on what I carried. My pack made creaking sounds as I strode alongside the highway.

I looked down at the footprints my boots had made in the sand and knew they would soon be erased by the Gulf breeze. The dunes to my right had pitches of grasses and sparsely set palmettos. There was a salty aroma of rotting seaweed that had washed ashore, now baking in the sun, and it was not entirely unpleasant. Tiny waves made a meek lapping sound as they reached the shore. They were nothing like the ones back in Southern California. And not a single surfer in sight I mused with a grin, taking another whiff of Gulf air.

Short wooden piers were distributed along the shoreline with tiny fishing boats tied up to them. To my left stood a row of grand looking southern homes with white pillared front porches and balconies. They were shaded by centuries old oak trees that reached out over the highway with their branches extending gracefully. Beards of Spanish moss dripped down from almost every branch, and the wind rustled musically through the leaves, a pleasing sound that I did not want to end. These southern plantation style homes were well groomed and appeared to have been freshly painted. They faced proudly out to the magnificent Gulf as though unafraid. I recalled from the evening news that hurricanes passed through here quite often, about every two or three years, so I knew that these homes were constantly being patched and restored. I hiked on.

Glancing over to my right, I saw an oil tanker steaming along in the direction of New Orleans, a city that I vowed to visit some other time. I didn't have the money to play tourist down on Bourbon Street, but maybe someday I told myself.

As this Gulf scenery moved slowly past, I thought about Michelle again. Maybe it was a preposterous idea to head all this way just to see her. I wasn't really sure just then. But my adventure had been real enough thus far, and that was enough for me. Every day had been a completely different experience. My pack kept on creaking as I strode along with it. Michelle had long, sandy brown hair that shimmered in the sun. I felt a warm glow in my chest and belly every time she smiled at me, and with each catching breath I'd want to let it out slowly to savor the moment. Yeah, I wanted to see her.

After about five miles of this, a dark bronze Ford Capri pulled over just ahead. It was a shiny gold metallic 3.0 GXL with a white vinyl top, the first one I had ever seen. (I later learned that they were made by Ford Europe, so this one had probably been imported.) The driver stuck his head out of the passenger window and made a gesture with his palm and fingers, I was welcome to approach. He looked a bit like David Bowie from the last album cover *Aladdin Sane,* with his medium length blond hair combed back and cropped at the bottom of the neck. A guitar riff from Bowie's song *Panic in Detroit* was playing inside my head as I walked up. 'Bowie' narrowed his eyes while he appraised me; his expression reminded me of Clint Eastwood in the movie *High Plains Drifter.* I must be getting a bit media starved out here on the open road, I realized. He gave an almost imperceptible nod and reached over to open the passenger door for me.

The humidity was becoming difficult to bear, and the air conditioned little car was beckoning. 'Bowie' was headed east in my direction, so I decided to take the chance. As I unshouldered my pack, he stepped out of the car to get a beach towel from the trunk. He arranged it on the back seat and then stepped aside to allow me to get in the car.

"Go ahead and set your pack down on top of that towel," he motioned. He must be a fastidious fellow, I thought to myself. That done, I settled into the cream colored leather bucket seat, knocked the sand off of my boots outside the car before swinging them onto the carpeted floorboard, and pulled the passenger door shut. Once again, I was committed to engaging another human being who I didn't really know at all.

We rode together in silence for a few minutes and I was just beginning to think that it would be a fairly easy leg of my journey when 'Bowie' decided to speak. "I assume you are heading to Florida?" He had a polished British accent with an upper crust, educated air about him.

"Yeah, as a matter of fact I am," I said, wondering to myself how far this guy was going.

"Why?" he prodded curtly.

"Well my father moved back to the states recently so I'm headed out there to Florida to see him. I'm also planning to see a girl I met there last summer while staying with him." The second part of my response seemed to displease him, but I wasn't sure why. 'Bowie' returned to his driving and I decided not to say anything more until he reinitiated the conversation.

We reached the town of Biloxi and drove over one of many causeway bridges that I would experience that day. Commercial fishing boats were clustered over to the leeward side, and I decided that they must be waiting for the afternoon tide before heading back out. We crossed over the bridge with the tires clacking rhythmically over concrete seams and entered the small town of Ocean Springs.

'Bowie' decided to speak again. "Tell you what, I'm going to make a quick stop at my house in Mobile, and then I'll be driving on to Pensacola. We could grab some sandwiches and sodas for the road; does that sound okay to you?"

I had to think about this before answering. Getting into a stranger's car was one thing, entering the man's home was quite another. I didn't want to leave the highway, although I was hungry and thirsty and the thought of a cold soda did sound tantalizing. "I'm not sure," I said.

"Suit yourself."

We drove on for another fifteen minutes, although it seemed more like a couple of hours in the stilted silence, until we reached the small town of Gautier. Somewhat to my relief, 'Bowie' reached down to the dashboard and clicked on a classical music station.

I was wondering how folks down here made their livings. Apart from fishing and tourism, the pace of life did not appear to conform to higher levels of commerce. Leaving Gautier behind, we passed a sign for the Gulf Islands National Seashore and I imagined myself walking on the beach at a slower pace, maybe even spending the night on the sand like I had done back in California. Considering this, I almost asked to be let out of the car, but decided it was still too early in the day for that. Anyhow the decision was made for me when we crossed over another bridge to Pascagoula, a sign that I initially mistook for Pensacola. I was thinking that I might have possibly dozed off but then we passed a road sign that said Mobile was 42 miles ahead, so I knew I was mistaken. I tried focusing on the classical music which I found to be a bit too structured but reassuring nonetheless.

The driver wore a pressed white shirt with blue silk tie and a matching blue blazer, creased khaki slacks and shiny penny loafers that looked like they were brand new. Or maybe he shined them daily himself.

I was relieved when he finally decided to break another silence. "I play church organ on Sundays for a congregation back in Gulfport. We had a funeral there this morning for a member of the congregation," he said, which explained the outfit. It was about the last thing I expected to hear and made me think that he might possibly be okay after all. Perhaps he was just a bit reserved because he was British. He was being a Good Samaritan to me though, I realized. "Thanks for the ride," I said, urging him to continue.

"I have a church I go to back in California," I said. Learning that 'Bowie' was a church going man, I thought it might stabilize the trust between us. He nodded. "I joined that church all by myself when I was about eleven years old," I continued. I had met the pastor during school recess. He was watering roses over behind the fence, next to the school, so I walked up and asked him if I could go to his church. My family didn't attend church very often back then but I wanted to go. The pastor told me it would be okay if I brought my parents along, at least at first, so that he knew I would have their permission. I got them to go with me about three Sundays in a row, and I continued going with or without them almost every Sunday after that.

"That's nice," he said, indicating that he was done with this particular conversation. Eventually we merged back onto Interstate 10 and passed another road sign. Now Mobile was 30 miles ahead.

"I presume you're English?" I asked, hoping it would not be too personal a question, and thinking that perhaps we'd established a connection considering we both went to church and all.

"Yes I am, just moved to the States a few months ago. I work for British Petroleum." I could feel he was beginning to open up and my shoulders finally unknotted as I settled back into the bucket seat. "I got my geology degree at Oxford. But I also studied classical music after college, so when I saw an ad in the paper for a church organist back in Gulfport, I decided to take the job. Many of the greatest composers in modern history got their commissions from the church."

"Perhaps I should take you up on those sandwiches," I said, hoping that I had made the right decision, "but I'll need to make it to Pensacola by mid-afternoon," I added, thinking a deadline might help my cause.

"That won't be a problem," he said. "I also need to stop by my house to get a few things for the rest of the afternoon. We should be in and out in less than fifteen minutes."

"Uh, okay," I said and settled back again.

Trees and farmland now lined both sides of the highway as we proceeded in a northeasterly direction up toward Mobile. I knew from my map that this was the route we needed to take anyway since it wasn't possible to cross Mobile Bay any further south. Eventually we reached the city of Mobile and left the highway, driving north along the river for a couple of miles until 'Bowie' turned left at a side street that was lined with oak trees draped in more of that Spanish moss, cascading down in bright shades of green. Each home sat on about two acres of property. They were all set back from the road with winding driveways leading up to them and had the appearance of venerable old southern mansions, although they looked to me like they had been constructed fairly recently. Their glossy appearance, and the relatively young landscaping gave that away.

"Here we are," 'Bowie' said as we turned into one of the driveways and drove up to a circular drive at the front of the house. It surrounded a fountain supporting a granite cherub that was emitting a stream of water from his lower extremity. The front entrance to the house had a balcony supported by white Romanesque columns. Apparently it had been designed to resemble a classic southern mansion out of *Gone with the Wind*, or at least it seemed that way to me. 'Bowie' set the parking brake and got out of the car, motioning for me to do likewise.

"I'd rather just wait out here in the car, if that's okay," I called out.

"Nonsense," he answered glibly, as though he had expected me to say this. "It's quite hot out here and my house is air-conditioned. You can wait in the kitchen while I go upstairs to change out of these clothes. I won't be but a few minutes." Waiting in the kitchen seemed harmless enough and indeed it was becoming unbearably hot inside the car with the motor switched off. Looking out the window I saw that the sun had now reached its zenith.

So I reluctantly got out of the car and followed him inside, crossing a white marble foyer into a great room that showcased a white Steinway grand piano. A beam of sunlight shone down upon it from an octagonal window twenty feet above, it was a carefully designed effect I assumed. We walked over plush burgundy carpeting into a large rectangular room lined with bookshelves that appeared to have been constructed from expensive cherry wood, highly polished with no visible dust at all. Two large stereo speakers stood in each of the back corners. They appeared to be very expensive, although I had never seen the brand before. Each was over six feet tall and I imagined they could fill the entire room with sound, but decided not to ask for a demonstration. I caught a glimpse of a beautiful flower garden through the back window, out in the backyard. The window had been decorated with cream colored drapes that hung down from the ceiling and were tied at each side with golden chord tassels. I thought they resembled Roman togas and then began to wonder where the kitchen was.

"I decorated the place just recently," he said. "Wouldn't you like to look around? You should see the master bedroom upstairs." This was certainly not something I was expecting and I didn't know what to say.

"It is much cooler here inside, don't you think?" he ventured further. "Why don't you and I go upstairs and take a quick nap? We'll feel much better when we get back in the car."

"Uh, I don't think that's a good idea," I said firmly. "I'd prefer to wait in the kitchen like you said at first. I can make the sandwiches while you change." A few seconds of stressful silence followed. "Anyway, I need to get going soon. My parents will be expecting me in Pensacola since I called them from Gulfport to tell them I was almost there," I lied, now wanting to get out of this house as soon as possible. It was pretty clear that the man was gay and I was being toyed with. This was not a good situation at all I told myself, and I resolved to be more careful in the future. "They will probably get worried if I don't arrive by 2 pm," I added for emphasis. "I wouldn't want to have them call the police or anything." It was about the only threat I could make in the era before cell phones.

Fortunately he decided not to press it and stepped abruptly out of the room. "Kitchen's through the side door to the left of the back window," he said. I could hear him stomping up the stairs, clearly disappointed. But to my relief it seemed he was not the type to coerce someone against their will. Perhaps my original assessment of him was not as far off track as I had feared. This apparent misunderstanding was partly my fault.

I entered the kitchen having no idea what to do next upon surveying it. It had been tastefully decorated with custom shelves and cabinets rising up to the ceiling. A platform counter stood in the center of the room, with a shiny black marble top and an array of pots and pans with shiny copper bottoms hanging above it. And everything looked like it was brand new. The stove must have been designed by a culinary institute, with two stacked ovens built into the cherry wood cabinetry beside it. Beyond that stood a large double door refrigerator with a burnished metal finish, also built into the cabinetry. Cherry wood shelves with cupboards and drawers wrapped around the adjacent wall where a three-well sink stood below French windows that opened out to the garden. The cost of this kitchen alone must have been more than the entire contents of my family's house back in California. It was a bit unnerving.

I walked over to the refrigerator and opened it to see whether I could find what I needed to make the sandwiches. 'Bowie' returned to the kitchen at precisely that moment to my relief. Now he was wearing black jeans and a white silk T-shirt that looked like it had been chosen to be intentionally snug.

"Here let me take that on, mate," he said as he walked over to the opened refrigerator door and started pulling out plastic container of deli meats and cheeses which he set on the polished marble counter behind. Then he retrieved a tomato, a head of iceberg lettuce, a jar of gourmet mustard (a brand I had never heard of, but it looked really good), and an expensive looking jar of mayonnaise. A loaf of rye bread came next from a special breadbox compartment. Then he set out a cutting board, knives and other utensils. Thus arranged, he said flatly "so make us some sandwiches," and strode back out of the kitchen.

I dealt out four slices of rye bread, bladed those with mustard and mayonnaise and stacked the meats on top. Next I added Swiss cheese, lettuce and tomato, thinking these would become my best sandwich creations of the summer. But they needed to be packaged for transport in the car, so I rummaged through the drawers until I found some plastic wrap and aluminum foil. I cut each sandwich diagonally and wrapped it with an outer layer of foil, so now they were all snugly wrapped and ready for the road. I stacked one on top of the other and waited, turning to gaze out the window where I noticed that some herbs, peppers and tomato plants were growing in the garden.

He walked back into the kitchen carrying a small Styrofoam cooler. "Well done," he said when he saw the sandwiches and opened the left refrigerator door to fill the cooler with ice. He added soft drinks and then grabbed the sandwiches, carefully placing them on top. Then to my relief, he put everything away, wiped down the counter and we were ready to go.

"Sorry if I made you feel uncomfortable," he said.

"That's okay." I reasoned that it was a fair misunderstanding, although I was still feeling twinges of anxiety in my stomach. I knew that this episode could have gone quite differently under slightly different circumstances, although I was relieved to find that I hadn't mistaken the man's character, just his sexual persuasion.

We walked back out to the circular driveway, me carrying the cooler and 'Bowie', as I still like to recall him, paused briefly in the foyer to key the alarm system. He instructed me to put the cooler on the backseat next to my backpack so that we could reach it while on the road. We settled back into the bucket seats of the Capri and shut the doors. I felt like I was a captive again. 'Bowie' revved the motor and switched the air conditioner to high, waited for the temperature to reach a comfortable level and then headed back down the driveway. I was relieved to leave this estate community with its "new money" opulence and return to the interstate, even more so when I saw the sign that pointed us in the direction of Pensacola.

We drove up a long expansion bridge over Mobile Bay. There were large shipping cranes beneath us standing ready to unload their cargo, and industrial fishing boats to the south of us heading out to the Gulf with frothy wakes behind them. After we returned to sea level the highway continued atop pylons over sandbars and inland marshes. I watched a Heron perched gracefully on one stilt leg, its head scanning patiently for sardines beneath the surface of the water. We then crossed a smaller bridge over the Tensaw River. There were large raft islands of silt below, deposited there from many decades of the river's passage.

Looking south to open water, I took in the lively display of sunlight flickering off wave crests that were rolling in from the Gulf. The lapping waves danced stochastically, colorful and alive. I rolled down my window and enjoyed the salty breeze as it entered my nostrils.

The highway left the marshes behind and we drove through a stretch of longleaf pines with densely packed palmettos fighting for space beneath them. Freshly mowed Zoysia grass lined both sides of the highway, casting a pungent aroma as their clippings dried in the sun. Not unexpectedly, a tractor mower came into view after we passed over the next rise; its driver was hunched over the wheel in no particular hurry. I found myself mesmerized by the endless green and brown textures, a blurred vision if I held my eyes steady. Brief snapshots would hold my attention for a second or two if I allowed them to lock on anything in particular, maybe a tree that happened to be leaning into another or a branch pointing in an odd direction. The rest of Alabama ran on through dense sand pines and small clusters of towns. I knew that the scenery was ever changing, yet on a macro scale it all looked pretty much the same.

By now it was difficult to see much further than a quarter mile ahead and the drive was becoming monotonous. Still we motored on without talking. Giving in to my growing unease, I decided to break the silence in a most awkward way.

"Sorry for not realizing that you were gay," I said at last. "I must have appeared a bit startled." He nodded slightly, pushing his chin out as a sign of determination, everything was now under control. "Anyway, thanks for understanding that I am not. I guess I was surprised because you said that you came from church before, and well I didn't think…"

"I'm not a member of that church," he broke in. "I just play there on Sundays and other events like the funeral this morning. It was one of the few jobs I could get while waiting for my green card. As I told you, I'm a musician," he laughed. The mood was lighter now.

"I studied baroque music, ten years in The Hague, that's in Holland, and played a lot of church organ music throughout Europe, some harpsichord as well. The UK tried to get me back in country for military service, which I decided to skirt by taking the job with BP and moving out here to the states. Wasn't about to get tossed for being a homosexual, it would have been a brutal pain in the ass, if you ask me." He laughed at his own joke.

"My mum made me study piano as a boy," he continued. "But I never really appreciated it until I was a student at Eaton. There was an old upright piano in the basement of my dormitory and I would go down there in the late evenings to decompress from my studies. I'd play it in the dark, trying to memorize all the keys. It was quite tactile and beautiful really, just me and that old piano.

"She died when I was at Oxford, my mum," he continued, gazing purposefully ahead. "So after I graduated, I applied to the Royal Conservatoire of The Hague and was happy to be accepted. During my time there, I developed a passion for early keyboard instruments and how they have been refined over the last three centuries. The modern piano is an exceptionally dynamic instrument, with a wide range of volumes and textures that can be produced by the keyboard and foot pedaling. But the early keyboard instruments were a lot more subtle in their responsiveness, and required more careful listening. I particularly love to play the harpsichord, since the texture of that music is much more subtle, but can be quite beautiful in its own right, you know?"

"I don't think I've ever heard a harpsichord played before," I answered. "But please continue." I wanted him to stay on this subject since he seemed to enjoy it.

"Music theory took a bit more work for me though, I must admit," he continued. "After a year of disconnected classes and a string of private tutors, most of whom I hated for their precision and arrogance, I eventually gravitated toward the Department of Early Music and Historical Performance. Perhaps it had a bit to do with the engineering side of me, but I truly loved learning how the instruments evolved, and how fantastically music composition evolved along with them through the centuries, from the Middle Ages and Renaissance to the Early Romantic Period.

"I had a small basement in my apartment where I could practice on a rented old baby grand piano. I also built a harpsichord from a kit, piece by piece during one particularly cold winter. I still have it, although I need to find a reliable way to ship it to the States."

"It must have been a difficult transition for you," I commented, "from the musical life that you had at The Hague to playing church hymns back there in Gulfport Mississippi I mean."

"Organized religion! If only people knew," he said, eyes squinting as he piloted the Capri down the interstate, shoulders squared forward as he gripped the wheel. His reaction was not expected.

"How do you mean?" I decided to press. I was having difficulty focusing on his musical musings anyway. A road sign announced that Pensacola was now just thirty two miles ahead. I had almost made it to the Florida state line! I waited for 'Bowie' to answer, not knowing what was coming. I would not forget the discussion that followed.

"Ever hear about Area 51 outside of Roswell, New Mexico?" he asked. I hadn't. There was no cable TV back in 1974. 24-hour sci-fi channels hadn't been invented yet and there were few if any documentaries on the subject. The country was still recovering from the Vietnam War and now the media was preoccupied with Watergate and whether or not Nixon would resign. I had no idea what "area" he was talking about, but then I remembered the bald bantam weight test pilot I had ridden with back in New Mexico mentioning Roswell and wondered whether these two things were connected.

"No," I replied.

"Well then, did you ever read about flying saucers as a kid?"

"Of course. They had always fascinated me growing up."

"Well they're real," he said with dark determination. I couldn't see how this could be connected to his comment about organized religion; perhaps he was trying to change the subject for some reason.

"Did you know that about one in ten people in this country claim to have seen UFOs?" he continued. "That's over twenty million people, including a lot of famous people throughout history. And many ancient historians recorded strange lights in the sky that could not be explained. The papyrus annals of Pharoh Thutmoss III mention circles of light in the sky. Hindu and Tibetan writings from that era also contain descriptions of shining disc like objects in the sky with incredible maneuverability. Roman historians from the third and fourth centuries, Pliny, Tacitus, Lycosthenes and Julius Obsequens, described fiery shields that swept across the sky. In 1492, Christopher Columbus described in his ship log a shimmering light moving back and forth across the sky. European astronomers from the eighteenth and nineteenth centuries reported numerous sightings of unexplained luminary phenomena.

"This brings us to 1947, Ken Arnold, while flying a private plane over the Cascade Mountains, observed nine glowing discs racing around Mount Rainier at speeds in excess of 1000 miles per hour. He later reported them to move 'like saucers skipping over water', so this fed the growing public interest in flying saucers, with more and more public accounts after that eventful report, and more and more news articles, studies, and analysis.

"Your government has been intentionally covering this up since the 1950s. But they have tens of thousands of pages of reports and analysis, photographs, even physical evidence. They just don't want us to know about it, because they don't think our fragile minds could handle the unknown, do you know what I mean? Yet it's perfectly fine for folks to believe in God and go to church on Sundays.

"I have a problem reconciling this," he said, "considering such cosmic phenomena are also described in the Bible, especially the Book of Revelation which I have read through many times."

"I don't see much of a contradiction there," I said next, "just a lack of comprehension."

"Exactly!" he said, turning his head toward me with a conspiratorial grin.

"I still don't understand the problem you seem to be having with organized religion," I ventured further, "the worship experience brings people together."

"I have a 'problem' with it because it conditions people to ignore the obvious. It *conditions* them to ignore all of the evidence that has been observed and written down through the millennia. It makes them closed minded to what is out there, makes them ignore all of the evidence, that we are not alone in this universe."

"I'm sorry," I said at last. "But I just don't see it the same way. I go to church and I've never felt closed minded about what I get out of the worship experience. I think God reveals as much as people can handle, and as they grow in their comprehension He reveals more. I believe in a universe that God created as both physical and spiritual. I think we need to seek both physical and spiritual truths in order to sufficiently understand the world that we live in. As far as I'm concerned, that extends to outer space and whether there is intelligent life elsewhere or not."

I could tell he was becoming agitated and I had an uncomfortable sense of where this discussion might be headed. I was poking a hornet's nest with a gay British geologist who apparently had God issues. I needed an excuse to get out of the car.

Soon after that we crossed over the state line into Florida, The Sunshine State. We drove on for about five miles and I finally got the nerve to ask for my dismissal. "Uh, would you mind letting me out at the next exit?" I asked. "No offense, but I need to take a break." Politics and religion are two things that should never be discussed with strangers, and I had just learned one of those lessons.

"That's fine with me," he said evenly. He must have also sensed the distance between us. No chance of camaraderie with such different points of view. "Hey, it's nobody's fault," he said at last.

"Yeah, I'm sorry too I guess," I said. "Look, I think I mentioned I'm heading to Florida to see about a *girl*," I said as bravely as I could, hoping it could provide a definitive close to the conversation.

We turned off at the Pine Forest Road exit and pulled into an Esso gas station. 'Bowie' set the brake and waited for an attendant to come out to the pump. Several black men in white Esso uniforms were bustling around other cars that had stopped at the station, wiping their windows and checking under their hoods. 'Bowie' shook his head impatiently and honked the horn. One of the attendants glanced our way but continued wiping the other windshield.

'Bowie' rolled down his window and shouted out to the attendant, "hurry on up and get over here, nigger!" This seemed to be out of character, even for him, especially in his British accent. The attendant shoved his windshield wiping rag into his back pocket and slowly walked over, eventually lifting the gas nozzle from its hook. He slowly shuffled around to the rear of the Capri and began to pump the gas but didn't say a word.

"Speed it up boy! I haven't got all morning here," 'Bowie' said. He looked over to me, his eyes narrowing with determination, and said definitively "you've got to keep these niggers in their place so they don't get uppity; they're just too damned lazy." I had heard all this the day before and did not want to hear it again, so I lowered my head and decided not to say another word. It seemed there was something uncharacteristic about someone berating a southern black man in a British accent.

I reached around and carefully lifted my backpack from the back seat, hoisting it over the bucket seat and stepping out of the car. I wanted him to just get his gas and go.

The Capri roared back to life with its belly now full. As it accelerated down the road, turning right onto the freeway onramp, I realized something. He never did explain exactly why he was driving to Florida.

CHAPTER ELEVEN

AN AGING CHEVY IMPALA SEDAN chugged and sputtered into the gas station and pulled over to the pump that the Capri had just vacated. The engine kept on knocking after the ignition had been shut off. Its gold paint job was badly oxidized and the crusty vinyl top was peeling in various places. There was also rust around the wheel wells and the tires were almost thread bare. I was amazed that it still ran. A battered New York license plate hung askew from the back bumper by a single bolt.

The two young men who were driving in this jalopy stepped out of the car. They appeared to be in their mid-twenties and were talking rapidly in a language that I couldn't understand, waving their hands for emphasis. One had a lean and well-muscled frame like a gymnast, and the other had a stockier build, perhaps a bit overweight. Both had olive skin and aquiline noses. They wore white T-shirts and khaki pants with oversized pockets, the kind you could buy from an army surplus store. Sturdy looking leather sandals were strapped to their feet.

The gas station attendant didn't appear to have any idea what these guys wanted. When one of them attempted to lift the gas pump from its hook, the attendant grabbed it and waved him away. This was his job. I shouldered my pack and walked over to offer my assistance.

"American?" one of them asked. His accent was not European and not Hispanic. I figured it must come from somewhere in the Middle East, possibly Israel, although my exposure to that part of the world had been limited to rebroadcasts of speeches by Menachem Begin on the evening news. Israel's prime minister was engaging in peace negotiations with Egypt at the time.

"Yes…" I said tentatively.

"Of course you are!" he belly laughed as though this was the funniest joke he had made all day. His brown hair was about two inches long and stuck out in every direction; it looked like a crew cut that hadn't seen a barber for several months. And his beard looked like it had been growing for about the same amount of time.

"You speak English?" I asked next, hoping that would not be funny too.

"A little, yes some. But as you see, we need help."

"How can I help?" It was the right question, probably my best one of the day.

"These people of your south, they don't understand we talk. We have very hard time to buy gas. We have very hard to rent room. We try to buy food to eat in car, we ask what in bags, chips you call it? What is this, chips? They wave us out of store. You need ride? You ride with us, help us to buy these things, is that how you say? You explain, very nice please?" He spoke in a guttural dialect that made all the words sound strange.

"Where are you driving to?" I asked.

"Florida!" he grinned a toothy smile.

"Uh, we're in Florida…"

"Cocoa Beach, Cape Kennedy, we go there! We see astronauts, space rockets."

"I'm going to Orlando; it should be on the way."

They discussed this briefly in what I was pretty sure now was Hebrew. Then one of them went into the gas station, presumably to ask something from the man behind the counter. He walked back out carrying a map of the State of Florida and unfolded it onto the hood of the car. They both hunched over it, tracing around with a finger and stopped. "Orlando!" the driver shouted enthusiastically. "Yes, we go through Orlando. You come with us, yes?"

"Yes," I said, nodding my head. This would most likely be the last ride of my trip across the country.

The pump attendant finished fueling the sedan and returned it to its cradle, walked over and looked at them and then looked at me.

"That'll be three dollahs, mistah." I turned to them and held up three fingers, then touched the palm of my other hand, thinking that should indicate money. The driver nodded and said something to his friend, who retrieved a small leather purse from his pocket and counted out three single bills. He held them to me and I nodded, then walked over and handed them to the attendant, who replied with a smile, "thanks and y'all have a good day now!" We were done here.

The stockier one pulled open the passenger door and motioned for me to get in back. I hoisted my pack onto the back seat behind the driver and climbed in over a pile of food wrappers that had been discarded there from various fast food restaurants around the country, including one from In-N-Out. That wrapper told me these two guys had made it all the way to Southern California and were now on their way back to the east coast. I settled in, fumbled between the seats to find the seatbelt and clipped myself in. My olive skinned companions slid into their seats and slammed the doors shut with wretched squeaks. The engine fired to life after several attempts and we motored back out toward the freeway.

"I am Dari," the driver said, looking at me from the rearview mirror. "This is Danni," he said motioning to the stockier one in the front passenger seat. Danni turned around and smiled at me, "howdy!" he said, laughing. These two guys had a warped sense of humor, but they were my kind of people I thought to myself.

"Dari and Danni," I repeated, nodding my head with what I was pretty sure was my best sincere look, fading to a humorous grin that I could no longer control.

"Yes. We come from Israel," Danni said enthusiastically. I congratulated myself on my Cracker Jack deductive reasoning skills and my mood quickly brightened.

"Why you come to this country?" I asked the obvious next question. For some reason when I'm speaking to someone from another country, I tend to talk the way they do. I've done it for years. With a Vietnamese refugee I would study with later on in graduate school, with my Mexican gardener gesturing toward a sprinkler that needed fixing, I mimic their speech patterns and word construction. I don't mean to be rude. I'm pretty sure it comes from genuine empathy. Maybe it's my crude imagination, but I sense that they understand me better when I talk this way. There seems to be more warmth between us when I talk the way they do. Or maybe they just think I'm being goofy but forgive me because, deep down, they know I'm being sincere, trying to listen and communicate without correcting them. Talking in a foreign language is hard enough without the person you're talking to correcting the words you've struggled to remember just as you get them out.

"We finish our time in national army," Dari replied. "We fly to New York City and buy this car. Amazing, such a big car for five hundred American dollars only!" he said.

I looked around. The ceiling liner had become unglued and was sagging down in various places, and there were dozens of cigarette burns in the upholstery. The left rear window handle had broken off and the interior smelled like extremely stale pipe tobacco.

"You smoke?" I asked, willing myself to be accepting regardless of the answer.

"No, sorry," Danni said. He looked back and studied my face, then smiling broadly. "Smells bad, no?" he laughed, understanding the reason for my question. He had a round face with bushy eyebrows over narrow eyes that looked like they had squinted for hours down the barrel of a rifle, but they were smiling at me just now. Like Dari, his hair had grown out about an inch and a half all around, and he had a cowlick thrusting its way up above his forehead. Unlike Dari, Danni looked like he probably shaved about twice a week.

"Yes," I said, reaching for the window handle and cranking it down a couple turns to allow some of the humid afternoon air to blow in. The air conditioner had been struggling mightily with little effect, obviously in desperate need of a Freon recharge.

Dari sloppily navigated the sedan up the onramp and accelerated into freeway traffic. He failed to notice an oncoming semi that had been honking loudly while veering into the fast lane to let us on. After we reached cruising speed I noticed that Dari needed to make frequent adjustments with the steering wheel to keep us pointed straight down the highway. Not only were the tires badly worn, they were completely out of balance.

"How long you in army?" I asked, hoping to break the tension I was experiencing regarding the questionable safety of the vehicle.

Danni turned around and gave me an appraising look, deciding again that I was okay. "Every man in Israel, we must serve on army two years. Then, two months free to go vacation any part of world, whatever. After that we return to Israel and take regular job, but must stay ready in case of war. This way, every man in Israel trained and ready to defend home country."

"So you decide to come to America," I said, curious to learn where they had been so far.

"Yes, Dari and me, we children play together same Kibbutz, we promise to see United States one day, a dream for us. In army, we save our money this trip. We fly to New York City, but cost too many staying there, so we buy car and drive to New Jersey. With car can stay motor hotel, motel you say it? We stay many motor hotels, very good," he said enthusiastically.

Danni studied the map and instructed Dari to take the next exit for Pensacola. I had hoped that we would continue on Interstate 10 since it would have been faster. "We drive down gulf coast," he said.

"Whoa, wait a minute," I said. "We need to stay on Interstate 10 to Tallahassee," I persisted. I struggled to recall the route from my own roadmap that was now tucked away in the flap of my backpack. I had studied it earlier that morning back in Hattiesburg, which seemed like a long time ago.

"No, we come to see Florida, we drive coast." It was pretty clear that his mind was made up.

"That's fine with me, so long as we don't drive around the entire perimeter of the state," I said, tracing a big "U" with my finger since I knew they probably wouldn't understand the word 'perimeter'.

"My final destination is Orlando; you see it on that map of yours?" I pointed again.

Danni hunched over the map some more and nodded his head, rising back up and straightening his shoulders. "Yes. We drive down highway 98, down gulf coast to highway 27, then through middle of state. That the way to Cape Kennedy! We stop at Orlando for you my friend." And that pretty much settled it. I was in for a tour of the western coast of Florida, and at least they would be going my way eventually. Stay with them or risk my chances on the side of the highway. I chose to stay put in the back seat of their beat up sedan, which was showing remarkable stamina I had to admit.

We took the Highway 95-29 exit and the tires squealed as the weighty vehicle slowed to make the turn. Then we headed eight miles south toward downtown Pensacola. The engine sputtered unevenly and I wondered what kind of gas mileage this jalopy must be getting, most likely less than 12 miles per gallon.

"We drive down gulf coast to Apalachicola," Dari said, studying the map some more, now with a glint in his eye as he glanced back at me from the review mirror. "You like oysters?" he asked. "We have oysters in New Orleans, very tasty, we love it. We ask where they come from and man behind raw bar say Apalachicola. We go there!"

"Well, okay," I said. "I've had them before, when I was in Florida last summer. Actually, I think I'm getting a bit hungry myself."

"Me too!" he said. Dari nodded in agreement.

"What did you think of New Orleans?" I asked, switching back into hitchhiking passenger mode, understanding my role here was to be sociable with these two young ex-army Israeli gentlemen, regardless of the language barrier between us.

"We drink too much there, maybe I think," Danni said, shaking his head a couple of times definitively, then once more for good measure. "We park on street, two blocks north of French Quarter, you say it? Just walking and walking all night long. Many people walk Bourbon Street stay up all night dancing in street. We buy many these drinks, very large glass, very sweet, 'hurricane' they call it. People throw plastic beads from high places to women dancing in street."

Dari smiled, glancing at Danni and nodding again. Danni smiled back, then shook his head a couple more times, shrugging his shoulders. "We make it back to car, sleep off alcohol for some hours, and then drive back to highway. So that's it, you know?" Somehow, I realized, these two young men had managed to make it out of New Orleans with their virtues intact.

The highway emptied into a city street and we made our way through downtown Pensacola. We followed the road signs for Highway 98, making a number of turns through town. At one point the traffic suddenly slowed to a crawl. We were approaching an intersection with a platform stage set up on the corner. Throngs of densely packed people were standing around it with their hands waving skyward. An albino guy with long white hair was shouting into a bullhorn in a heavily punctuated, almost epileptic voice. He looked about my age with torn jeans and a white tee shirt, about six feet tall and rail thin, possibly 120 pounds dripping wet. We drove by slowly, careful to give the crowd a wide berth. Danni rolled down the window to hear what was going on.

"Jesus DIED to free your SOULS!!!" the young man was shouting, arching backward as he spoke, his long hair whipping wildly. After he said this, his whole body jerked convulsively and it took several seconds for him to compose himself. He raised the bullhorn back to his mouth. "Accept JEsus as your lord and SAvior!! He is the WAY, the TRUTH and the LIFE, my friends!" The crowd bellowed their affirmation and waved their hands skyward once more. The young man jerked convulsively again. He repeated the process several more times as he spoke into the microphone. Taking care to avoid people standing out in the street, Dari took a right and headed down 9th Avenue, finally able to accelerate back up to 25 mph.

Danni shrugged over to Dari, and Dari shrugged back at Danni. Then they both looked back at me and I shrugged in response. How could I explain to them about Southern Baptists? Did I understand what this albino guy was doing? I thought I did but decided to let it go, remembering the new hitchhiking rule I had made for myself after my last ride. I smiled, nodded and shrugged one more time for good measure.

We eventually approached the Pensacola Bay Bridge, a long expanse of concrete spanning three and a half miles over the bay to a long narrow peninsula that served as the final land barrier between Florida and the Gulf of Mexico. The balding tires made rhythmic "kuh-clack" sounds as they rolled over rib sections between the poured concrete slabs, with their pitch rising as we approached the parabolic crest of the bridge. I rolled the window down a few turns and took in another breath of the humid salt air. Looking down, I studied a sailboat crossing underneath as we passed the bridge's apex, and I listened to the pitch of the tire clacking fall again when we descended to the opposite bank. The water was choppier out here than it had been back in Alabama, and the breeze was considerably stronger as well, hinting that another storm could be coming soon.

We left the bridge and made our way onto Santa Rosa Island, just a strip of land about 1500 feet wide that paralleled the mainland. Dari decreased speed as we motored through a small fishing town named Gulf Breeze. We passed by a green bait and tackle shack shop, a white clapboard Baptist church, and several other small buildings that quickly faded in the distance.

Another bridge led to a narrow stretch of land with clusters of stilt houses perched in the wetlands beside it. They were painted in bright contrast colors such as lime green, turquoise and mustard yellow.

After 10 miles we crossed back over the causeway toward Gulf Islands National Seashore and Navarre Beach. I looked to my right and was almost blinded by the whitest sugar sand I had ever seen. The water to my left was a texture of lime-greens and dark emeralds. And the gulf water was a much deeper turquoise. The wind sculpted sandy beach appeared to be alive; with its features gently rising and falling as we passed.

Then we drove by another cluster of stilt houses. As before, most of them were painted in soothing pastel colors. But one had been painted in mauve, which was particularly striking and completed the scene.

By this time I was feeling a sort of bond with Dari and Danni as I watched them taking in the landscape along with me. Here we were out on the perimeter of civilization viewing coastal areas unlike any I had ever seen before. I wondered what it would be like to camp out there on the beach, wading into the water with a fishing pole to catch my dinner, building a fire and barbequing it up on the sand. Considering I only had a quart of fresh water in the side pocket of my backpack, some wax covered cheese that I hoped was still good (and no fishing line), I realized again for the second time that day that it was an impractical idea. Still I desperately yearned to camp on the beach and resolved to do it another day.

Danni and Dari seemed to be intent on following the outermost island roads wherever possible, crossing bridges when they ran out of road and crossing back again at the next opportunity. This was getting a bit frustrating for me but the salt air smelled fresher out here somehow.

When the road rejoined Highway 98, we made our way through Windhaven Beach and took a short bridge to an outer bank where a sign directed us to Fort Walton Beach Park.

"Two hours Apalachicola to maybe," Danni said after consulting the map. My cross country trek had been as much about eating different types of food as it was about meeting different types of people, so at this point Apalachicola oysters seemed like a perfect new adventure. I nodded back enthusiastically.

A sign planted in a thicket of palmettos told us we were entering the city of Fort Walton Beach. My father had been stationed here at Eglin Air Force Base shortly after returning from Korea. My sister was born here about twelve months later. He built a small two-bedroom house for our young family just south of the main entrance in an unincorporated community called Shalimar.

Our small house had been built near a shallow beach. I would often run down there whenever my mom wasn't watching me closely. Then she would chase after me and snatch me up into her arms. The thrill of capture always made me giggle, but it would usually result in my banishment to the small bedroom that I shared with my sister.

I do remember one time when my mom let my sister and me play in the water while she watched us from the beach. I was about three years old and my sister was still in diapers. It was a bright sunny morning and we were sitting there happily in the warm shallow water. My sister's diaper had gotten so saturated with seawater that she could barely stand, which was quite funny to me. I would help her stand up and then let go of her hand, giggling at the spectacle of her plopping back down in the shallow water. But she was not about to be subordinated. Every time I splashed water at her she splashed right back with her tiny arms. It was a really good day, and I was pleased to remember it now.

The house had cement block walls. I remembered this because my mom would take me down to the construction site when she brought my dad his lunch. These lunch visits were often my only opportunity to see him, since he worked on the house whenever he got time off between flight assignments. When the block walls were done, he proceeded to frame the roof and interior walls. This was my favorite part of the process since there had always been piles of sawdust for me to play with, and small scraps of lumber that I could stack on top of each other. I pretended that I was building a little house of my own. One thing I particularly remember was watching my dad build the 'joists' that would support the roof of the house. I would proudly repeat the steps back to him as he explained them to me, making sure that I was a safe distance away before he moved on to the next step. He built a jig to hold the pre-cut pieces of lumber while he hammered them into place, using nails and metal strips with shiny metal shark teeth poking down from them. My dad hammered until the tiny teeth sunk into the wood to secure the joists together. It was a tedious process and took longer than I had the patience to watch, but eventually I could recite every step from memory and frequently did over the dinner table. Conversation at the dinner table must have been challenging for my parents when I was that age.

I have a picture of me "helping my dad", carrying small scraps of wood around in the unfinished garage, with my dad leaning down and watching me. I also have a couple of super 8 movies of us playing together in that house, one during Christmas time. These represent the scattered memories of a childhood that my dad was still a part of.

As we drove through Fort Walton Beach, I thought about my childhood house and wondered where it was exactly and whether it was still standing. I would learn later that it is indeed still there, just a few miles north of where we were driving. Glancing around, I realized that the entire area had probably grown substantially since 1959. Nothing looked familiar so I let my memories suffice as we drove out of town.

As we proceeded over the Pensacola Beach Bridge with our threadbare tires still slapping rhythmically over another stretch of concrete seams, I watched oyster fishermen stacking baskets of shellfish on the dock below. The sea water was seeping out as they hoisted them out of the water.

The clacking sounds stopped when we left the bridge and drove down another narrow finger called Oskaloosa Island. The sand dunes here appeared to be sporting sea grass hairstyles. They rose and fell as we drove along, like they were vying for my attention.

We continued over the East Pass Bridge to the small harbor town of Destin, another coastal town that supported industrial fishing. Shrimp boats were slowly dieseling back to the dock to unload their holds. We passed a small seafood restaurant and I remembered that I was hungry, having not eaten much of the sandwich I had made for myself that morning in Alabama. I pushed away thoughts about the gay British classical keyboardist who had driven me from Mobile down to Pensacola.

Danni and Dari were consulting the map again but I couldn't understand what they were saying. It was late-afternoon and they still seemed determined to take the outermost stretches of navigable road. Again I briefly considered asking them to let me off but decided not to take the risk. These guys seemed pretty happy to have me along for the rest of the ride. And I had to admit that the scenery was amazing. I consoled myself that we were still headed in the right direction so long as the Gulf was still to our right.

Unfortunately Highway 98 veered eastward soon after that and the Gulf was no longer visible. We were passing through a stretch of pine forest and I was starting to panic, but thankfully the Gulf came back into view. Florida was such a flat state. It was difficult to know which way we were going without waterway landmarks.

When we reached Panama City Beach Dari pulled over at a gas station so that we could use the restroom. I fished out some change from the outer pouch of my pack and bought three bottles of orange soda from the vending machine. I handed one each to Danni and Dari and they gladly accepted. We stood there underneath the awning to stretch our legs.

I waited a minute or two and then asked, "How far do you plan to go today?" I was thinking that these meandering side routes had most likely diminished our chances of making Apalachicola by nightfall.

"That is great thing about this trip," Dari said. "We don't know until it happen!" This was not a surprise response.

"Oh," I said. "But you did say that you want to get to Cocoa Beach, yes?"

"Yes, but it could be maybe another some days."

"And we will go through Orlando, still okay?" I wanted to make sure that they had understood me before. "Orlando is where I want to go." Why did I feel like I had to keep making that clear?

Dari opened his map on the hood of the car again, studied it some more and smiled. I wasn't sure if he was being coy with me or if he was just unwilling to commit to a plan. "Yes, we take you there," he said for what I hoped would be the final time that day.

"Then I ride with you there tomorrow okay? We must to find a place to stay tonight along this way," I pointed.

"Yes let's go!" I had to admire these guys for their enthusiasm. They may have just completed a two year stint in the Israeli army, but they had gentle hearts and seemed keen for adventure. I finally decided to just let go and put my faith in them.

We crossed over Saint Andrew Bay to the inland harbor and followed the signs for Highway 98 through Panama City proper, which took us back over the East Bay to the outer peninsula headed southeast. My spirits lifted when we entered the seaside resort town of Mexico Beach just around 5 PM.

"We should probably find a place here to stay the night," I commented, trying not to seem too obvious about my desire to stop for the day. I could see several motels just ahead that abutted the highway and faced the water. It would feel great to stretch my legs and go for a walk on the beach. Dari and Danni resumed talking in Hebrew and then nodded affirmatively to my relief. We pulled over at the entrance to the El Governor Motel, a multi-story stack of rooms with every balcony facing the Gulf. There should easily be some vacancies I reckoned; the parking lot was only half full. Danni went into the office to ask about the rates. When he returned to the car he asked me to go back in with him. Evidently he was having trouble communicating and needed my help. I accompanied him to the office and smiled at the woman behind the counter, asking politely about a room for the night.

"We only rent by the week honey," she said, "a lot of folks come down here to Mexico Beach for their vacation you know," she added.

"Well we're just passing through," I pressed. "Are you sure it wouldn't be possible to rent a room for just the night? We've been driving all day and quite frankly we're all pretty tired." I kept on smiling to reassure her as she pursed her lips and considered. Finally she answered. "You'll have to ask the manager hon'. He's tending bar out at the poolside cabana just now," she nodded toward the north end of the building. That would be our only recourse.

Dari joined us now, having grown tired of waiting in the car and we walked back to the pool area and approached the cabana. "Dave", according to his nametag, was standing behind the bar and polishing beer glasses with a towel that hung from his belt. "What will you fellers have?" he asked.

"I want here, very please," said Danni. "For just the night," I added.

"Um hmm," he muttered, inspecting us while he continued polishing glasses with the towel. "Well … we don't usually rent out rooms by the night," he said. It didn't sound like a "no" to me, so I decided to press some more. "We'd be out first thing in the morning," I said, thinking this might make a difference for some reason. "We're traveling around the state," I whispered to Dave, wanting him to know that we were doing some serious traveling here, but certainly not wanting Dari and Danni to hear that part.

Dave slow talked a tentative reply in his Florida southern drawl. "Well like I said, we usually just rent out our rooms by the week, but I guess I could charge twenty five dollars a night for three people. That'd be about fair, considering we charge $125 dollars for the week, and considering the sheets and towels would have to be changed out after you leave."

I explained all this to Dari and Danni and they looked at each other. "No, it is too much," Dari concluded. "We drive on."

"Well I'm sorry about that but I just can't go any lower than $25 for the night. This is a popular vacation destination you know," he said. "Lots of tourists come here every year. I couldn't set that kind of a precedent. Sorry that it won't work out for you. But hey, it's now happy hour so the drinks are half price! What will you have?"

I explained his response slowly to Dari and Danni while Dave stood there and waited patiently.

"Okay!" Dari exclaimed. "We have Mexican beer on Mexico Beach!" He seemed to think this was funny.

"Well Mexican beer it is!" And with that Dave produced three cans that had a triple X on the label, setting them before us on the bar. "Tres Equis," he said. "Try it and I think you'll like it."

I gripped the can and enjoyed its coolness as the drips of condensation rolled down over my fingers. Then I brought it up to my lips and took a sip of the frothy and refreshing brew, resisting a temptation to swallow it down all at once. I would need to keep my wits about me, at least until we figured where we would be staying. Gazing out to the mile long stretch of pristine sand, it was one of the most beautiful beaches I had ever seen, almost too perfect it seemed. A few small groups of tourists were out there on the beach, sitting peacefully in wicker beach chairs and staring out to the gulf. A young couple sat there with two small children playing beside them, they were digging in the sand, apparently constructing fairy tale castles from their imagination. And for a brief moment I was three years old again, sitting in the sand along shallow water somewhere back in Fort Walton Beach. Yes, I told myself. I would return and find that house one day.

Dari turned his attention to Dave our bartender. "Where we can get oysters?" It was still his end goal for the day.

"Well there's a small restaurant just up ahead that serves them up pretty fresh," he said. "But you really should head straight on down to Apalachicola, if you don't think you'll be staying here with us that is. It's only about thirty miles further down the road, and they've got a place on the waterfront that serves them up fresh right off the boats. The freshest oysters you'll ever find."

I explained all this to Dari and Danni and both of them nodded emphatically. It seemed that we would soon be underway once they had finished their beers. I took a final sip of mine and a satisfying belch made its way back up, making my sinuses tingle.

Feeling generous, I left a couple dollars on the bar for the three of us and we walked back out to the parking lot. The old sedan reluctantly rumbled back to life after several unwilling cranks of the starter motor, it probably had been wishing the day was over just like I had. Dari coaxed it forward anyway and we headed southeast down the highway.

The water was glassy after we had crossed over to Saint Joseph Bay. We followed its perimeter down the landward edge in a southerly direction. The harbor was shaped like a harp and appeared to be man-made. A narrow strip of land about two miles out formed the outer barrier of the bay. I imagined the size of the barge mounted dredgers that had been used to dig up the sand for that. It must have been quite a feat of engineering.

Highway 98 hooked off in an easterly direction when we reached the bay's widest span and headed inland. We continued following the meandering highway in a southeasterly direction for another fifteen miles or so. I was starting to worry that we might be headed in the wrong direction, but a road sign appeared reading that Apalachicola was eight miles ahead. We would make it after all.

A brilliant sunset had settled onto the gulf horizon by the time we reached the town of Apalachicola. We made our way along a cozy downtown street, and to my surprise Danni decided to pull over in front of a stately looking hotel. It was a Victorian era three story building, with wrap around verandas on the upper and lower levels. Several guests were rocking away on the porch; no doubt enjoying the cool breeze that was blowing in from the Gulf. A painted wooden sign that hung over the porch entry said this establishment was the "Gibson Inn / Rooms – Dining Room – Bar / Est. 1907". Danni went into the office to ask about the price. Dusk had fallen by the time he returned.

"Also twenty five dollars that one," he said, looking somewhat discouraged. He had probably pleaded our case the way I had done with Dave back in Mexico Beach, but clearly it hadn't worked. "Okay maybe we stay here tonight, but first we eat". I wasn't too excited about coughing up the eight plus dollars for my share of the room, but I was most definitely hungry, so first things first I decided.

We cranked the engine over once more and drove slowly down to the water's edge, making a left onto Water Street where to Danni's delight a brightly painted cinder block restaurant appeared. There was a painted sign on the wall that said this place was "Moe's Oyster Shack". It was lit up from red and green floodlights planted down in the sand, a festive sight if there ever was one, and this made us instantly hungry. Several dozen cars had already parked in a sandy clearing next to the building. If this was the place that Dave had told us about, we knew it should not be missed. Dari pulled into a space next to a rusted VW bus with a string of seashells hanging from the rearview mirror. I could see as we exited the sedan that the restaurant had been built right next to the causeway, and it had a boat dock behind it, right on the waterway just as Dave had said it would be. It was beer and oyster time.

I stepped onto the soft sand and stretched my tired muscles, breathing in the moist salt air and listening to the now familiar rumbling of cicadas in the trees, once again cooling their wings as darkness settled in. Their droning made a lively backbeat to what I later learned was Zydeco music filtering out from Moe's Oyster Shack, right here in Apalachicola Florida.

"Let's go, we eat now, okay?"

"Yeah let's," I said easily, following Danni inside with Dari close behind.

The music was loud when we entered the restaurant, and I could hardly understand what the waitress was saying when she directed us over to the raw bar. Danni found an empty stool and we shouldered our way on in, eventually pulling stools over to either side as other customers left. Danni sat with his larger bulk, raised his hand to the barmaid and ordered a frosty pitcher of draft beer that quickly appeared. The barmaid reached underneath the bar and pulled up three frosty mugs to set in front of us. Danni poured and handed a mug to Dari and then to me.

"To Florida adventure, and to new friend," he shouted above the Zydeco music as our glasses clinked together. A platter of oysters was waiting when we turned back to the bar, freshly half-shelled on crushed ice. The barmaid returned with a squeeze bottle of ketchup sauce spiked with horseradish and said "Enjoy!" Then she turned to help the next customer and left us to it.

I watched Danni pick up a half shell, add a dab of the ketchup sauce and then slurp away, marveling at how he knew what to do. They must have oysters in Israel I realized. My hunger pangs had been awakened by the foamy sip of beer, so I decided to dig in, curious to find out what one of these fresh Apalachicola oysters tasted like.

Oysters became one of my favorite delicacies that evening. I still remember the briny sweet and meaty taste as I sucked the first one down. With a tentative slurp, the ice cold morsel slides past your teeth and tantalizes the tongue. The flavors become more complex when you chew it. And the swallow is your throat's way of getting in on the tasting, an all-around satisfying experience. There was a hole in the bar with a metal trash can below it. Suspecting what it was for, I tossed my empty oyster shell down the chute and reached over for another. We were on our second tray of oysters before long and our second pitcher of beer as well. At one point, a busboy walked around the bar with an empty trash can and dragged the full one through the back door to a dumpster outside. A moist breeze blew into the bar, carrying with it the sound of seagulls who were snacking away out there on the oyster trash. It made me feel more alert in a pungent sort of way, but then the door swung shut.

I glanced around the bar while tapping on my thigh to the Zydeco beat. The man shucking oysters was engaged in a lively discussion with several of the patrons, and a woman was shouting back to him with similarly energetic hand gestures. She was wearing a pale blue, loose-fitting cotton blouse that didn't quite conceal her ample bosom, and tight fitting denim jeans tucked inside a pair of alligator boots. Her long blond hair bounced animatedly as she spoke. The man shucking oysters had on stained painter's pants with red suspenders pulled over a faded denim work shirt. He had a long bushy beard that I would remember years later while watching ZZ Top play live at the Hollywood Palladium. And when he turned around, I noticed his long rope of braided red hair. Other patrons were seated at tables in the next room facing the water, leaning into their buckets of steamed shrimp and sides of coleslaw with Zellwood corn, or plates of grilled grouper with dirty rice and okra. Their manner of dress was casual at best, and most of them wore shorts and T-shirts with fishing logos on the back, and flip-flops or athletic shoes with no socks. The band took a break and someone put a few coins in the jukebox, now it was playing an eclectic mix of blues and southern rock.

Our beer sipping and oyster slurping kept going unabated for another hour, at which point Danni, Dari and I collectively patted our bellies and nodded to each other in agreement that it was time to leave. I raised a hand to the oyster shucker and he came over and told us that our bill would be ten dollars and ten cents (someone must have had one extra oyster). I reached into my front pocket and counted out fifty cents, then unfolded a thin wad of singles from my back pocket and peeled off three of them, relieved that I had enough money into my pocket to pay for my share. Most of my cash was still rolled up in a pair of jeans that I had shoved into the bottom of my backpack that morning, but I was careful not to mention that to anyone. Danni made up the difference from a leather money belt under his shirt and we all stood up, steadying ourselves as we prepared to leave.

CHAPTER TWELVE

DARI WAS PONDERING WHAT TO DO as he walked back out to the rusty sedan. "That hotel too much cost," he said when we reached the car. Danni stood there for a moment and reflected on this, then smiled. "No problem, we drive on!" he said with as much enthusiasm as he had every other time that day. It was not exactly what I wanted to hear, but I would need to get some more money out of my backpack if we went back into town. So I reluctantly agreed to drive on until we could find a cheaper motel. The Impala's old motor refused to start at first, but it fired to life after Dari's third attempt. The weary sedan was ready for bed time, and quite frankly so was I. Dari coaxed the gas pedal and he eventually got the vehicle moving back to the roadway. But the engine continued to sputter in protest. We made our way down Water Street, circled around Battery Park, and took the ramp to a three mile bridge crossing over the East Bay, hoping to find a cheaper motel on the opposite side. Unfortunately we didn't see one in Eastpoint, a small fishing town that obviously didn't cater to tourists. Once again Danni said "we drive on," but this time his enthusiasm seemed to be waning.

I decided not to worry, ready to accept whatever fate would give us. I was pretty sure that we were still headed in the right direction, and every passing mile would mean one less mile tomorrow, so I rolled down the window and tried to enjoy the cool evening air as it blew over my face. We followed down the rim of Apalachicola Bay for another twenty minutes.

Fatigue was settling into our weary bones by this time and none of us felt like talking, so Danni decided to switch on the radio and fiddle with the knob until he found a country and western station. It was a cowboy-cowgirl duet and they were singing a sad song accompanied by a weeping steel guitar. "That nice," Danni said. It seemed he'd never heard this kind of music back home in Israel and was finding it pleasing, although I was pretty sure he couldn't catch much of what they were singing about. He bopped his head in time with the music nonetheless, and smiled like this day had been the best day ever, which indeed it had been in many ways. So we drove on with our bellies full and a nice beer buzz, not much caring anymore how much further we would have to go that night, at least as long as Dari could stay sufficiently alert to drive. I made a mental note to pay closer attention to his driving from here on, but he seemed to be okay at least for now.

A spotlight appeared out of the darkness and blinded us temporarily. It was coming from an old lighthouse just ahead and was making a slow 360 degree rotation. A waning moon was also rising with a dark bite out of its side that looked more prominent now. As if ignoring this annoyance, it proudly cast a beam on the bay as it rose skyward. We reached a small fishing village called Carrabelle and followed Highway 98 down to the water's edge, quietly making our way through the darkened and sleepy town. Then we took an inland route which caused me some concern. I was starting to think we may have made a wrong turn somewhere when the Gulf finally reappeared, this time with no land barriers obscuring the view. A wide expanse of dark water was shimmering before us, reflecting the moon's silver light.

An announcer came on the radio with details about a rodeo that would be held the coming weekend up in Tallahassee. "Rodeo!" Dari cheered, glancing at Danni and then back at me. Danni switched on the overhead light and consulted the map. "Maybe forty miles north of here," he said.

"Yeah, but that rodeo's not until this weekend," I tried to explain, hoping they would rethink the plan that was obviously brewing inside their heads. "That's two days from now. What are we going to do in Tallahassee for two days? And oh by the way, it will probably be expensive. Big city," I said emphatically.

"Yes, you may be right", Dari's voice quieted back down. "Okay, we drive on!" I exhaled slowly, relieved.

We continued east on Highway 98 for another twenty minutes or so, listening to 50s era country and western songs that I tried to tune out. But Danni seemed to enjoy them unfortunately. The highway bent north away from the Gulf and we passed a sign announcing the entrance to Bald Point State Park. I could hardly make out the dense forest of scotch pines to our right, but the silhouettes of the trees made a dark jagged contrast to the moonlit sky. I held my breath and was relieved when Dari did not make the turn. There could be wild pigs hereabouts and I had no desire to sleep another night out on the hard ground.

We crossed over the Ocklockonee Bay, our final bridge of the day, and continued north until we got to a fork in the highway. Dari braked and studied a pair of road signs illuminated in the headlights. The one to our left pointed in the direction of Tallahassee, and the one to our right directed us to the continuation of Highway 98, which happened to be the direction I was hoping we'd go since it took us closer to Orlando. Danni clicked on the ceiling light and tried to study the map, but it was obvious by his sagging posture that he was about ready to nod off. Upon seeing this, Dari pulled the car over to the side of the road and shifted into park, letting the engine idle as he turned back to me.

"You drive?" he asked. He was clearly finished for the day also.

"Sure," I said, knowing it was either that or we would most likely wind up someplace sleeping in the sedan next to the highway, probably not a desirable option for any of us. I got out of the car and walked around to the driver's side. Dari shifted into neutral and stepped out so I could take over, more than happy to let me have the wheel. I settled into the seat and fidgeted with the rearview mirror. Once Dari had closed the rear passenger door, I put my foot on the brake and shifted into drive, easing us back out onto the road in the direction of Highway 98. The steering wheel required frequent adjustments to keep the car pointed more or less straight down the highway. I knew these tires were badly worn, but it became a constant concern now that I was behind the wheel. I hoped that we wouldn't have a flat out here in the dark.

Danni and Dari were fast asleep now and Danni was snoring badly. I toyed with the idea of turning the radio back on but decided against it. Instead, I took a few deep breaths and steeled myself to continue driving for as long as I could stay awake, or at least until a decent looking motel emerged.

It was a bit past 10 pm according to the dimly lit clock on the dashboard. I took a brief glance at the gas gauge while continuing to make steering adjustments.

We only had about a quarter of a tank left which was not a good omen. A 25 mph speed limit sign emerged from the blackness and the small town of Hampton Springs came out of the gloom with little warning. Its only street light glimmered from a pole next to a phone booth at the town's only gas station. Unfortunately the gas station was dark and closed. I couldn't find a motel here either so I drove slowly out of town, uncertain what to do next. Then I passed another sign for the town of Perry, just four miles up the road.

When we got to Perry, population 6253, I was relieved to spot a sign for the Sun-n-Sand Motel just ahead with an arched neon sign flashing the word "vacancy". A marquis beneath it spelled out "free breakfast" in removable black letters. I pulled up to the office and shifted the transmission into park, turning off the ignition. Dari and Danni awoke immediately, probably an instinct drilled into them from their army training. We walked into the office to ask about a room.

A repurposed shop light was flickering overhead. It was dark on the other side of the counter except for a small reading lamp, casting an amber glow over a messy office desk that was stationed against the back wall. Dari rang a bell on the counter and we stood there uncomfortably, wondering what would happen next. Out of the gloom from the back door came a rumpled looking man in his mid-fifties, with a few bumps and other such noises. He had on a dingy grey bathrobe with a trucker's hat pulled down over his greasy hair that read "Let's Rodeo". This seemed fitting somehow.

"Y'all want a room, I suppose?" he asked in a gravelly voice, and moved his big head slowly from left to right as he stared each one of us down.

"Yes please," I answered, deciding to take charge of the situation. He studied me for an uncomfortable moment and then slowly nodded.

"We've only got one cottage left," he grumbled at last. "It's got just a single full sized bed though, and it'll be eight dollars for the night." I glanced over to Dari and Danni and they nodded that it would be okay. I figured I'd sleep on the floor, hoping that the room would at least be carpeted.

"Okay, that will be fine," I replied to "Rodeo Man".

"Can you tell us about the free breakfast?" I ventured, trying to verify that we could save some money the next morning.

"Come back to the office tomorrow and I'll give you some free breakfast coupons when you check out, tell you where to go." Danni paid and I promised to give him my share of the money tomorrow. "Rodeo Man" handed Danni the key to room number 8, then turned around and returned to his sleeping compartment behind the office, hitting the light switch as he shut the door, leaving us in darkness.

We got in the sedan and I drove slowly down to the third small cottage on the left. With tires crunching over the gravel, I eventually saw a rusting number 8 nailed to the door, illuminated from a bare light bulb screwed into a socket just above. I pulled over and killed the engine. It finally died after several more diesel hickups. Danni inserted the room key into the door latch and it opened with a loud click. A musty smell wafted out once the door creaked open. He reached in and found a light switch, revealing a rumpled bed with a badly worn brown comforter draped over it. Stepping inside, I saw the light was coming from a floor lamp standing next to a lime green Naugahyde chair, over in the right front corner of the room. A framed picture was hung over the bed of a cowboy about to lasso a steer, and a battered oak dresser stood against the left hand wall, completing the décor.

I motioned down at the green shag carpet and said I would sleep on the floor. Danni was having nothing of that however, and shook his head emphatically. As I began to get concerned, he and Dari pulled the comforter off the bed and lifted the top mattress, setting it on the floor next to the bedframe. After arranging the comforter on top, Danni announced "we sleep here", and nodded over to the box spring mattress and back at me. Apparently I was to sleep on the box spring, which still meant that I would need my sleeping bag, but I concluded it would be a better option since the musty shag carpet looked like it had never been vacuumed.

We stepped out into the foggy mist to retrieve our bags from the car. I propped my backpack next to the Naugahyde chair and took off my boots, placing them next to it against the wall. Then I removed my bag of toiletries and made my way over to the small bathroom so that I could wash up a bit. After I had cleaned the day's grime off my face and relieved myself, I returned to the room. Dari and Danni were already fast asleep by this time. I stripped to my shorts, draped my clothes over the chair armrest, switched off the lamp, and crawled into my sleeping bag. I started thinking about the day I had had, but it didn't last long. Gravity took me down and my tired body fell into a very deep sleep.

I awoke abruptly to a flash of light that startled my eyelids. A clap of thunder quickly followed, deep and vibrant, and a heavy rain began pelting the window like a snare drum. The rain was coming down hard now. I looked at my watch and saw that it was already 8:02 AM. Dari and Danni were still fast asleep, even after a second flash of lightning and … a thousand one, a thousand two, crack-thunder-rumble! Good thing I wasn't sleeping outside just then. I decided to take a shower in the small bathroom before they awoke.

The hot water invigorated my body as I scrubbed down completely for the first time in several days, deciding to use the single use shampoo bottle that I found on the glass shelf over the sink, next to a tiny bar of soap in a white paper wrapper that I decided to leave for Dari and Danni since I had my own. I toweled off, pulled on my jeans, and continued drying my hair as I walked back out to the main room. The rain had stopped by this time, and a ray of sunshine now was beaming into the room. Dari and Danni were stretching themselves awake. Dari motioned that he would take a shower while Danni arranged his travel bag, once again pulling out the individual State of Florida roadmap that he had purchased the day before in Pensacola. He unfolded it and placed it on top of the box spring mattress, studying it while I rolled up my sleeping bag and strapped it to the bottom rail of my backpack. Then I came over to inspect the map along with Danni. Dari emerged from the bathroom in olive cargo pants and he was still shirtless. He had an exceptionally hairy chest and back. "Ah!" he said while toweling down his hair and beard. "Where we go today gentlemen?" he said with a chuckle. Apparently the word "gentlemen" was a new one that he was having fun with.

"Well, like I said before I'd like to get to Orlando today…" I said for probably the fourth time, pointing to a black dot with bold letters in the middle of the state. Dari came over, looked down at the map and then pointed to another dot on the opposite coast.

"Cape Kennedy, Cocoa Beach…the astronauts, yes?" he seemed to remember.

"Yes," I replied, "But I don't think they launch many rockets these days, and no astronauts, just satellites." NASA no longer had an active space program, a disappointing thing to think about since the final Apollo mission was still fairly fresh in my memory. "But you can visit the space center. I hear that by itself is worth the trip out there."

"Cocoa Beach…beautiful beach girls, yes?" Dari had obviously heard about bikinis. "OK, we can make there by tonight! We drop you in Orlando on way across state." And there it was; this was going to be my final leg of the journey.

So we studied the map some more and planned out the day's drive. We would follow Highway 27 southeast to Ocala and then take old Highway 441 down to Orlando. I pointed my index finger to the dot that said Altamonte Springs. "You can drop me off here,"

I said. "There is a shopping mall where I can call my father to come get me. Then you drive down to Highway 50," I traced the route with my finger, "and take Highway 50 east all the way to Cocoa Beach." It would be another fairly long day of driving for them. We all nodded in agreement and decided to get going; packing up the rest of our gear and loading the bags back in the Impala.

I walked the key back to the office and set it on the counter. "Rodeo Man" still had the hat pulled down over his greasy hair, a more unpleasant sight in the daylight than it was the night before, but at least he had managed to dress himself and seemed to be in a bit better mood. I asked about the breakfast and he pointed to a building next to the parking lot that faced the street, it was a diner called Joe's Place, conveniently located right next to the motel.

He handed me three blue meal coupons about the size of credit cards. They looked like they had been circulated a fair number of times between Joe's Place and 'Rodeo Man'. But the words "one free regular breakfast entree, juice or coffee" were still legible on them. My stomach told me that I was hungry so I returned to the car and told Dari and Danni about the free breakfast, then handed them each a coupon and pointed in the direction of the diner.

This didn't take much convincing. Dari locked the car and briskly walked over to the diner, keen to get going but unwilling to pass up a free breakfast. Danni followed him in close pursuit. I walked into the diner right behind them and glanced at my watch, seeing that it was already past nine AM. We chose to sit at the counter, hoping to make it quick.

The only other customer was a fiftyish man of impressive girth with a grey flattop crew cut who had been sitting over in the corner booth. A cigarette dangled from his lips as he read the newspaper, not much caring to look up when we arrived. I turned to the counter and observed a short order cook shuffling back and forth behind the service bay. There was an order slip dangling from the metal carousel that must be the old guy's breakfast order. He unclipped and studied it for several seconds, then clipped it back onto the carousel and tossed a handful of shredded potatoes on the grill, adding a dab of lard and stirring it around with a spatula while he shook salt and pepper over the sizzling spuds with his other hand. I watched the steam rising from the grill.

A round woman in a red striped apron obstructed my view and this startled me to attention. "Trudy", according to her plastic nametag, wore black horned rim glasses, with frizzy salt and pepper hair pulled back in a severe bun. Her mouth made a bit of a scowl as she stood there waiting impatiently with her order pad. I quickly inspected my plastic menu and ordered two eggs over easy with sausage and hash browns, since they smelled pretty good from the grill just now. I also decided to order a glass of orange juice having foregone that luxury the day before. This would probably be my last day on the road, and I was in Florida after all. Danni and Dari simply gestured that they would have the same, "but coffee for me," said Danni. "And me too OK?" said Dari. Trudy scribbled out our orders on her pad and ripped off the top sheet, clipping it to the carousel. The short order cook studied it and then added more potatoes and sausage to the grill, along with a fresh dab of lard. He cracked and fried the eggs, flipping them nimbly with an oversized spatula. Trudy returned with the juice and coffees and turned back around to get our plates when they appeared from the kitchen, setting them before us in a fluid motion. She moved pretty quickly for a woman of her girth, even though we were the only customers sitting there at the counter.

I gently tapped the salt and pepper shakers over my plate of food, pounded an inverted ketchup bottle over the hash browns until a generous dollop came out, and tucked in, stirring the egg yolks around into the potatoes. I enjoyed the medley of flavors as they entered my stomach. Soon my plate was empty when I glanced side to side I could see that Danni and Dari had finished theirs too. I placed my coupon on the counter and Danni and Dari put theirs down as well. Trudy glanced at the coupons and made a slight nod with her pressed lips curled downward. I got the message and pulled out my wallet, pulling out a worn dollar bill and placing it on the counter next to the coupons. She nodded again, this time to me directly with just the faintest hint of a smile that quickly left her face after I had acknowledged it. Now that our bellies were full again, we decided it was time to head back to the car.

My attention span soon faltered after we had rejoined the highway. The Florida landscape was so intensely green that I was having a hard time taking it all in, having traversed over 1500 miles of arid landscape through the Mojave of California, Arizona, New Mexico and Texas. Another Scotch pine forest made strobe flashes against my eyelids as the rising sun blinked through them. The ground was saturated with vegetation competing for what little light got through, with palmettos, ferns and vines wrapping around and draping over almost everything. This scenery was subliminally hypnotic, a type of Morse code that I could almost comprehend but didn't really care to. And it went on like that for miles and miles.

I realized I hadn't remembered to call my father to let him know that I was coming. I hadn't called Michelle either, which seemed pretty dumb at the time considering she was the reason for my trip. At least I had thought she was the reason when I started on my journey six days before, back in the smoggy Pomona Valley. I rolled down the window and breathed in the morning air. It was moist and warm, with a pungent medley of molding pine needles and palm fronds. The gentle turbulence invigorated me as it blew against my face, once again flapping the hair against my neck.

In one of Michelle's letters she had asked whether I would be coming out again this summer. I hadn't replied to that and was hoping it would be a nice surprise. But my father... why had I forgotten to call him? I mused about this as the dirty Impala sedan clattered down the highway.

The trees yielded to an open clearing and I watched several longhorn cattle standing out in the grassy meadow grazing. They looked like Texas longhorns to me except that their hides were ivory, probably a special breed adapted for the Florida climate, which made quite a striking contrast to the green background. Bright azure sky was dominating the horizon, with puffy clouds shifting around slowly and changing shape as they moved. They would probably reach critical mass again later that afternoon, releasing another rain shower onto the landscape. I hoped to be in Orlando by then.

My father wouldn't approve of my chosen mode of transportation, I was thinking. Having ridden with Dari and Danni for the past two days, I decided to say that I had connected with them through a ride share ad back in California, but only if he asked.

The countryside continued to alternate between stretches of pine forest and clearings planted with corn, with occasional lakes and meadows and more of those white long horned cattle standing out there in them. It went on like this for another half hour with none of us talking. Danni had not yet decided to turn on the radio, so the only noise came from our balding tires as they rolled along the hot Florida asphalt. We had been motoring along at 70 mph with nary a car in sight, but then we reached another series of speed signs instructing us to decelerate to 45 mph, 35 mph, and then 25 mph.

"Those signs mean must slow down," I said, reaching my hand over the seat and motioning with my thumb downwards. Danni hit the brakes, and had slowed just enough when we passed a sign announcing the entrance to Cross City. There was a white sedan parked directly behind it. I could see his "Smokey the Bear" hat pulled down over the man's eyebrows, although there weren't any lights on top of the car. The patrolman turned his head as we moved past, but he didn't follow. We were doing 35 mph and we were still slowing down.

"This must be our lucky day," I said.

"What?" Dari asked.

"Next time watch those speed signs," I said, "or one of those patrol cars will pull us over, give us ticket." Danni nodded his head in understanding, an expression of relief now on his face.

As we rolled slowly into town, with Danni glancing repeatedly at the speedometer to maintain a steady 25 mph, we passed a few small houses set back from the highway with sand driveways leading up. One had a tire swing hanging from an oak tree in the front yard. Small businesses lined the road as we approached the center of town. A woman in curlers was entering Thompson's general store. Two wagon wheels were nailed to either side of the sign over the store's front entrance for some reason. I studied an aging white two story building with a water tower standing next to it that had the town's name painted on the tank in black letters. Then we passed the Dixie County Courthouse, a white stately looking building with a gabled roof. The pleasant little park on the opposite side was shaded by another one of those large oak trees. Did that moss stuff really come from Spain? I didn't know. A pair of old men were sitting at a concrete picnic table under it, with their heads bowed over a game of checkers. Just like back in Mississippi, I mused, must be like that all over the south. The "business district" gave way to more small houses, and soon we encountered another array of speed signs granting us permission to accelerate back up to 35 mph, then to 45 mph. I saw a sign for the Cross City Correctional Institution and was glad that we hadn't been pulled over by that patrol car back there. We passed the town's final speed limit sign and returned to open highway.

I was just getting used to this when another series of speed signs came into view. Danni was more alert this time and dutifully slowed down. The gateway to Old Town was a proud little Methodist church with a white steeple. Danni decided to pull into the town's only gas station to refill our tank. Just past the post office, the curving Suwannee River came into view and we began to follow alongside it.

A friendly looking motel appeared on the left with a blue neon sign out front announcing the Suwannee Gables motel and marina. A man in a fishing hat was roping down suitcases on a rack atop his Rambler station wagon. His wife and two small children were trying to help, another leg of their summer road trip was likely done and on to their next adventure.

We kept following the river for several miles. The sun's reflection made ripples on the emerald water as drove along. While studying cottontails that lined the banks I wondered what geological reason could explain the river's frequent bends and turns through the flat landscape. I had read the Florida soil is made up of ancient sea floor sediments with fragments of shells and fossilized diatomaceous sea creatures long ago extinct. This sandy composition floated on aquifers and sink holes were not uncommon. Maybe that explained the shifting sands which had created the river's meanderings. We crossed over a bridge that spanned the river and I caught a glimpse of two black teenagers who were fishing along the bank. Each wore a dirty sleeveless T-shirt with tattered jeans rolled up to their knees. One of the boys was startled when his bobber disappeared underwater jerking down his fishing pole. Rings of sunlight were reflecting on the water around the line. He had just begun to reel in the line when I lost sight of him. I hoped he would have a nice fish dinner with that.

The highway proceeded in a southeasterly direction after we left the town, and the speed signs reversed their order permitting us to accelerate back to 55 mph. I borrowed the Florida road map from Dari and noted that the next town of Chiefland was only ten miles away. We would head east from there on Highway 27, to the town of Williston and then southeast to Ocala, at which point we would then take Highway 441 down toward Orlando.

The ride from Chiefland to Ocala was uneventful, and to be honest there isn't much that I still remember. I tried to retrace that leg of the trip with my son many years later, but by then a construction boom had transformed the landscape and nothing looked quite the same. I do remember a road sign for Cypress Gardens with a row of attractive young women on water skis gliding side by side through the water and waving down to us. I also remember the scent of orange blossoms as we passed through the groves lining the highway. Most of those groves are no longer there, having been replaced by businesses, neighborhoods and shopping malls. And I remember a seemingly endless procession of lakes, some smaller and some larger as the highway made its way down toward Orlando. Those lakes are still there, however many of them are obscured from view now.

Neither Dari nor Danni said much during this leg of the trip. It had been a struggle for them to find the English words for what they wanted to say. But a bond of friendship had formed between us by this time, and we were content to ride on without talking, settling into the rhythm of the road. I was grateful for their generosity, realizing that I would soon be safely deposited at my final destination.

"Thank you," I said.

Dari turned around and smiled at me. "You are very welcome, my friend," he said. I hoped that I had also been helpful to them on this leg of their journey.

I regained my bearings when we entered the town of Apopka and then made our way southeast, down Semoran Boulevard toward Altamont Springs.

When we finally got to the Altamont Springs shopping mall, having stopped at countless traffic lights along the way, I asked Danni to pull into the parking lot.

"You can drop me off here and then continue down to State Highway 50. Take that east and it will take you all the way to Cocoa Beach."

Danni pulled into the lot and found a parking space, shutting off the struggling and overheated engine with another gasp and a sputter. He walked around to the trunk, opened it with his key and lifted out my backpack, handing it over to me. "Best of luck to you, my friend," he said in his best English, struggling to make sure it came out right.

"Good luck to you as well, my friend from another country!" I replied, and then repeated the directions down to Highway 50. I said the words slowly to make sure they would understand. "I hope you have a good time in Cocoa Beach tonight, my friends, and also the rest of your trip. I enjoyed getting to know you both."

"Me too!" Danni said, grabbing my hand and shaking it firmly.

I walked up to the passenger side and Dari rolled down his window, extending his hand out to me as well. I took it and he shook back vigorously, his smiling eyes locking onto mine. "You must come to Israel," he said, continuing to pump my hand. "We show you Tel Aviv, the most beautiful beaches in world!" He opened the glove box and scribbled onto a pad of paper, tore off the top sheet and handed it to me. It contained his address and phone number and I folded it carefully before sticking it in my wallet. I might still have it somewhere, stashed away in a box of memorabilia that my mother packed up when I left for college.

Then Dari decided to step out of the car, extending his hand to me once more. I offered him mine and he pulled me toward him in a bear hug, patting my back as he did so. When he finally released, he stepped away and smiled at me one more time. It was an effective goodbye.

Danni decided to do the same, patting my back just as vigorously. The two young Israeli men settled into the sedan, fired up the engine and slowly made their way out of the parking lot, waving back to me when they turned right on Highway 436. I watched them drive away until the sedan was no longer in sight.

CHAPTER THIRTEEN

I WAS AT THE END OF MY CROSS-COUNTRY JOURNEY now. Here I was standing in a shopping mall parking lot in the blazingly hot mid-afternoon sun, and it was unbearably humid. The sun's rays baked down on the pavement and cast shimmering reflections off the car hoods as they radiated its heat. I tried to focus, grasping the rail of my pack and walking slowly but deliberately toward the mall. I was trying not to break a sweat but my shirt was already soaked by the time I reached the entrance. I stepped onto a ribbed rubber entrance mat that caused the sliding glass door to open automatically, and a cold stream of refrigerated air wafted over me when I walked inside. I decided to look around for a bench where I could sit and wait for my body temperature to return to normal. Locating one, I sat down and rested the pack against my knees while trying to ignore the shoppers who would cast nervous glances in my direction when they walked quickly past.

The bustling atmosphere inside the shopping mall was a bit overwhelming as I sat there listening to a brass medley of songs from hidden mall speakers. Shoppers were busily walking around and most of them ignored me. I recognized a tune from Herb Albert, also known as "The Dating Game" theme song from TV. I tried to ignore their curious stares.

After a few minutes had passed, I saw that my shirt was showing patches of dryness and noticed that my hair was no longer sticking to my face or my neck. I decided to walk down the mall way to find a restroom where I could wash up a bit. I was carrying the pack beside me like a suitcase, as though it would be less conspicuous that way. It was probably a false assumption, but I didn't seem to be attracting much attention. Still I was relieved when I saw the sign and opened the door to the men's room.

I washed up and changed into the clean Hang Ten T-shirt that I had been saving for this occasion. This time I decided to shoulder my pack when I walked back out into the mall, feeling a bit more confident now.

As I was making my way to the center of the mall, I passed by a record store, a novelty gift shop, a See's Candy kiosk, a women's dress shop and a shoe store. Stopping to get my bearings, I correctly chose the right hand corridor and followed it down to the Farrell's Ice Cream Parlor, the place where Michelle worked. I stood outside in the mall way watching the waitresses move efficiently between the tables. And there she was, carefully lowering a tray loaded with sodas and ice cream sundaes onto a corner table. After distributing them to the customers who were seated there, she quickly turned around and returned to the service counter to refill her tray for the next table. There was a restrained sense of urgency about her, pausing just long enough to smile at the customers and take their order. Most of her money came from tips which encouraged her to move the tables pretty quickly.

She wore a red and white striped dress and a ruffled pink apron decorated with brightly colored buttons, some with phrases like "Are you ready for sundae?", or "Have you been good? Have some ice cream!" There was a button with a picture of Albert Einstein, one with W.C. Fields sitting at a poker table in a bowler hat, one with a peace sign, and a yellow "smiley face" button. The management encouraged the waiters and waitresses to wear lots of these buttons, which seemed kind of silly and perhaps it was, but evidently it helped with the tips so everyone embraced the idea in a competitive sort of way. I enjoyed watching her lithe body moving gracefully with efficient purpose. Then she glanced out into the mall and froze when she saw me. Her expression changed quickly from startled, to surprised, and then a smile. It was the most beautiful smile.

A wave of perplexing emotions coursed through me as I stood there with my feet glued to the floor. There was a warm and nervous sensation in my chest and stomach, but what I remember most was the clear feeling of relief. I had made it and she was actually happy to see me. I was at peace with myself for the briefest of moments.

Michelle carried her tray back to the kitchen and spoke briefly with the manager, apparently requesting a short break. He looked at her sternly, glanced at his watch, and then nodded. She walked out into the mall and motioned for me to follow her down to the entry way where her workmates would not be able to see us.

"Hey," she said at last.

"Hey," I replied, enjoying the physical reality of her standing there before me, with those almond eyes that I remembered, and with her lips curled into an uncertain smile, how pretty she was.

"Brett, I thought you said you weren't going to be able to make it back to Florida this summer, that you needed to work your summer job to pay for college," she paused, thinking of the obvious next question. "What are you doing here?"

"My job starts in little over a week." My step-father had pulled some strings to get me a summer job at the wire mill in Etiwanda, back in the Pomona Valley where I was destined to return. I would be making $6.85 an hour, which was considerably more than my previous part time movie theatre job. I needed this money for college. Yet here I was in Florida. Could I stay? Did I have to go back?

"But I had to see you," I said, having no idea what else to say.

"Well I have to get back to work," she replied with those captivating yet unreadable eyes looking into mine, probably searching for what to think next just as I was.

"What time do you get off work?"

"Five o'clock."

I looked at my watch. It was about three thirty in the afternoon.

"Cool. Can I see you later?"

"I'll be meeting some of our friends down at the lake this evening," she said, her face now showing the hint of a smile. "Maybe I'll see you there?" She seemed even more beautiful now.

My three thousand mile journey had led up to this moment and it had been worth it.

"I'll be there!" I beamed back at her. I watched her go, her lean and graceful body striding back to the ice cream restaurant with graceful purpose. Then I started to notice that people were glancing a bit too long in my direction as they entered the mall, me the long haired kid in grass stained jeans with a backpack on, standing near the entrance of a major shopping mall. It was time for me to go.

I went outside, found a telephone stall and inserted the dime that I always kept in the watch pocket of my jeans. After taking a breath, I dialed my father's number and my stepmother answered.

I wasn't quite sure how she would react to my unannounced appearance in town. I didn't know her very well actually. I remembered from last summer that she was a fastidious housekeeper with lots of rules that I seemed to keep forgetting. She had not had children of her own, but I knew that she wanted my sister and me to feel welcome when we were visiting my father. It was still a work in progress.

"Oh Brett!" she said. "Your father will be so happy you called. Where are you?"

"Well, actually I'm here in Orlando." Silence on the other end as she digested this.

"I managed to catch a ride with some friends who were planning a cross country road trip," I ventured, thinking that if I came out and admitted that I had been hitch hiking this would not have gone over well. "They just dropped me off at the Altamonte Mall and are now heading on out to Cocoa Beach," I said. At least that part was true.

"Well I hope you're planning to stay with us?" she said expectantly.

"Of course," I answered, and then added "I'm sorry that I didn't call ahead. I didn't know how many days it would take for us to make it to Florida," which was also true. "Anyway I'm here now and I am excited to see you and Father," I added hoping to make a good impression, which I wasn't sure was possible just then under the circumstances.

"I suppose you need a ride?" My father's house was about fifteen miles from the pay phone where I was talking now with my stepmother. It would have been a long hike, especially during the muggy Florida afternoon heat of summer. "Yes please, if that's not too inconvenient for you."

"Sure Brett, I'll be there in about thirty minutes."

"Great, I'll be waiting outside the east entrance to the shopping mall."

I found a bench and sat down, clutching my pack against my knees while customers walked by on their way into the mall. The pack was much dirtier now than it was when I started this journey, having collected considerable amounts of dust from El Paso, grease from outside of Dallas, and clay from Mississippi along the way. I reached down and tried to swat off the dirt as if my pack were a throw rug. The humidity of the southern afternoon permeated my formerly air-conditioned clothing, causing my pores to open up once again. There was no escaping this, it seemed. Once again the beads of sweat were oozing out of my pores, a familiar reminder of the hot and sultry weather I had endured over the past six days.

I smiled at the few departing mall customers who were brave enough to make eye contact. Some of them smiled back, evidently trying to recall whether they knew me, or maybe they just felt sorry for the dirty hippie kid who was sitting there. I thought about how good it was going to feel to take a shower and crank the water down to its coldest setting. I would rinse off the sweat and grit that clung to my eyelashes and lined the creases of my neck. I still had a relatively clean pair of jeans and the corduroy shorts stashed away at the bottom of my pack, along with a pair of running shoes and flip flops. I contented myself with the thought that I would soon be wearing clean clothes again, clothes that didn't stick to my skin.

Just as I was thinking about going back into the mall to cool off, my stepmother pulled over to the curb in a new Cadillac Eldorado, a four door sedan with bronze metallic paint and a roof trimmed in imitation leather, the type of car that real estate agents like her seemed to prefer.

"Oh Brett!" she called out to me as she lowered down the electrically controlled driver side window. She made this exclamation a lot when she saw me, or when I called on the phone, as though it were always a surprise. I felt the cool air billowing out from the open window as I approached the car. "There you are. What a surprise to see you!" She smiled through oversized sunglasses that hid her displeasure with my disheveled appearance. "How are you?" she asked at last.

"I'm great! Thank you so much for coming to get me." The trunk popped open. My backpack was not welcome on the backseat.

"Brett, would you please get one of those beach towels in the trunk?" I knew what to do and laid it over the passenger seat before settling in and fastening my seatbelt. Then I shut the passenger door and enjoyed the air conditioning as my stepmother eased out of the parking lot and drove down highway 436 to the north I-4 onramp.

Here I was riding again with someone I actually knew, someone who was taking me to a house that had a guest bedroom with an attached bathroom and shower. I would be sleeping in a real bed tonight. Not the desert sand. Not on some wet grass behind a gas station. Not the lower box springs portion of a squeaky hotel bed. It was a bit overwhelming to realize that this hitchhiking journey had truly ended. I wasn't quite sure if I was ready for the predictability of a regular day, however I wanted to see my father, and I appreciated my stepmother for trying to make me feel as welcome as she was able.

But as I rode in the air-conditioned Caddie to my father's house, I thought again about Michelle, the girl who had sent me letters every week during the past school year, who had lifted my spirits as I struggled through my senior year of high school, the girl who I would be seeing again that very evening. A wave of imaginings, a quiver of hope, and a growing sense of relief coursed through me as I rode along in my stepmother's comfortable vehicle. We were heading up the interstate to Sweetwater Oaks, a master planned subdivision of upscale executive homes. My father, a custom homebuilder, had designed and built a considerable number of homes in the area and now he lived proudly in one of them, just four houses up from Lake Brantley.

We took the Highway 434 exit and headed west to Wekiva Springs Road, then proceeded north into the nestled community. As advertised, there were mature oak trees lining both sides of the road, again with that now familiar Spanish moss hanging down from the branches. Their shade gave a feeling of permanence and grandeur to this newly constructed community. We passed Husky Realty with its colonial style building standing proudly behind an elaborate water fountain. Old man Husky had brokered virtually all of the lots in this community and had grown considerably wealthy in the process. His gold Cadillac convertible stood out there in front along the circular drive like a trophy.

We turned off the main road and made our way down a few side streets until we reached Palmetto Drive. My father's house was on the left hand side and I could see the lake and the artificial beach where I would be meeting Michelle that evening. It looked like the perfect place to live out the rest of one's days; however he was planning to build himself an even bigger house as soon as he had sold some of the others now being built. He had already purchased the lot from Mr. Husky in Sweetwater Estates, a new subdivision that was just being cleared.

As we approached the house, my stepmother reached over the sun shade and pressed a button on the remote which activated the garage door's automatic lifter. It was a relatively new experience for me since none of the houses back in my Southern California town had such a convenience. I figured that they must need these electronic wonders here in Florida since it rained so much, almost every afternoon over the summer months.

Another wave of heat and humidity swept over me as I stepped out of the Cadillac. My stepmother quickly lowered the garage door and pressed another button under the dash to pop the trunk. I carried my pack inside and entered my father's air-conditioned house, letting out a sigh of relief. Standing there in the laundry room, my stepmother looked down and I "thoughtfully" unlaced my hiking boots and set them back out in the garage.

"Did you want to take a shower?" It was not really a question.

"Yeah that would feel great, actually." I was right with her on that motivation.

"Bring your dirty things back to the laundry room after you're done. Please put them directly into the washing machine if you don't mind." I understood. She did not want to touch them.

"Have you got anything clean to wear?"

"Yeah, I've got one clean pair of shorts left. I've also brought a clean pair of sneakers and flip flops. They haven't been worn yet either." I didn't want her to think they were dirty.

"OK then. Your father should be home around five."

Walking past a great room that opened out to a fully screened-in back porch complete with swimming pool, I continued down a side hall to a guest room that was strategically located on the other side of the house. Each of the guestrooms had its own bathroom, which seemed like quite a luxury to a young man who had grown up in a house with four kids and only one bathroom to share.

Standing beneath a brass showerhead in the cool spray of water, the encrusted sweat and grime slowly surrendered as I lathered and rinsed, alternating the water from cool to warm and back again. I used one of the travel shampoos that my stepmother had left on the vanity and worked it into my scalp, then rinsed some more and spun around under the shower dial's coolest setting. I cupped my hands and splashed the water around to rinse soap suds off the tiles, then turned the shower off and used a squeegee to remove the droplets of water from the tiles and glass door. It had been an important directive from my stepmother the summer before, and I understood that it was necessary to prevent mildew.

That done, I went back to the bedroom with the towel wrapped around my waist and retrieved the clean pair of shorts from the bottom of my pack. My Hang Ten T-shirt was still okay so I put that back on as well. I laid the dirty clothes in a pile to the right and sorted through the remaining items in my pack. The half-full baggie of pot would have to go: my father would have a fit if it were found in my possession. I made a mental note to get rid of it. I thought about tossing the rest of the waxed cheese I had forgotten about but decided to wait. I would give the can of tomato sauce to my stepmother who most likely would take it to the pantry without comment.

After returning to the vanity to comb my wet hair and shave for the first time in two days, I strolled out to the great room, a bit more confident now and a lot cleaner, and settled into one of the black leather captain's chairs. My stepmother was in the kitchen preparing dinner.

"Would you like something to drink?" my stepmother called out from the kitchen.

"Sure, a cold beer would taste really good if you have it." She walked out and placed one on the lampstand next to my chair, sliding a coaster underneath before she set it down. She had these special coasters that held disposable cocktail napkins to absorb beads of condensation from cold drinks, something which happened quickly here in Florida.

"Thank you so much!" I smiled. She smiled too and walked back into the kitchen. The ethos between us seemed better now that I had showered and changed. My stepmom was okay. She always treated my sister and I like members of the family whenever we visited. It was nice, although I was careful to never press it.

I found the remote and clicked on the evening news. There was a sinkhole in Winter Park that had gobbled up a small house. Emergency crews were constructing a barricade around it. The camera view from a helicopter hovering overhead showed a live feed of the sinkhole as it continued to widen with slivers of earth breaking off and falling into the abyss. The crater eventually reached and consumed the back wall of a foreign auto garage. Now I could see its cinder blocks falling into the abyss as well. After several more minutes of this evolving destruction, the drama intensified as expensive sports cars began to fall into the crater one at a time. The camera feed switched to an announcer standing behind the crowd of people who had gathered there to watch this disaster unfold. They made a collective gasp every time one of those expensive sports cars fell into the hole. Later on, coverage would show that the owners had hired their own helicopters to retrieve these precious vehicles from out of the abyss. It was a desperate act and some would not succeed, however their insurance would not cover this type of loss apparently.

As I was taking another sip of beer, I heard the garage door open automatically. My father had arrived and I was excited to see him.

"Well hello there young son!" he called out excitedly from the laundry room as he washed up. My stepmother must have called on his Motorola car phone to let him know I was here. The call must have cost several dollars which was a lot of money back then. Our embrace took a bit of effort since he was about the same height as me but a lot bulkier, most of it hardened muscle except for his sizable belly. He walked over to a bar in the corner of the great room, took out a crystal tumbler and filled it with bar ice to make himself a scotch and water. Then he settled into the black leather swivel chair next to mine and set his drink on an identical coaster.

My stepmother walked out carrying a tray of hors d'oeuvres, cheese dip with sliced vegetables and crackers and some mixed nuts. She left it on the lamp table between us and went back to the kitchen to finish preparing dinner. In her other hand was a crystal cocktail glass with Fleischmann's Gin and lots of ice, her usual drink. She kept the gin bottle under the kitchen sink but never cracked it open until after 6 pm.

I watched beads of moisture dripping down my beer can and tried to think. How should I explain this unexpected visit? Indeed I was happy to see my father and stepmother, but Michelle was the reason I had decided to come out so suddenly. I thought it might solidify our relationship somehow. And I only had a week to find out if it had been a good reason or not. I dipped a cracker into the cheese dip and pondered my challenge.

"So how long are you planning to stay? We didn't think you'd be coming out this summer," my father was about as surprised to see me as I was for having made it all this way.

"I'm still planning to work at the wire mill back in California, the job my stepfather got for me. It starts a week from Monday so I should plan to fly home next Saturday." I still had close to $160 dollars remaining for this contingency. The one way flight would probably cost about that much, maybe a little more, but I decided not to mention it since I didn't want to be dependent on them. I made a mental note to call a travel agent the next day. Travel agencies back then could get you a cheaper airfare than you would by calling the airline direct. The airlines didn't have the sophisticated call centers that they do today.

"Hmm, that doesn't give us much time, now does it? Well anyhow, it's good to see you Brett."

"Yeah, you too," I smiled back and let it settle for effect.

"Well I'd better go shower and change. You know how your stepmother is," he said.

"Yeah, I know."

He hoisted himself out of the chair and took his drink with him.

Meanwhile on the evening news, a zoom shot from a helicopter hovering over the sinkhole was focusing on a black Porsche sports car falling into the abyss. As I watched, my father walked into the great room wearing a red golf shirt and navy slacks and sat back down next to me, resuming our conversation.

"Think you might like to help me out at the job sites this week?" he asked.

"Yeah, I'd like that Dad." He seemed pleased.

It was time for dinner and I was both grateful and hungry, having not had a proper balanced meal in several days or maybe more, I wasn't sure and didn't care just then.

He talked about his job sites over dinner, about subcontractors who were messing up or getting behind, and about a new lot that he was planning to make a bid on. My stepmom ranted about a client that she had driven around looking at houses the day before. She had spent close to ten hours in the car with him already, showing house after house that he consistently found something wrong with. This particular gentleman, an executive who happened to be relocating for one of the local defense companies, had made the mistake of commenting about how glamorous it must be to be a realtor. It had been after 6 pm and he didn't seem to think or care that she had a home to go to.

"So I told him he had no idea what it was like to work such long and unpredictable hours. Other people's wives were already home by then. They'd already had their drink; they'd already had their dinner!" She slapped her free hand on the table for emphasis, but the other hand was still cradling her gin on ice. "Finally he apologized and suggested that we call it a day. We're going back out tomorrow morning to look at more houses." She could be direct but most people liked that about her, and if they didn't, well she didn't damned much care. I found her abrupt manner to be a bit uncomfortable at that stage in my life. But I like it now.

I struggled to find a way to tell them that I wanted to go down to the lake after dinner to see my friends. I just mumbled something about wondering what the local kids were up to.

"Oh Brett, you know they're probably down at the lake by now. Why don't you go on ahead?" I smiled and returned to my room to get the pair of flip flops that I had carried all the way from California, not really wanting to see my boots again until it was time for my flight back home. Fortunately, I remembered about my bag of pot and retrieved it from my pack, shoving it into my pants to conceal it before I walked out.

The local kids were congregating under the picnic shelter down by the boat launch. Jimmy was their ringleader. He had graduated from community college the previous June and was still living at home with his rich parents, generally smoking pot and drinking beer during the afternoon when they were away at work. I guessed that he was unable to find a job, or maybe he just wasn't in much of a hurry to grow up. Michelle had written that he was thinking about enlisting in the army come September. He had a rebel sense of urgency about him, this being his last summer unfettered by responsibilities. Pete, his second in command, was reaching into a cooler to pass beers around when I got there. He handed me one. Over on the swing set sat Kyla and her sister Annie. They were ignoring the boys, dragging their toes through the sand and talking in whispers as they swung back and forth.

I remembered the good times I had spent with Kyla the summer before. At least they were good until her college boyfriend came home and she decided to introduce me to Michelle. She was wearing her blond hair longer this summer and looked even more drop dead gorgeous than before. I felt myself blush when I waved in her direction. Fortunately it was getting dark. Then there was Nick, Michelle's younger brother, standing quietly with both arms crossed while listening to the other guys boast about the partying they had done over the past week.

I turned to Nick and gestured that I had something to share with him privately. We walked over to an oak tree and I pulled out the plastic baggie of pot that I had carried with me from California. "Need to get rid of this, man, can you help?"

Nick grinned. He was growing a moustache and it made him look conspiratorial. "How much?"

"Can you give me ten?" I had bought it for fifteen.

"I've only got five on me."

"Fair enough," I said, happy to get it out of my father's house. The fragile relationship I had built with him could not be jeopardized. He would not accept the typical excuse that other kids did it. His son was a high school valedictorian. His son was an athlete. His son was an Eagle Scout. His son was darned near perfect. Well I might have been those first three things but I was certainly not perfect. At that stage in my life, I still had a number of emotional puzzle pieces that did not quite fit together. And I kind of liked it that way.

"Maybe you can share some of that with me later?"

"Sure thing," Nick nodded as he stashed the baggie down his pants. We walked back to the guys and retrieved our beers from the picnic table.

We were illuminated briefly as a blue Chevy Malibu approached and pulled into the sandy parking lot. Recognizing that it was Michelle's car, I felt a sudden wave of nervous energy. She had a friend with her who exited the passenger's side and walked over to the guys while ignoring the other girls. Paola, a jaw dropping beauty from Venezuela was a good friend of Michelle's. When she reached the guys she grabbed a beer from the cooler and started to flirt with them. Michelle stepped out of the car and walked over toward me. Then everything faded around her; all I could see was her. I caught my breath and realized that she was actually here. I instinctively took a step forward as she approached.

"Hey," I said, enjoying her body close to me for the second time that day.

"Hey," she said, wanting me to make the next move. She appeared somewhat impatient, could she be nervous? I tried to think of something epic to say but nothing came to mind in the uncomfortable silence. I remembered a tip I had learned from one of my teachers in speech class: relax your shoulders and breathe. It seemed to encourage her to do the same.

"So I've been thinking about you, a lot over the past school year as a matter of fact."

"Yeah?" she said. "Well like I said before, you weren't supposed to be coming out here this summer, so..."

"Sorry I didn't tell you I was coming," I said. "My folks left for Utah a week ago with my brother and sisters, but I didn't want to go. I needed some time to myself before starting work at my stepfather's wire mill in a couple of weeks. I knew I needed that money for college in the fall. At least I was thinking that way at the time.

"But when I woke up last Sunday I felt this overwhelming restlessness, like I had no idea where I was going with my life and was about to explode. For some reason I went out to the garage, saw my backpack and just started packing. I hiked to the freeway onramp and started hitching rides. And so now here I am, six days later. I had to see you..." I decided to stop there. There'd be more time to tell my story later if she'd let me.

"You actually hitchhiked across the country to see me?" She looked at me dubiously, but then a smile began to form on her beautiful face. Without thinking I pulled her close and she tentatively wrapped her arms around me, returning the embrace. A warm glow coursed through my body as I felt her breath. Sometimes it's best to simply be, I thought to myself. I had made it this far. The rest would be OK.

"Want a beer?" I said at last.

"Sure." She smiled again, and we walked back over to join the others. Paola was talking rapidly and waving her arms for emphasis as she spoke. She appeared to be winning whatever discussion they were having.

We all stood around the picnic table and the rest of the evening was filled with laughter and teasing. It felt good to be back together with the gang and feel accepted by them. Kyla and Annie stopped their swinging and came over to join in on the lighthearted conversation. I decided to stop drinking at this point, not wanting to say anything stupid that I might regret later. The puzzle pieces of my mind had not yet formed a cohesive picture that I felt I could communicate or describe.

The moon returned and broke through the clouds, casting its waning quarter beacon on the lake in rippling shimmers. I walked down to the beach and stood there to watch. It had been a long week. A peaceful feeling settled in with the awareness that life was happening all around me and every day was a gift. Had I felt this way before? I couldn't remember.

Michelle walked down to join me. "Beautiful," she said with a sigh.

"Yeah," I said doing the same, pleased that she had come down to join me. I put my arm around her and she relaxed against my body. No words came... I just wanted to enjoy the quiet as we gazed out to the lake.

Eventually Paola shouted over in her Latin accent that she needed to go, so I walked Michelle back to her car. Paola was already waiting in the passenger seat by the time we got there.

"Can I see you tomorrow?" I asked Michelle, shutting the car door for her after she had buckled in.

"I have to work in the afternoon but there's a party at Pete's house tomorrow night. His parents are on vacation in the Caribbean."

"Great, I'll see you there!" I said.

After she drove away, I walked back to the picnic table to help Pete crush the empty beer cans and toss them into the waste container. I thanked Pete for the beers and then went over to Jimmy, remembering that I didn't have a car.

"Hey Jimmy, do you think you could give me a ride to Pete's party tomorrow night? I left my car back in California. It's a bit indisposed at the moment," I laughed.

"Sure buddy," he said. "I'll pick you up at six."

The house was dark except for a lamp that had been left on for me in the living room. I stepped quietly over to turn it off and felt my way down the hall to my guest room. Finding the light switch and closing the door, I stripped to my shorts and went to the bathroom to wash my face and brush my teeth, using the hand towel to dry around the sink as my stepmother had reminded me countless times to do. I fell into a dreamless sleep as soon as my head hit the pillow.

CHAPTER FOURTEEN

BRIGHT FLORIDA SUNSHINE PEEKED THROUGH the mini-blinds. Its mini-beams were rocking back and forth across my eyelids as a cool morning breeze blew in from an open window that I had forgotten to shut the night before. I was lying in a comfortable bed with clean sheets on a Saturday morning and I did not want to get up, but then I started wondering about the time and fumbled for my watch on the nightstand: it was seven AM. The coolness of this early morning would not last for long I knew. I sat up slowly, massaging my temples. A slight headache but not too bad, I was glad that I had not decided to have that last beer the night before.

My backpack still rested against the side wall but the flap had been left open and a stack of neatly folded laundry had been placed next to it. My stepmother must have done this for me the previous evening while I was out. I was grateful for the transaction I had made with Nick. She would have found the baggie otherwise. That would not have been good. But I had forgotten about the cheese and tomato sauce. All the food I had carried was gone.

I showered, put back on the tan corduroy shorts and powder blue Hang Ten T-shirt I had worn the previous evening, and walked out to the kitchen where my stepmother was sitting at the dining room table. She was poring over house listings, getting ready to take her client out again.

"Oh Brett! You're up. Did you sleep well?"

"Yeah, it felt great to sleep in a normal bed again. Guess I must have been pretty tired. Sorry, I must have missed Father. Did he go out already?"

"Yes, your father left early to check on his job sites. But he said to let you sleep."

I felt a bit guilty about this but decided to shrug it off. "Yeah, thanks. And thanks also for washing my clothes, by the way. Could have done it myself, but yeah thanks so much."

"Not a problem," she said with a lilting voice that sounded almost kind, I wasn't sure. Then she turned her attention back to her listings. "By the way, I found spoiled food in the bottom of your pack. I threw it out, I hope you don't mind." I decided not to ask about the tomato sauce.

I got a box of cereal from the pantry and settled onto a stool at the kitchen counter for breakfast. A morning news broadcast played over the house intercom. President Richard Nixon's impeachment hearings were underway and his private tapes from the Oval Office were about to be subpoenaed. Just then the electronic garage door opened and my father made a quick stop in the laundry room to wash up before striding into the kitchen. He smiled when he saw me sitting there.

"Well hello there, young son!" he said, glad to see me. "Haben Sie gut geschlaffed?" He and my stepmother had spent a couple of years in Wiesbaden Germany before he retired from the Air Force. His German was not the best but he had fun with it anyway.

"Yeah, it felt really good to sleep in a nice clean bed," I nodded. "Thanks again for having me on such short notice. Sorry that I didn't manage to let you guys know sooner. I wasn't exactly sure I'd make it, to be honest. Those Israeli guys were a little hard to understand sometimes." I had been somewhat elusive about this, sticking to my plan to create the impression that I had ridden with them all the way from California rather than hitching most of the way myself.

"Well I decided to stop by the house to see whether you might want to go back out with me. Would you like to help me check on some of my job sites?" he said expectantly.

"Sure Dad. Am I going to be okay in these flip flops?" I had been about to head down to the lake after breakfast. Nick was going to take his father's boat out and he had promised to give me some skiing lessons. I wasn't keen about putting my badly worn hiking boots back on.

"I don't think it will be a problem," he said after an initial pause.

For the next couple of hours I rode next to my father on the bench seat of his white Ford work truck, shuttling from one job site to the next to check on his "subs". They were pouring a concrete footer at one, which would form the perimeter of the house, laying pipe into a foundation at another, and framing the inner walls at a third since the outer concrete cinder block walls had already gone up. He typically kept between one and five job sites going at any given time depending on which way he thought the economy was headed. He had been a pretty good forecaster up to then and he was still in business when other builders had gone under. Being an independent contractor and ever cost-conscious, he made damned sure that his subs were well orchestrated among the job sites, moving them from one to the next rather than let another builder have access to them. Time was money which explained why he drove out to every job at least twice a day, every day except Sunday. Even then he could be found bright and early working at the draft board in his home office, sitting there in a T-shirt and boxer shorts working on a new set of blueprints before church.

We pulled up to a new lot that he was planning to have cleared. Standing at the corner of this lot, we watched the surveyor stake out the perimeter of the house while my father consulted his blueprint to make sure he had everything registered correctly. With that done, we trudged through the sand scrub and tagged trees that needed to be cleared with blue plastic ribbon. While we were doing this, a large Caterpillar tractor rumbled up the road and pulled to a stop in front of our site. A large man climbed down and strutted purposefully over to meet us. "Cutter" wore a camouflage commando shirt that had the sleeves torn off to accommodate his bulging ex-football player biceps. A towering man, my father and I stood up a little straighter when he approached even though we were both over six feet ourselves.

"Y'all about ready for me to clear this lot?" Cutter asked in a deep bass voice. He had thick black hair sticking out from underneath his camouflage hunter's cap, with bushy eyebrows and keen hunter's eyes, the pupils were a dark shade of hazel that looked almost black. My father had informed me earlier that Cutter could keep six or seven girlfriends going at a time across that many counties. Studying his massive physique standing there before us while he waited for an answer, I believed that it was true.

"Yep it looks like we're almost ready," my father said after carefully checking the lot and walking around one more time to make sure that everything had been properly staked out. He nodded at the surveyor who walked over to give him an invoice on a clipboard to sign. My father fingered a checkbook out of his bulging shirt pocket and wrote the man a check right there on the spot, pocketing the invoice. He would record the payment in a ledger as soon as he got home.

"Well alright then," Cutter grinned, patting me on the shoulder. "Good to see you again Brett," he said before climbing back onto the tractor. "It's time for me to make some money," he said producing a toothy smile. My father was popular with the local subcontractors because he always paid them promptly when they were done. On the other hand, it was also known that he wouldn't pay for something unless the job had been done according to his exacting standards, often making subcontractors come back to redo the work until it had been done right. That didn't happen too often these days.

When Cutter set to work we climbed back into my father's pickup truck and drove on to the next lot. We slowly motored down a new subdivision road that still had dense patches of Scotch pine and scrub palmettos to either side. Wooden stakes with blue plastic ribbon had been pounded into the ground at regular intervals to designate the lots that still needed to be surveyed. He pulled the truck over to a stop at the end of a cull de sac and we inspected one of the lots that he was planning to buy from Mr. Husky. We trudged through the scrub until we found the wooden stakes with blue tape that marked the perimeter of the lot. After locating the stakes he decided which trees would need to be felled for the foundation of the house and which could stay. He wanted to minimize tree loss as much as possible. He would keep this picture in his mind and start sketching ideas on his drafting board as soon as he had closed the deal with Mr. Husky.

As we were driving back up the road, a lunch truck appeared and my father waved him over. At that time of year in Central Florida there would always be a layer of sweat between your skin and clothes that refused to evaporate in the high humidity. Only way to cool down was to drink something cold at every available opportunity. This was one of those times. We both got a large paper cup and filled it with Pepsi and lots of ice.

When we returned to the first lot, Cutter was waving excitedly which seemed out of character for him. He had stopped his Caterpillar tractor at the corner of the lot and was standing there inspecting the front fork at a respectable distance. A nest of rattlesnakes dangled from it, having been recently dug out of the ground. Realizing that we had been standing on that spot just forty minutes ago, I looked down at my flip-flops and resolved to wear my boots from then on. My father smiled at me as I was doing this, reading my mind.

"Whoo boy!" said Cutter. This pretty much summed it up.

By mid-afternoon I was sitting in a lounge chair by the pool, this being a Saturday and not one of my father's full work days. We had come home and made sandwiches, and then taken cold showers to rinse off the sweat and grime. Now he was in his home office working away at the drafting board, no doubt working on ideas for the lot that he was about to buy from Mr. Husky. My stepmother was off with a client showing houses and I had a can of cold Stroh's beer standing next to me on the plastic table. When beads of sweat began to drip down my chest, I would dive into the pool and return to my lounge chair, take another sip of beer and repeat the process as needed. Cicadas rumbled from the trees, reminding me of my first serenade three days ago back in Mississippi. Eventually I decided to go back into the house, since it was just too damned hot out there on the patio.

Air conditioning is very important to Floridians who can afford it and probably even more so to those who can't, especially during the mid-afternoon heat of summer. It was a good excuse to go for a drive in an air-conditioned car or visit a shopping mall as a last resort. Ice skating was pretty popular this time of year but it cost nine bucks to get in, which was a small fortune for a young man trying to impress a date. I thought about these things as I sat in the front room and reflected on the people and places I had experienced over the previous six days.

I heard my friend Jimmy drive up to my father's house in his sea blue Pontiac GTO and kill the throaty engine. By this time we were finishing dinner on the back porch since it had cooled down somewhat in the early evening. He rang the doorbell and my stepmother got up to let him in. I followed her. "Hello Mrs. Roberts," he said with sincere politeness, and upon seeing me he also said "we're going to a party at Pete's house if that's okay."

"Oh hi Jimmy," my stepmother smiled. "We were just finishing dinner on the back porch. Why don't you come back and join us. Would you like a cold beer?" She was in a pretty good mood I noted. Apparently she had negotiated a good offer for her prospective buyer.

"Sure Mrs. R. But we can't stay long. Our friends are waiting for us." Jimmy had a knack for being persuasively polite.

My father and stepmother were friends with Jimmy's parents. Jimmy's father was a senior executive at Martin Marietta and had referred a lot of clients to my stepmom since his company was growing so rapidly. Although they had heard about local kids "using marijuana", they were pretty sure that Jimmy was okay. After finishing off his beer, Jimmy thanked them and we turned to go.

When we had turned the corner and were out of earshot, Jimmy popped the clutch and peeled rubber down the street, braking hard at the next corner. With the monster 454 engine rumbling on idle, he reached into the ashtray for a joint that he lit with the cigarette lighter and handed to me. He selected a cassette tape from the glove compartment and put in into the player, turning up the volume. A guitar riff opened to *Communication Breakdown* by Led Zeppelin and with that he revved the engine and popped the clutch again, forcing me back in my bucket seat as we rocketed forward. "Want another beer? There're some cold ones in the cooler on the back seat," he said as he took the joint from me and took another drag. I pulled a couple cans from the icy water and handed one to him. A rush of adrenaline had hit my system and I felt that it was now time to party.

The song *When the Levee Breaks* was playing as we pulled up to Pete's house, which seemed a bit ominous. Jimmy killed the engine and the Goat gave a throaty sigh from out of its back mufflers.

Annie met us at the door with cocktail glasses containing a brown liquid on crushed ice that I didn't recognize. Each glass had an orange slice garnishing the rim. Jimmy took a greedy gulp from his and I took a tentative sip from mine. It had an earthly sweet taste that reminded me of a bit of pepperoni and mushroom pizza after swallowing it.

"What is this?" I asked as Annie took my hand and led me into the kitchen where a large pot of brownish liquid was steaming away on the stove. The stew had dozens of mushroom buttons bobbing up to the surface.

"Magic mushrooms!" Annie announced giddily with a conspiratorial smile. I took another tentative sip and Jimmy's glass went bottoms up. He set it next to the sink and opened the fridge to get another beer. I hesitated, took another sip and then dumped the rest of my drink in the sink when no one was looking. Grabbing a beer for myself, I clinked cans with Jimmy in a show of solidarity.

Annie then led us back to the living room where my favorite *Ziggy Stardust* album was playing on the turntable at high volume.

My body got taken over by Mick Ronson's masterful guitar riffs as I entered the room. I crossed my legs and settled onto the shag carpet with the others, feeling one with the music. Paola was sitting there opposite me, with her attractive long legs crossed in a lotus position that hid them from view and I felt it a shame, preferring to see them fully extended. They were beautiful legs, so beautiful; Paola was beautiful, so beautiful, no she was, voluptuous. The buzz was taking hold and I shook my head, trying to clear it. I felt the space closing between me and Paola and I decided to let it happen. She rested her head against my shoulder and then put her arm around me in a quick embrace, and when her soft hair gently touched my cheek it caused goose bumps to form on the back of my neck. But it had been intended to be a friendly embrace and it didn't last long. She smiled at no one in particular and turned back to re-engage the music.

Then Kyla came over and sat cross legged next to me. She too put her arm around me in an affectionate embrace and with a knowing smile. "How are you, Brett?"

"Um, good. Yeah, I'm really good," I replied, pausing between sentences to verify. Kyla smiled back, a genuine smile, it had some kind of meaning that I was struggling to discover. I couldn't, but it was no matter I decided at last. Her arm felt good around me and I decided to enjoy it. It was a good lesson.

Ziggy played for time, jiving us that we were voodoo. I thought I understood what that meant, at least at the time.

Suddenly, Michelle appeared and Kyla shifted over so that she could sit next to me. The person I had hitched three thousand miles to see was now sitting here beside me, on the shag carpet in Pete's living room listening to Bowie, and my attention was now on her. Pete and Jimmy joined our circle to engage Kyla and Paola which felt well-orchestrated and maybe it was.

"...now Ziggy played...guitar!" I grimaced internally, because the song reminded me of the night I had crashed my car into a curb back in Montclair, but I took a breath and decided to shrug it off. Then the song *Suffragette City* came on and it brought us to our feet so we started dancing.

A Journey with Strangers

Paola may have been voluptuous but it was Michelle who was truly beautiful, a tanned five foot eleven with sandy brown hair that had naturally sun drenched highlights, and with a lean yet well-endowed figure that I found to be both sexy and athletic. I couldn't help gazing into her beautiful eyes. She was not an easy one to read, and yet here she was dancing with me, her eyes roving side to side as though she were on a fashion runway, briefly finding their way back to me with a faint smile, then off again on the catwalk. She moved so fluidly with the music that I could not help but move along with her. I felt she had a thin emotional crust that would require patience, and I also knew I had less than a week but that it could not be rushed.

I walked Michelle to her car later that evening, with the music fading behind us. I felt my head begin to clear as I collected my thoughts.

"So…hey…" I said at last.

"So hey again yourself," she responded, grabbing my shoulders and looking into my eyes with curiosity. "So like I asked before, what are you doing here Brett? I thought you had a summer job back in California."

"Well yeah like I said, it starts a week from Monday."

She pressed her lips together as she considered.

"I thought we had decided to move on," she said with a hint of finality.

"Did we?" I felt my heart sink.

"We'll both be starting college in the fall, me here and you back in California. Who's to say where we'll both wind up?"

"Yeah, who's to say," I replied, tentatively. "But I had to see you!" I rallied at last, releasing a suppressed smile that could no longer contain itself.

I think she could tell. The faintest glimmer of a smile was tugging at the corners of her lips, wrestling for control as her eyes struggled to maintain their serious composure. At last her whole face brightened; and that became my second lesson of the evening.

Sometimes you don't have to use a lot of words; you just have to mean the ones that you choose to say.

"I've got a double shift tomorrow and a pretty full work schedule the rest of the week," she said, reading my mind. "But I'm off Thursday evening and all day Friday."

"Please, let's spend that time together," I nodded my head for emphasis feeling an irrational sense that everything would be okay. "This world will always be filled with choices, and right now my choice is to be with you. I've just got this feeling I can't explain."

She considered tentatively as I stood there gazing into her eyes. "Call me tomorrow," she said at last. Then she got into her Malibu and drove away. And I stood there watching until her taillights faded into night.

It was another Sunday morning, exactly one week since I had left the smoggy Pomona Valley behind for my trip across America. The sun was shining through the mini-blind, rocking back and forth over my face again as I lay there in bed. I glanced over to my watch and saw that it was almost 9 am. They had let me sleep in again this morning. I swung my feet down onto the carpet and stood up slowly, my head still fuzzy from the previous evening. I needed another cold shower.

When I returned to the bedroom, I saw that my stepmother had left for me a pair of khaki slacks and a white short-sleeved oxford shirt with blue stripes. They were folded neatly and had been stacked next to my pack on the side wall, just as the stack of clean clothes had been the day before. Clearly I was supposed to put them on.

My father and stepmother were out on the back patio finishing their breakfast by the pool.

"Your father and I thought you might like to go to church with us this morning, okay Brett?"

"Yeah, sure, I'd like that." I added, knowing that it would be expected.

Breakfast was fresh fruit atop a bowl of granola with skim milk. My stepmother must be on another diet, I mused while crunching into it.

"How do your slacks fit?" my stepmother asked after I had stopped crunching and taken a sip of freshly brewed coffee.

"Um, the length is okay but they are a bit loose around the waist..."

She looked over to my father who we both knew was reluctant to throw anything away. "I might be able to rustle up a belt for you Brett," he said, "I think my waist size was about the same as yours is now when I was back in flight school." He got up and walked over to the master bedroom, and after a few minutes of rummaging through their walk-in closet he came back out with a skinny black leather belt that didn't look like it had been worn since the fifties. He handed it to me and I tried it on. It would have to do, although I had to cinch it up to the last available belt loop.

The parking lot was almost full by the time we pulled into a space at the newly built Presbyterian Church, a modern building with vaulted ceilings and brightly colored stained glass windows. My father introduced me to a dozen or more of their friends as we walked from the parking lot toward the narthex, but I lost track of their names. "This is my son Brett," he would say. "He'll be attending college next fall." "Brett is visiting us from California," my stepmother would say. I gave them all a firm handshake with a nod and a smile. We walked in and sat near the end of a pew five rows back on the right hand side of the sanctuary.

The service was pleasant and I noticed that the children were quite well behaved, with everyone standing and singing and sitting again in almost perfect unison. The choir members performed as if they had been trained by a drill sergeant. Everyone stood and opened their songbooks as if the choir was a single organism, singing in perfect harmony with not a single voice standing out among the rest, and they sat back down the same way when the song was over. The preacher's sermon was direct and everyone paid strict attention. But the sanctuary became livelier when it was time for the song of the day, and my father and I had fun singing together in our baritone voices. It made him smile and I smiled too.

We returned to the house and had sandwiches on the patio.

"I think I'll head down to the lake," I said when we were finished.

"Sure Brett go on ahead," my stepmother said.

So I changed into my shorts and walked down to the pavilion. I shaded my eyes and looked out to the lake, hoping to locate Pete and Jimmy who would probably be boating again today. There they were pulling a water skier who appeared to be Annie. I waved when they saw me. Annie let go of the tow rope as they approached the shore and motored to the beach to pick me up.

It was a sixteen foot "Glaspar" speed boat, a new design with a 100 horsepower Mercury outboard motor.

"Come aboard!" Pete said. "I assume you're ready now for that water skiing lesson?"

"Yeah, I guess so," I said. Pete nodded to Jimmy. They must have thought this would be amusing.

As could be predicted I failed to get up on my skis over the first five or six attempts, falling sideways or backwards and one time spilling forward, having forgotten to let go of the tow rope that time. A bubble of water splashed over my head until I remembered to let go of the handle. On my last attempt, I managed to stay erect on both skis after the boat had pulled me up. I was wobbly at first and almost fell this time too, but then I decided to give Jimmy a thumb up to go faster after gaining my balance. He happily complied and gunned the Merc engine, yanking me forward and almost causing me to fall again. The skis jarred my body as they bounced over the water. Pete motioned for me to turn out of the wake and I leaned to my right, catching a couple feet of air as my skis cleared the wake and splashed back down. I was not about to steer back over to the other side, so Jimmy decided to wheel the boat into a turn that whipped me around fiercely. This was scary but also thrilling. Fully spent, I let go of the tow rope and my body slid back down into the water.

Pete and Jimmy took turns towing each other around the lake and I enjoyed the spray blowing over the bow when the boat bounced through the waves. After several turns around the lake they returned me to the beach and I waded ashore on wobbly legs. I was done for the day.

"Thanks guys," I said, waving back to them when I reached the sand.

"It was fun having you with us!" Pete said. "Maybe we'll see you tonight." Then Jimmy hit the gas and they sped back out to the lake for another run.

I returned to my father's house and walked around back to take a dip in the pool. As I toweled off, my stepmother called out to me from the kitchen. "Oh Brett, Kyla called a while ago and asked to have you call her back when you got home."

"Thanks," I said, making sure that I was dry enough to enter the house.

"And oh by the way, I bought you a pair of swim trunks since it didn't look like you had any. They're in the laundry room. I washed them since they're new." The woman was psychic.

"Thank you so much!" I said.

"You're welcome, Brett." I was genuinely beginning to like her.

I went into my father's office and called Kyla. She was having a pool party barbeque and asked if I would like to come. Michelle would be there. I was grateful for my new swim trunks. I borrowed a beach towel and rolled a change of clothes in it for later. My father let me borrow the truck.

"Thanks again," I said as I was leaving.

"You're welcome, young son," my dad said. Funny, I was starting to think of him as Dad now.

The music was loud coming from Kyla's house as I drove up, it was coming from the back of the house, "Ziggy Stardust" again, it was one of their theme albums that summer. A sign on the front door instructed me to go around to the back patio where I found the usual suspects hard at play. Nick and Annie were splashing each other in the pool. It was hard not to stare at Paola in her sequined black bikini, sitting there at the edge of the pool and leisurely kicking her legs back and forth in the water. Jimmy was helping Kyla barbeque burgers and dogs. And there was Michelle, even more beautiful in a blue bikini that complemented her athletic figure. She was playing a vigorous game of ping pong with Pete, keenly intent on winning every point. I grabbed a beer from the cooler and played the spectator. Michelle smashed a backhand landing a final point and Jimmy raised both arms in surrender. Pete decided that it was time to drink beer and walked to get one from the cooler. It was then that Michelle noticed me with a Mona Lisa-like grin.

"Hey," she said.

"Hey yourself," I said back, and smelled a hint of jasmine perfume when she stepped over to me. Then surprisingly she reached her arm around me and softly kissed my cheek, tentative, lingering, and then she pulled away. Kyla glanced over in our direction with a smile and turned back to her grilling with Jimmy. She put her arm around him in a show of solidarity.

"Grab a paddle, California boy," Michelle said nodding over to the ping pong table. Michelle called out for Nick and Annie to join us for doubles. They toweled off and came over, clearly up to the challenge. Nick, athletic like Michelle, could return her forehand shots with an equally skilled backhand. Annie, like me, was less skilled but equally enthusiastic. The four of us played back and forth games of table tennis, cheering every winner and laughing at every missed shot, joking and sipping beer between the sets. Michelle hugged me in celebration when I hit the occasional winner, boosting my confidence. Maybe it was just because of the point we had just made, but it felt good nonetheless.

"Food's ready!" Kyla announced triumphantly. She and Jimmy were already on their fourth beers, based on the number of empty bottles I could see on the tile counter next to the grill. We headed over and loaded our paper plates with burgers and brats, squirting ketchup and mustard onto them. Kyla had also sliced some fresh watermelon. I held our plates while Michelle pulled out a couple of cold beers and we walked over to a pair of sea green Adirondack chairs at the back corner of the patio enclosure and behind the Jacuzzi. I set our plates on a small glass table between us and twisted off the beer caps, setting the bottles onto the table as well. The sun had begun to set and it was now coloring the horizon in orange and red hues. It didn't look like it would rain today.

"So it's really great to see you, again," I said as Michelle settled into her chair.

"Why," she said.

"Um, what do you mean?" I said carefully. She had appeared to be in good spirits just a minute ago, or so I thought. Her hugs had felt genuine and I was confused.

"I mean, why is it so great to see me? What do you want from me Brett?"

"Um, to be honest, I'm not exactly sure. I guess I don't have any expectations, really." I let that sink in, taking a bite out of my bratwurst and chewing it slowly. Michelle continued looking at me with a mixture of suspicion and expectation. "It's just that … you've been on my mind a lot lately," I continued, "ever since the morning after graduation when I woke up with a wicked hangover, I'll tell you more about that later. Anyway, something felt unresolved. I started thinking about you, and then I couldn't stop thinking about you. I spent the afternoon re-reading the letters that you had sent." I took another bite and a sip of beer, and then set the bottle back down.

"So like I said, I made a spontaneous decision last Sunday to see if I could make it out here hitchhiking. I carried enough money with me to get back home from pretty much anywhere if I had to. And I figured that if I made it, it would be a sign that I had made the right decision."

"Wow, you really are crazy Brett…" she said with a smile.

"Yeah, maybe… Anyway, it was an awesome trip. I met so many different people along the way… Maybe I'll write a book about it someday," I said.

"Will I be in it?" she said.

"I guess that depends…" I teased, hoping I was not reaching too far.

Her smile brightened into a smile but she quickly suppressed it, still trying to decide.

"I work double shifts tomorrow through Tuesday and single shifts on Wednesday and Thursday afternoon," she said, "but if you invite me to dinner Thursday night, I just might say yes."

The money I had left might barely be enough to cover an economy class plane ticket back to California on Saturday, but I didn't care just then. "Michelle," I said without hesitation, looking into her eyes, "will you have dinner with me on Thursday?" smiling at the end.

Her face brightened once more. It felt like I had won something I was not expecting. "Yes!" she said.

We finished our dinners and rejoined the others for more games of round-robin table tennis.

CHAPTER FIFTEEN

I AWOKE TO THE SOUND OF A BRISK KNOCK at the door.

"Wake up Brett!" my father called from behind it. "Time to earn your keep young son," he said it in a pleasant tone, letting me know that he would be happy to have me along. I had enjoyed working with him the summer before, so I was looking forward to it as well.

"Yeah okay, that sounds great!" I said. "Give me a second to take a quick shower and I'll be right out."

A pair of new work boots was waiting outside my door. I picked them up and walked out to the kitchen where a bowl of corn flakes and a hot cup of coffee were waiting.

My stepmother had already left to show a house and I made a mental note to thank her later for the boots.

My father was back in his office assembling blue prints and other items that he would need to bring with him to the job sites. He fully supported my college plans but I could sense that he wanted me to work for him after I graduated. I had no idea what I wanted to do and had tried to express as much. Anyway he seemed pleased to see me strap the tool belt back on, even if it would only be for a few days.

When we pulled up to our first work site I could see that the footer had been poured and a plumbing crew was busy laying pipe. We stepped out of the truck into the bright sunshine and walked over to Luther, an affable black man from Eatonville with a bright smile who directed his crew with positive energy and efficiency. "Well hello there Mistah Roberts," he said in a deep voice, probably hoping that he would receive an advance from my father's checkbook so that he could pay his crew later. My father wore a poker face as he walked around the footer, inspecting the demarcation of interior walls that had been made with taught string tied to wooden stakes. The crew kept bustling around while he inspected their work. Satisfied, he walked back to Luther and pulled out his checkbook.

"OK there Luther," he said. "You and your crew got here on time like you said, and it looks like you've got everything in order. Here's a five hundred dollar advance," he tore the check out and handed it to Luther. "You'll get the rest as soon as you finish this job, which had better be tomorrow. I've already scheduled the slab to be poured on Tuesday and your pipes have to pass inspection first."

"Well now of course I know all about that Mistah Roberts. Don't you worry none, my boys and me will have everything done by the end of the day and I'll meet you back here first thing tomorrow morning. That sound about right?"

"Outstanding. I'll stop back by this afternoon to see how you are doing. Have a good day."

"Why thank you Mistah Roberts!" Luther said with another smile. "By the way, good to see your boy Brett here" he said, turning to me. "You back for another summer Brett?"

"Just for the week," I replied, shaking Luther's firm calloused grip.

"Going to be a college boy I hear," he nodded with full enthusiasm.

"Yeah, that's the plan," I said.

"Well good luck to you!" I knew that Luther was saving up some money so that he could send his own kids to college. He had about five or six of them according to my father, which probably explained why he worked so hard.

"Luther has the best damned plumbing crew here in Central Florida," my father confided to me as we drove away to the next job site.

When we got there, I could see that the cinderblock sidewalls had already been cemented and set. A huge pile of lumber and pre-assembled joists had been delivered and a framing crew was fast at work building the interior walls. A second crew was arranging and assembling the trusses that would be sequentially nailed into place to construct the roof. They would get this whole process done within the next few days and then the lot would look like it had a house on it.

My father reached around behind the seat to get a roll of blue prints and walked out to Sam the foreman.

"You got your funnies Sam?" he asked. Sam walked over to his work truck and pulled out his own set from the toolbox in back. They both rolled them out on the hood of Sam's truck and leaned over inspecting them. My father pointed to several key areas that he wanted to inspect before the joists went up.

For my father, even the smallest detail was extremely important. Another builder in the area had gone belly up by failing too many inspections. My father cautiously built on spec using his own money and then put his houses on the market, whereas this other builder mostly did his work under contract, on tight deadlines, and could not absorb the loss when things got behind. My father knew every structural detail of the houses he designed, from the required thickness of crossbeams to the spacing of the joists. Nothing was left to chance and he would come back multiple times to this job site over the next few days until the framing was done to his satisfaction.

We drove to our third and final site for the day. Here the framing was done and the sheetrock had been nailed into place. It was time for trim carpenter work, a job that my father prided in doing himself. The care that went into trim carpentry would showcase the quality of the entire house, and he wasn't about to leave this job to anyone else but himself, unless it was me working under his careful supervision. I felt trepidation mixed with pride that I was allowed to help out with this artistic endeavor. And I wanted to do everything right the first time, but one thing that I learned pretty quickly was that it is almost impossible to get trim work right without making a few mistakes along the way. I had made a number of them during the previous summer, so by now I was feeling a bit more confident. My father knew the fine balance between adding to the scrap pile and teaching a carpenter his craft. Sometimes the scrap pile would win and he would lose his patience. Although several of his previous hires had failed to measure up, he was probably more patient with me and I was determined to improve under his direction.

He liked to nail the trim boards along the ceiling as well as the flooring. When he started out in the home building business he would do this all by hand, but these days he used a nail gun which was powered by a 5 HP gas compressor. He also had a skill saw mounted waist high on a metal tripod that we moved with us from room to room with its electrical cord running out to a power box at the corner of the job site. Part of my job was to move this equipment around while trying to anticipate where it would be needed next. My father decided which room to do next depending on how many 12-foot long trim boards would need to be cut, often redoing those calculations in his head as he went along in order to minimize scrap.

We used the skill saw to make opposing 45 degree cuts so the trim boards would fit together in the corners of the room without any gaps. In some cases we used a hacksaw to carve out the contours of the first trim board so that the second trim board would fit cleanly against it. Both methods worked pretty well if done correctly. If not, then at least one of the boards would have to be recut which fed the scrap pile. "Measure twice and cut once," my father would say.

I was allowed to cut and mount the floor trim boards given my current skill level since they were less visible to the prospective home buyer. But for my father, the ceiling trim had to fit perfectly together, thus I was content to hold the boards in place and watch while he secured them with his nail gun.

The floor trim had to be nailed a half-inch above the slab to allow room for the carpet that would be tacked down later. I marked the height every two feet or so with a carpenter's pencil, checking carefully every time before using the nail gun. The force of the nail gun would usually set the nails about a quarter inch into the wood. Any nail heads that still protruded were set manually with a special metal die and a few taps of the hammer. I began to enjoy this process as I became more confident. It felt good to survey a room that had been "trimmed" and know that it had been done right.

I also learned how to mount and trim interior doors which required a considerably higher amount of skill and agility. One needed to know how to hold a levelling tool, support a door frame, and nail at the same time. If the door did not close without "binding", it would simply have to be ripped out and remounted. My father taught me how to use shim boards to support the frame as I nailed it in place, an essential skill without which the whole process would be nearly impossible to get right.

Trim carpentry can be a hot and sweaty job, especially during the Florida summer months. Our clothes were drenched and clung to our bodies as we worked. The only relief came during our short breaks with a trip to the back of my father's truck where he kept a five-gallon igloo cooler filled with ice water. We were wearing work scarves that we rinsed in the ice water and tied around our heads. We also kept beach towels in the truck to sit on between job sites.

I was relieved to hear the lunch truck make its way down the road toward our job site, tooting its horn as it came to a stop. The driver and proprietor of this mobile enterprise made it a point to know which job sites were in progress and he would stop at each one of them in his regional area between 11 am and 1 pm. We knew that we had to hurry out there since he would not wait long. As we approached, he walked around to the side of his truck and lifted the aluminum side panel, revealing wrapped sandwiches and cold drinks on a bed of crushed ice. Water was dripping fast from a drain hole onto the pavement. I wondered how long the ice would last out here in the Florida heat. We each grabbed a sandwich and soda and my father paid.

As the driver sped away to his next stop we dragged cinder blocks to sit on underneath an oak tree that had been spared, near the front of the house. This particular tree would remain a permanent fixture when the property was fully landscaped. There was a light breeze, although it was scarcely enough to encourage evaporation from our drenched clothes that were now soaking into the cinder blocks we were sitting on.

"I guess you've been seeing Michelle again now that you're here?" my father asked after swallowing the last bite of his sandwich.

"Yeah, I have. I guess I thought she would be more excited to see me though."

He considered that, nodding. "Be careful son. Don't make any commitments you can't keep."

"Yeah, that I know," I replied, letting it linger for a moment. "She'll be working double shifts most of the week though so I probably won't be seeing much of her after all. Although she agreed to go out to dinner with me on Thursday and also said that she's got Friday off."

"Well then I suppose I've got you for the next several days."

"Yeah, I guess so. It's good to work with you again Dad. I'm going to miss this when I'm off at college."

"Me too. Come on let's go finish those back bedrooms."

After another couple of hours of nailing trim boards we swept up and I carted the 5 gallon drums filled with scrap wood and sawdust out to the dump bin. My father always left the job site cleaner than he found it, something that his subcontractors needed to heed if they wanted to be hired again.

Then we drove to check on Sam the framing foreman. My father walked through carefully and checked the beams and joists, gesturing as he spoke. Sam just nodded in agreement. I was standing there with arms crossed and Monroe, a member of Sam's crew, walked over to keep me company. "You're Brett, right? I've been hearing a lot about you from your dad. Going to college in the fall he told me, back there in Southern California." He looked at me through keen eyes set in a weathered face that had spent many years working under direct sunlight.

"Yeah that's right, although I'm pretty sure my father would have preferred that I go to college out here and help him with his construction business part time."

"Don't you even think about that right now," he said with determination. "You've got a good opportunity back there with the college thing. There's no way I'd be working here right now if I had that chance. You take it, son, and follow whatever profession your heart desires, you'll never regret it."

"Thanks. I'll remember that."

"You do that."

My father walked back to join us.

"Everything all right, Mr. Roberts?"

"We should be in good shape for an inspection tomorrow, Monroe. You guys do good work." Monroe smiled at that, revealing yellowed teeth that didn't look like they had seen a dentist in many years. My father knew the name of everyone who worked for him.

We got back in the truck and drove to the first job site. The plumbing crew had left for the day so we walked around and inspected their pipe work. Everything appeared to be properly aligned with where the interior walls were supposed to be constructed after the slab had been poured which my father was planning for tomorrow. He spent a lot of time pacing around and inspecting every detail while checking with his tape measure. Now satisfied, he announced that it was time for us to go home.

When we arrived at the house my father led me to the back yard and we both used the garden hose to rinse off, using old towels that my step mother had left out by the pool to pat down our wet clothes. Then we changed into our swim trunks which my stepmother had thoughtfully hung on a rack to dry in the pantry. Jumping into the pool felt like the best sensation ever. "Ahh!"

My stepmother returned after we had showered and changed.

"Thanks again for buying me those swim trunks," I said. "And thanks also for my new work boots. That was really thoughtful."

"Well the work boots were your father's idea. But I do like having excuses to shop!" My dad nodded with pained amusement.

As my dad and stepmother were sitting in the living room discussing their days, I asked to use the phone in my father's office.

"Sure Brett, go right ahead."

I located a phone book in the second drawer of the desk and found the number of a local travel agency, seeing that their hours were from 9 am to 6 pm. I checked my cheap waterproof sports watch and saw that it was now 5:20 pm, so there was still time to call. I dialed and was able to reserve a flight for Saturday morning at 10 am, with a connection in Atlanta and then non-stop to Los Angeles International. I gave the agent my name, birthdate and home address. Back then it was still possible to make a reservation and pay for it at the airport just prior to the flight. The airlines sent a fee back to the travel agency after the fare had been paid. This particular one-way ticket would cost me $125 plus a $5 booking fee. I thought about my date with Michelle and wondered whether my father might be willing to pay me for helping him out this week. I vowed to work harder tomorrow.

Then I found a phone number scribbled on a piece of paper in my wallet and called Kyla. Fortunately it was she who answered.

"Hey Kyla, it's me Brett."

"Hey Brett, thanks for coming to my pool barbeque yesterday."

"Yeah ... it was good seeing everyone again. Listen, Michelle isn't free until Thursday. I was wondering if I could come by tomorrow evening to talk."

"Sure, I guess. My folks are gone this week so I'm housesitting with my sister. Want to come over for dinner tomorrow? They left steaks in the fridge that need to be barbequed."

"I'll bring a bottle of red wine."

"Good answer. See you tomorrow Brett." She hung up.

I returned to the living room. It was cocktail time with another plate of cheese dip and appetizers to pass around, the "poo poo platter" as my stepmother liked to call it. I went straight to bed after dinner and soon fell into another sound and dreamless sleep.

Bright sunlight pierced through the blinds again the next morning. This was becoming a bit too predictable, I thought to myself, but I was relieved to have awakened this time before my father came to knock on the door. Checking my watch, I could see that it was already past eight o'clock in the morning. Thinking I had probably overslept, I quickly showered and made my way out to the kitchen where a note was waiting. My dad had already left to check on his job sites and would be return around 8:30 am to get me. I was finishing off a bowl of cereal when the automated garage door opened.

"Sorry about that, Dad," I said as we exited Sweetwater Oaks and headed down Wekiva Springs Road toward the next subdivision.

"Not a problem, young son. Always happy to have you along!" he said cheerfully. He seemed to truly enjoy building his houses and was continuing to buy more lots with the profits. Other than the house he was living in now, he rolled pretty much every cent he made back into the business.

"You can do anything you put your mind to," he would tell me. He believed it, and despite his many absent years as a parent, this lesson has always stuck with me.

A grading crew was busy working in tandem to clear and shape the first lot. The only remaining trees were those that were to be spared for final landscaping.

We arrived at the second job site as a large concrete truck was emptying its gooey contents to pour the slab. A black work crew was pushing their concrete squeegees around on long poles to flatten and smooth out the surface. A second concrete truck was waiting its turn at the end of the street, its diesel engine still running to maintain the mixer rotation.

We spent the rest of the day finishing up the trim work at house number three. Charlie the lead painter was now busy at work in the rooms that we had completed the day before, plastering the drywall seams and puttying over set nails in the trim boards.

Upon returning to the house, I rinsed off in the backyard and then showered and changed into my corduroy shorts and a flowered Hawaiian shirt that my stepmother had left hanging in the closet for me. I went out to the great room to thank her and asked my father if I could borrow the truck. Feeling more presentable and catching my second wind after the day's work, I drove out to the Winn Dixie on Highway 434 to purchase a bottle of Mateus wine, and also a bouquet of flowers for some reason. I presented them to Kyla when she opened the door.

"Why thank you Brett!" she said in her lilted southern accent that always seemed to convey a hint of trouble. Kyla was a compulsive flirt who clearly knew what she was doing, considering she could be so incredibly sexy while doing it. A still small voice inside my head reminded me that she had a boyfriend and I was here to discuss Michelle. Songs from the "Tea for the Tillerman" album by Cat Stevens came softly from the stereo in the living room as I crossed the threshold into Kyla's house.

"Where's your sister?" I asked while glancing around, hoping to locate her somewhere.

"Annie's out with Nick," she whispered conspiratorially, "but please don't say anything about that, I'm covering for her." That southern accent again, with her long blond hair parted down the middle, shaping those doe-like eyes. I felt my heart rate rise involuntarily.

Kyla's family had moved into this house the previous summer but it was still sparsely furnished. Her parent's preferred modern Scandinavian designs and were evidently taking their time to find just the right pieces. The living room had only two chairs and a coffee table in addition to the stereo and its accompanying wall unit; all were built from teak wood. An expensive cream colored Berber carpet drew my attention. Kyla found a vase for the flowers in the kitchen and arranged them on the coffee table. Then she sat cross-legged on the carpet and smiled, giving a slight nod for me to join her. The sliding doors were open to the back patio and a ceiling fan pulled the cool early evening air into the house. A light rain began to fall through the patio screen enclosure, making circular ripples on the pool surface that coalesced as the drizzle turned into rain.

"You said you wanted to talk," she said. "So why are you here?"

"Was that two questions or just one?"

"You tell me," she answered. Could I really confide in her? I wasn't sure. Frankly, I didn't even know how I still felt about her. I did know that Kyla had asked her sister to introduce me to Michelle the previous summer. Kyla and Michelle both worked at the ice cream parlor. I probably would never have met Michelle if not for Kyla. But then again, although my feelings for Michelle were growing stronger with every moment I spent with her, I knew deep down that I still had a crush on Kyla. I hadn't learned how to master such emotional uncertainties, nor did I want to exactly.

"Well first of all, thanks for introducing me to Michelle," I ventured forward. "The times that she and I spent together last summer were amazing."

"Good," she said. "I thought you two would get along."

"How do you mean?"

"Well, you're both athletic for one thing. I knew that you would enjoy playing outdoors together. And to be honest, you're both kind of nerdy in an endearing sort of way."

"Okay," I tried to laugh. "So what do you mean by that exactly?"

"Exactly? I'm not sure. It's just how I perceive both of you, I guess. Frankly I sense that you both tend to overthink things. That's why you're perfect together." I wasn't sure if she meant it or was just teasing me.

"You mentioned something about two steaks that needed barbequeing?" I said, changing the subject. The rain outside had finally stopped. Kyla led me to the kitchen and we seasoned the steaks, arranging them on a plastic platter. Washing my hands, I opened the bottle of Mateus and poured us each a glass.

"Thanks for having me over, Kyla," I said as we clinked glasses. I carried the platter along with my glass out to the patio and started the grill. Kyla busied herself in the kitchen arranging place settings. That done, she went to the living room and put on a fresh album, this one from Roxy Music, an early bootleg containing a live performance of *Out of the Blue*, which seemed perfect for the occasion. I busied myself with the steaks on the grill while taking in the evening breeze, moist and cool.

Kyla came out to join me, bringing her wine. We clinked glasses again and took another sip, enjoying the quiet until I heard a faint rumble of thunder from far away. Another storm was approaching on its way westward.

"It's nice out here. Wouldn't you rather eat on the patio?" she asked.

The sun was setting on the western horizon. Florida is almost completely flat and the sunsets can seemingly take forever to fade into dusk. I wanted to stay out here and watch it.

"Yeah sure," I said, forking the steaks off the grill onto a fresh platter. Kyla opened a side patio door and selected a beach towel from the adjoining bathroom, using it to dry off the patio table and chairs. I carried the steaks and wine glasses over to the table while she retrieved the place settings from the kitchen. She motioned for me to get the bottle of Mateus and I also found a tossed salad that she had prepared and left on the counter. I brought them out to the patio table and pulled out a patio chair for her to sit. Once I had joined her, she extended her glass and we toasted the dinner we had made together. The temperature had dropped into the low 70's by this time and we enjoyed the cooling outdoor breeze as we sat there under the screened patio enclosure that protected us from bugs. We could hear the sound of river frogs coming from a small creek behind the property that fed into the Wekiva River. I decided to just enjoy the peaceful quiet and sip my wine as Kyla did the same.

"Something's bothering you Brett," she said at last. "What is it?"

"I guess it's the disappointment of a reality crashing into a dream." Kyla waited patiently for me to continue. I wanted to trust her, I needed her advice. So I continued.

"Michelle wanted to end our relationship at the end of last summer," I said. "Neither of us thought I'd be back this summer, and she knew we'd be applying to different colleges. She said that she didn't want to hold me back, that she wasn't sure how she felt about me anyway, and that we should part as friends."

"And yet here you are."

"And yet here I am." I took a breath.

"I decided to write her a letter last February. She sent me one back saying that she missed me, that she missed my 'gift of gab' as she called it," I reflected out loud, taking in another breath.

"Maybe you're right," I continued. "Maybe Michelle and I both think too much. But I really loved talking with her all last summer, sharing our thoughts and dreams. They didn't have to make any sense, yet somehow we understood each other." I paused again, trying to figure out what I meant and deciding that it didn't really matter. "I could just talk with her for hours you know? It was easy."

"So, you hitchhiked back here to find, what exactly?"

"I'm not sure. I haven't been able to get Michelle out of my mind. I wanted to see her again. Something felt unresolved between us. The letters…"

Kyla bit lightly on her lower lip, considering what I had said. "Michelle's afraid to love you, Brett," she said.

"Yeah I can see that, but why?"

"Why do you think? You don't live here, Brett!"

"I can make it work somehow," I said, having no idea whether it was true.

"Uggh! Men! You guys can be real idiots sometimes!" she said over her shoulder while carrying the plates and silverware back to the kitchen. I grabbed the rest of the table items and followed her in, deciding to wash the dishes to prove her wrong.

"Thanks," she said. We busied ourselves with putting things away and then carried our refilled wine glasses out to the living room, setting them on the coffee table and settling back down on the carpet. Dusk had fallen and the garden lights clicked on, the pool reflected them with shimmers of amber light. We took another sip of wine and Kyla smiled, looking at me.

"I like you Brett," she said. "You're smart and good looking, but you don't really know that much about women do you?"

"It's something I'm still working on," I confessed. "I guess I want to have a relationship as well as a friendship, is that possible?"

"Yes Brett, I think that it is," she replied. "But that's only half your problem."

"What do you mean?" I asked. She pressed her lips together, deciding.

"Are you sure it's not just sex that you want?" That took me by surprise and my expression probably showed my confusion, not so much by the question but by how it made me feel.

"Look at you!" she said. "You know what I mean. You're only here for a few more days, Brett! What are you hoping for exactly?"

I reached for my glass of wine and drank half its contents with one swallow. "I guess I want a relationship first," I said definitively, hoping that I meant it.

"Well I wish you luck," Kyla demurred, uncrossing her legs and extending them to lie on her side facing me, with her arm propping up her head as she looked back at me, maintaining eye contact…

"There is one more thing you should know Brett," she said. "Well two things actually."

"What?" I said, settling into a similar position opposite her.

"Michelle's still a virgin Brett. You do know that don't you?"

This touched my feelings on a number of different levels. I felt relief because it told me that Michelle had not yet given herself to another guy. I also realized that Kyla was probably not a virgin by the way that she had said this. And I felt conflicted because being a virgin was not exactly something a guy was comfortable talking about or sharing, especially with someone as beautiful as Kyla.

"What's the other thing?" I asked.

"A couple of weeks ago I was with Michelle and some other girls. We decided to go canoeing down the Wekiva River. It was a hot afternoon so we decided to paddle into a cove for a quick swim. Most of the other girls stripped down to their bras and panties, but Michelle took off all her clothes. The way she swam up to us… Brett, I think Michelle likes girls. She may not know it yet; it's just a feeling that I have about her." She reached over and lightly touched my cheek.

Unformed, conflicting possibilities crept into my subconscious mind, but the effects of the wine were taking hold and I decided to let them go. Kyla's hand gently moved down my cheek and I was feeling attracted toward her again. There was tingling warmth when our lips touched that was soothed by her returning embrace.

"That felt like electricity," she whispered softly as our lips parted. It wasn't exactly how I remembered it from my dream, wrong girl for one thing, and I knew she was just toying with me. But still, I didn't want the moment to end.

"I think you better go," Kyla said finally. Her words were not what I had wanted to hear just then but I knew that she was right. I was unprepared for this lure of passion that would lead nowhere, and there were no words left to say. I took one final look at Kyla lying there on the carpet as I stepped outside, and carefully shut the door behind me.

On that Wednesday morning, I got up of my own accord and got ready for work with nothing planned that evening. My father was surveying the framework that had been completed the day before and I stood there waiting for him to give me instructions. One of the ceiling beams had been cut too short, he had decided. He called Sam over and instructed him to have his crew rip out that section of framework and redo it.

"It's going to take some additional lumber, Mr. Roberts," Sam said slowly. "I could probably have it delivered to the site tomorrow."

"Keep your crew on site Sam," my father answered. "Brett and I will drive down to the lumberyard and pick up what you need." He made a list on a small notepad that he kept in his shirt pocket and we climbed into the truck.

"Time to go see Mister Thomas, Brett," he said. "Every day costs us money." As we drove south on I-4 headed for downtown Orlando, my father explained that Mr. Thomas was a member of his

Shriner's organization. Both of them wore funny hats and drove miniature cars down Church Street every year in the Christmas Parade. We exited at Gore Street and turned into Thomas Lumber Company. My father pulled the truck up to the loading dock out back and we stepped up into the warehouse.

"Well hello there Mister Roberts!" Mr. Thomas was a confident and vigorous man whose business was booming with all the new construction happening north of Orlando. My father tore off the sheet of paper from his notepad and handed it to Mr. Thomas. He called to a couple of his workers and they efficiently loaded the lumber into the truck while he and my father chatted away, catching up on local events. After it had been loaded, my father wrote a check for the amount due and returned to the truck holding the invoice. He wanted me to drive back so that he could study the blueprints and make sure that we had everything we needed.

By the time we returned to the job site, Sam and his crew had already torn out the section of ceiling joists that needed to be rebuilt. My father and I unloaded the lumber and promised to check back by the end of the day. We returned to the house and hitched up an old trailer that he preferred to use for dump runs. We would spend the rest of the afternoon hauling building scraps from the jobsites to the dump, about four trips in all. It was just one of many jobs that my father did himself to save money on a project. He worked hard every day, and he was glad to have me along.

When we returned to the house, following our usual rinse off with the hose and dip in the pool, I decided that I needed to go out for a run before dinner, thinking it would help to clear my head. A lot of thoughts were rattling around inside, like pieces of my soul were struggling to find balance and peace.

I laced up my powder blue Nike Marathon running shoes, glad that I had brought them along. "I'll be back in about forty five minutes," I announced to my stepmother, who was busy preparing dinner while holding her cocktail glass of gin on ice in the other hand. "OK Brett, I'll tell your father. Have fun!"

This was not exactly fun, more of a compulsion. I hadn't been running in several days and was feeling the effects of withdrawal from the "runner's high" that I usually got after a nice long run. I started jogging down Sweetwater Boulevard and broke into a full run when I hit Wekiva Springs Road, heading west toward the state park. I was curious to find out about canoe rentals at the marina; Jimmy had given me the idea at Kyla's pool party last Sunday. They were just closing up as I arrived at the kiosk, jogging in place. Canoe rentals were five dollars and the marina opened at 10 am.

A light mist began to fall as I jogged back down to Wekiva Springs Road and headed toward my father's house. Just as my mind was adjusting to this, a crack of thunder foretold the heavy rain that quickly followed. Its fat raindrops were now pelting my skull in rapid succession, and they drenched my hair and rushed down my neck into my saturated clothes. My soaked Nikes made squishing sounds as they fought through sheets of rain to gain traction with the pavement. Raindrops painfully smacked my face, chest and belly as I leaned into the oncoming torrent. Flashes of lightning came down from the sky and I knew that I needed to get back under tree cover as soon as possible. With my arms pumping in determination, I settled my mind into a Zen like state.

I remember feeling vividly alive in that moment. It was kind of a purifying experience that calmed me down despite my struggle against the rain.

There was a misty rainbow overhead when I got back to my father's house, diffracting the waning sunlight in brilliant colors as it arched over Lake Brantley. I knew the scientific explanation for this, having taken high school physics, but it felt like a miracle had happened just then.

I sipped a cold beer in the living room later that evening after dinner, joining my father and stepmother to watch the evening news. A fence had been constructed around the block where the sink hole had fallen several days earlier; the buildings had been condemned and would be torn down once the ground had stabilized. Years later, that sink hole would become a pond surrounded by a city park.

The news anchor then reported that Leon Jaworski, a special prosecutor who had been appointed by the justice department to investigate the Watergate scandal, had requested that President Nixon release the tapes that had been recorded in the Oval Office around the time of the Watergate break in. Transcripts of the tapes had been released that spring, and revelations were being discussed almost daily in the news. A court ruling was expected in several weeks.

"Terrible how those damned liberal democrats are trying to take this country down," my stepmother commented.

"Those dumb shits don't respect the presidency," my father commented in reply.

It was time for me to go to bed. "Thanks for dinner," I said. "I'm pretty pooped. See you in the morning."

"Nighty nightshirts Brett!" my stepmother said with a lilt to her voice, returning to the news.

CHAPTER SIXTEEN

I HELPED MY FATHER the next morning with odd jobs around his building sites. He had driven back to the first house the evening before and inspected the roof joists, deeming them to now be acceptable. A roofing crew was hard at work, moving nimbly along the roof and whapping their two pound hammers in rapid succession, they were nailing one-inch plywood sheets into place. Next came thick waterproof sheeting followed by the shingles. The finished roof would last for twenty years, hurricanes notwithstanding. There was a pile of lumber scraps that needed to be taken to the dump, so he had hitched the trailer back up to the truck and this would be our first task of the day.

Painters were busy at work inside the second house, the one that we had finished trimming two days earlier. There was a pile of scraps, discarded masking materials, and paint buckets out in front of the house.

"Go get the hose from the truck and hook it up to that faucet behind the house," my father instructed. He wanted me to rinse out those empty five gallon paint buckets. I knew from the previous day's work that they would be used for hauling scraps back to the dump trailer.

We spent the rest of the morning building a fenced in area outside of the master bedroom that would be used for a garden, a two foot side door opened out into it. It was another one of my father's signature touches and he was very proud of his solariums as he called them. We sunk the fence posts and constructed the fence and gate ourselves. He left the perimeter fencing to his subcontractors, but this was his way of showing them the quality standard he expected.

That afternoon, my father walked me to the side of the house and gestured how the mounds of sandy soil would need to be smoothed out to create a gentle slope down to the curb. It would be my most difficult job that entire week. Armed with two shovels, a rake and a wheelbarrow, I must have moved a ton of sandy Florida dirt up and down that forty foot span. It was too narrow for a Cat tractor to maneuver according to my father. The five gallon igloo cooler in the back of his truck was almost empty by the time I returned for my final drink, having now finished the grading to my father's satisfaction.

"You do good work young son!" he said as he walked out to the truck carrying his tools. "But we're going to have to hose you down before you get back into the truck," he laughed as he looked me up and down. I was covered in dirt. He led me to the other side of the house where the painters had left a hose, turning on the water and handing the hose to me. As I was still rinsing the sand out of my hair he returned with a towel.

"Michelle has the day off from work tomorrow and I'm planning to take her canoeing, is that still okay with you Dad?"

"Sure you can Brett," he said.

When we returned to the house, after a more thorough rinsing in the backyard followed by a dip in the pool, my father walked out and handed me eighty dollars. "That's for four days of good work, son. Come back next summer!" Unfortunately this was not to be, something that I regretted years later.

Returning to my room to shower and change, I saw that my stepmother had set out a new pair of clothes for me to wear on my date with Michelle, black Levis jeans and a blue button down silk shirt, short sleeves for the summer evening. This time she had gotten the size from my work jeans and everything fit perfectly. A new pair of black suede leather shoes had also been set on the floor next to my bed. My stepmother had a much better sense of style than I had.

I thanked her once again after I walked back out. "You can't take a girl out in those ratty clothes you had hanging in the closet. I hope she likes what I bought for you." She smiled as I politely spun around.

I was sitting by the pool on the back patio having a drink with my father and stepmother when Michelle arrived, ringing the front doorbell. I met her at the door and invited her to join us on the patio. My father offered her a drink as she sat in one of the patio chairs, crossing her legs and looking relaxed. Michelle was wearing slim pastel blue chinos and a flowered blouse with a lapis necklace and matching earrings. She was also wearing a touch of eye makeup that she didn't really need. The effect was stunning though, and I was glad that she had been willing to meet my parents. Maybe it would help explain why I had travelled three thousand miles to see her.

"I love what you are wearing Michelle," my stepmother said.

"Thanks," Michelle said with a smile. Soon she and my stepmother were talking easily about their clothes and jewelry, seeming to hit it off quite well actually.

My father asked whether she would like to have dinner with us. "I would love to, but perhaps another time," Michelle said. "Brett promised to buy me dinner and I'm taking him up on it." She seemed pleased.

"Well okay, I guess it's time for us to go," I said. As we walked out I looked back at my stepmother and mouthed "thank you" while gesturing to my clothes. She nodded and smiled back.

"You drive," Michelle said as we climbed into her car. Her father, still in Germany on a six month work assignment, had left it for her to drive. It had already received several dents to the front bumper and rear passenger door.

"I'm always crashing in the same car," Michelle said as we drove away, parodying an obscure David Bowie song. I drove carefully nonetheless.

We drove down I-4 to downtown Orlando and exited at Church Street. I pulled into a space at the public lot underneath the freeway overpass and walked around to open the passenger door for Michelle. She seemed impressed by this gesture and took my hand as she stepped out. We walked arm in arm up Church Street to Rosie O'Grady's. I had called ahead and reserved a table on the indoor patio facing the street. I held the seat for Michelle and sat opposite her. A tiffany lamp provided soft illumination as we inspected our menus. A waitress arrived and we ordered drinks, a gin and tonic for me and a J&B on ice with a splash of water for her. I couldn't suppress a chuckle after the waitress left.

"What?" Michelle asked after the waitress left to get our drinks.

"It's just that I feel sort of like a 'grownup', although not really."

"Well, you keep working on that Brett," she nodded with an amused look and returned to her menu. Then she let out a giggle as well. The ice had been broken.

The waitress came back with our drinks and we ordered food. Thankfully Michelle went straight for an entrée, deciding against an appetizer. She worked as a waitress and had probably served many couples just like us. I decided to keep it simple and order the pork chop.

"So you woke up one day and decided to hitch hike across the country just to see me," Michelle said, folding her hands in front of her and waiting for my reply. She looked amused.

"Yeah, well as I said it's a long story, or maybe just a painful one. I was originally planning to drive my car out here, but I got pretty drunk the night of my high school graduation, and well, I crashed my car."

"You crashed your car?" she said, somewhat surprised that a generally careful guy such as myself would do such a thing.

"Yeah, as I said a long story."

"Or maybe just a painful one," she replied with twinkling eyes. "Exemption granted on the details," she said.

"Thanks," I said, relieved that I would not have to elaborate.

While we talked over dinner, I shared some of the experiences from my trip across the country. Michelle was interested in my encounter with the grand wizard of the Ku Klux Klan while driving through Louisiana, the traveling shoe salesman in Mississippi who had a girlfriend at every stop, and the gay church organist who propositioned me in Mobile. She particularly liked my descriptions of Dari and Danni and their perceptions of America, especially their reaction to the albino evangelist who had been preaching from a street corner just outside of Pensacola.

"Wow, you really crammed a lot of experiences into just six days," she said.

"Yeah, well there's another experience on my mind that I was planning to ask you about," I said. "Would you like to go canoeing with me tomorrow? We could launch from the Wekiva Marina. I've already checked into canoe rentals."

"Yes! That sounds like fun," she said enthusiastically.

I paid for the dinner and we strolled along Church Street, enjoying the street performers. Michelle clapped as a juggler completed his flaming torch routine and I put a dollar in the hat, grateful for the money that my father had given me earlier that evening. Michelle kept her arm around me as we walked back to her car. When we got there she kissed me, just a quick one, but it was a nice surprise and it made me very happy.

I pulled up to my father's house and turned off the ignition, walking around to open the passenger door for Michelle. When we got back to the driver's side, she pulled me toward her and kissed me again, this time more softly, lingering. I felt my heart race and held her close, exploring her body energy and sensing its warmth. "Thank you," I said as I released our embrace.

"See you tomorrow at 9 am, California boy," she said. I stood there watching her tail lights fade into the night.

My father and stepmother had already left when I awoke to those now familiar beams of light shifting back and forth across my eyelids. It was Friday morning, my last day with Michelle, I would be leaving tomorrow. I fumbled for my wristwatch to learn that it was already eight o'clock. I had better get moving, I told myself, and decided to take a cold shower, enjoying the sensation and knowing that it would be another hot and muggy day once I went outside.

I found a large plastic bag in the hall closet and stuffed it with the items that we would need for the canoe, towels, a couple of visors, and a bottle of sunscreen. I was finishing off a bowl of cereal when Michelle rang the doorbell. I grabbed the plastic bag and walked out with her to her car. She wanted me to drive again which I didn't mind.

We headed back up I-434 to the Winn-Dixie supermarket to get a few things for lunch. Michelle also grabbed a bag of fresh cherries and a six pack of Pearl beer from Texas. I wasn't sure how they would go together but it seemed like a good idea at the time. When we got back out to the car, Michelle put the cherries and beer in a small cooler that she had filled with ice. She had also filled an empty 2-liter plastic soda bottle with water and stuck it in the freezer the night before; it was already about half thawed sitting in the trunk of her car. We would survive our canoe trek.

We drove up the dirt road to Wekiva Marina and pulled over at a grass parking area. Several vehicles with boat trailers had already been left there for the day, their owners were now far upriver. I carted the cooler and other essentials over to the dock and set them down. A row of green fiberglass canoes bobbed up and down in the water, still tied to the dock and waiting for customers. Near the end of the dock, a black man in worn coveralls was fishing with a bobber for catfish while chewing on an unlit cigar. He spit some of the tobacco juice into the water and watched the bobber intently.

Michelle was standing by a green kiosk that sold sundries and fishing supplies, talking to the man behind the counter. He had on a sleeveless athletic jersey from Tulane University and was also wearing a dirty camouflage hunting cap. He looked like he hadn't shaved all week. I came over and told him that we'd like to rent a canoe for the day, letting him know that we were together.

"Looks like you went to Tulane," I said stupidly, attempting to direct his attention away from Michelle.

"Yeah," he said, suppressing a smirk, "Philosophy major."

"What brings y'all out here?" I said, trying to sound like I was from here.

"Helping my father out over the summer," he said, ending with another smirk.

I looked back to the river, taking in the scenery that he probably looked at every day. "Really beautiful here," I said.

"Yes it is," he said, loosening up and smiling broadly, revealing white teeth that seemed to have seen a dentist regularly.

Once I had filled out a form and handed over my California driver's license as collateral, he hollered back to the main building behind the kiosk. It housed a rustic catfish diner that was open nightly, a local draw according to my father. A younger man with long stringy hair came out to help us with our canoe, rubbing his hands on a dirty apron as he approached the dock. He fetched two flotation cushions from behind the kiosk and carried them over to the canoe, tossing them onto aluminum seats that were suspended from the gunwales. Then he untied the canoe and walked it over to the dock area where I had stacked our cooler and other items, holding it in place as we stepped in and positioned our things. I held the canoe steady against the dock while he retrieved a couple of paddles and handed them to us. He gently shoved us away from the dock and we started paddling upriver.

The marina soon disappeared from view as we paddled the winding Wekiva River in a northeasterly direction. After my ears adjusted to the quiet I became aware of subtle sounds such as the rustle of river grass in the wind, the occasional croak of a river frog, a few birds chirping. The water was surprisingly clear and I could see all the way to the bottom, observing an occasional fish swimming against the current. We paddled by a log extending out into the river with a row of turtles perched on top in a linear formation; their heads were extended upward to soak up the sun. Native palms, new growth cypress and pine trees lined both sides of the river. Water hyacinths and water lettuce also floated on the water, extending outwards from each bank with strikingly textured shades of green that almost interlaced. It would have felt as though we were hundreds of miles from civilization had it not been for the occasional shack, they were built right up to the bank on either side of the river.

All of them had been painted a dark shade of green, apparently an effort to match the scenery, but they were still a bit of an eyesore. Most of them were shuttered. I would later learn that environmentalists had been fighting for years to get these "squatter cabins" torn down.

We also passed through sections of dense hardwood forest that sheltered us from the sunlight. I was getting more comfortable piloting the canoe, using the J-stroke that I had learned as a boy scout and was now coming back into my muscle memory. Michelle was an experienced canoeist and skillfully maneuvered the front of the canoe around bends in the river. It was enjoyable to paddle along quietly together.

The river widened after we navigated around one of the bends, and we saw a blue heron standing near the shore. It was extremely still, watching the water intently for a fish to swim by.

"Can you paddle by yourself for a while?" Michelle asked.

"Sure," I said.

She lifted her paddle into the canoe and positioned it behind her. Then she pulled her T-shirt up and over her head, changing into a string bikini top while I paddled. I couldn't help but stare at her graceful back and the fullness of her breasts hanging there from either side. The canoe began to turn sideways; and I pulled strongly with my paddle to get it pointed back straight upriver, still a bit flustered as I imagined her paddling the rest of the day naked. "Get a grip Brett" I told myself silently, hoping that she could not hear my thoughts. After securing her bikini straps, she reached back for her paddle and smiled as she caught my expression.

"Uh, could you do that again?" I asked, trying to sound as if I were joking.

"Maybe later," she teased, and resumed her paddling.

By midday the humidity had begun to drain our energy. Paddling was getting to be a bit more of a chore. "Let's pull over to that cove," Michelle said, pointing with her paddle. The water was fairly deep over there with a bubbling spring feeding into it. As our canoe reached the bank, Michelle dove into the water. I stepped out of the canoe and pulled it up onto the sand, jumping in after her. We waded there together in the cool spring water.

"I really love it out here," she said. "It's just so peaceful."

"Yeah, I can't imagine a more perfect day," I answered, enjoying her closeness. She dove under the water and came back to the surface, spraying me with her wet hair as she shook her head, laughing. I decided to do the same. She swam back to the bank and stepped out of the water, reaching into the canoe for the cooler and plastic bag and carrying them over to a small patch of grass in the shade beneath a red oak tree. She was arranging our picnic as I came over to join her. We sat together and leaned against the tree, eating our lunch and sipping our ice cold beers. The cherries did seem to compliment the beer, I mused, tossing a small pebble into the river.

"It was worth it," I said.

"You mean this?" Michelle said, gesturing with her thumb.

"Hitchhiking was a fantastic adventure," I said, "but it doesn't compare to being here with you."

I chewed a couple more cherries, tossed the pits into the water and took another sip of beer. Michelle cut a piece of cheese and handed it over to me on a cracker.

"Michelle," I said, looking at her, "I think I'm crazy about you."

"I'm pretty sure you're right about that Brett," she said, "the crazy part I mean."

"Maybe you're right," I said, tossing another cherry pit into the river.

"But..." she said, hesitating.

"But?" I asked, turning back to her.

"I'm happy with you Brett." She smiled, nodding her head as she said this.

"Well look, I know I'm flying home tomorrow, and college is coming up. I know I've got a lot of things to work through. But the feeling that I have for you is real and..." she put her fingers to my lips. "Let's not talk about that," she said looking away.

We loaded our things into the canoe and pushed off, paddling again upstream. I looked back at the beach where we had sat together and took a picture in my mind.

After paddling for another hour, we decided it was time to turn the canoe around and drift back downstream. Michelle placed her paddle in the canoe behind her and I kept mine in the water mainly for steerage. She reached into the cooler for another beer and handed one to me. A breeze approached us from downriver, causing ripples in the water. Large cumulous clouds were coalescing in the sky and I could see that the weather was about to turn. I decided to paddle while Michelle continued to lean back slightly against her arms, with her hands grasping the gunwales. She pulled her shirt back on when the breeze picked up which made me a little sad. I reached down to get my beer and took another sip.

"So what would you like to do this evening?" I asked.

"Let's go back to my place, I'd like you to meet my mom," she said. "Maybe we can barbeque out by the pool.

"I'd like that," I said.

Michelle resumed paddling when we passed the first of the river shacks and soon we made the final turn headed back to Wekiva Marina. The long-haired kid stepped out to meet us at the dock. "Did y'all have a good time on the water?" he said.

"We sure did," I said as I maneuvered the canoe alongside the dock. He took Michelle's hand and helped her out of the canoe and then walked back to give me a hand which I waved off, stepping onto the dock on my own. I went over to the kiosk to retrieve my driver's license and Michelle carried our things out to her car. It was just beginning to rain again when we rolled up the windows and pulled out of the lot, heading back down the dirt road to Wekiva Springs Road. I turned on the wipers and at first they made a mess of the windshield until enough raindrops had fallen to rinse the dirt away. Michelle turned on the air-conditioner to keep us alert, we were both pretty tired. Then she found a rock station on the radio and turned the volume up, *Rebel Rebel*, a new one from Bowie.

"So tell me about your mom," I asked as we headed up highway 434 toward Highway 17-92.

"She's from Germany," she said, turning the volume back down. "My father met her over there when he was serving in the Army."

The song *Killer Queen* came on the radio next and she turned the sound back up a little. "She didn't speak any English when they met," she said. "But I guess they hit it off pretty quickly. They were married in a small town outside of Frankfurt and I was born six months later."

The rain was falling heavier now and I turned the wipers up to full speed.

"Anyway, after my father got discharged from the Army they moved to Milwaukee where he grew up. They lived with his parents until he managed to get a job with a shipping company. There were a lot of German families up there so my mom was pretty happy. Then my father got transferred to Orlando, which happened about four years ago. Fortunately my mom's English has gotten much better since then."

Michelle directed me to make a left shortly after we had passed Highway 436 and we turned into a relatively upscale neighborhood of single-story ranch homes. She asked me to park in the driveway of her house and then led me in through the garage. We went through a door in back that opened directly into her bedroom; it was a new addition that her father had built after her eighteenth birthday so she could have some privacy away from her brother. Another door from there led out to the pool. The main house had been built to elbow around the opposite sides of the pool, giving it a feeling of intimacy and privacy. The rain had stopped.

"My parents picked this house because they like to walk around naked," Michelle explained. We passed over to the main house and found her mother Ursula in the kitchen. Fortunately she was wearing clothes at the time.

"You must be Brett," she said. "Michelle has been talking about you all week." Michelle turned away, embarrassed. Ursula walked toward me and took my hand affectionately. "He is very handsome," she whispered to Michelle.

"Very pleased to meet you Mrs. Wagner," I said, trying to be charming. Whereas Michelle seemed careful and reserved, her mother was carefree and high energy. I liked her straight away.

Nick walked into the kitchen in his boxer shorts, still toweling off his wet hair from the shower. "Hey Brett," he said smiling broadly, trying to embarrass me as well. "I see you've met my mom."

"I've been looking forward to it," I said, recovering my composure.

Ursula seemed somewhat displeased with Nick's walking around in his underwear, which I found encouraging. "What are you planning to do Nick?" she asked.

"Annie's coming over," he said. "We were going to go out."

"Well then let's all go out together!" Ursula said enthusiastically. "It will be my treat."

"What am I going to wear?" I whispered over to Michelle, standing there in my swim trunks and T-shirt.

"You look like you're about my dad's size," Michelle said. "Let's go find something for you to wear in his closet."

"You go right ahead Brett," Ursula said. "Russell's not coming home for another couple of months." I could tell that she missed him deeply.

Michelle led me into her parent's walk-in closet where she picked out a pair of powder blue denim jeans and a black silk shirt. "My dad brought this shirt home from Thailand," she said." She also selected a pair of webbed leather sandals which fit my feet perfectly.

"You sure all this is okay?"

"I'm pretty sure he won't notice," she said. "Don't worry," she added, "I'll wash them tomorrow." Then she led me back to her room. I tried to be a gentleman by not peeking while we both changed into our clothes, but it was pretty hard not to. Michelle had selected a pair of white jeans and a rainbow colored tube top that accentuated her bare athletic shoulders. A pair of blue sandals completed the look. Fashion had not been something that I thought about very often, but it was becoming clear to me that I needed to pay closer attention.

I noticed a small wine rack over in the corner of her room with a single bottle of champagne collecting dust in the bottom slot.

"That was a gift from my grandfather before we left Milwaukee," Michelle said.

"Looks like it's been there for a while," I commented.

"Well, I've been saving it," she said.

"For what?"

"My first time," she said, obviously regretting it and turning away so that I couldn't see her face. "Let's go."

Nick drove the five of us to the club in Annie's mom's new Oldsmobile. He and Annie were under eighteen and would not be drinking while we were out; at least as far as Ursula was aware of anyway. I rode in the back with Michelle and her mother.

We drove up to a local rock club on Highway 17-92. The sign on the marquis out front announced that a band called Foghat was playing there that evening.

"No way," I said as we entered the lot. "Is that the band from England they've been playing on the radio?" Their version of Willie Dixon's "I Just Want to Make Love to You" had been getting a lot of local airplay on the FM dial.

"Yeah a lot of great bands have been coming through Orlando," Nick said. The population had increased considerably in Central Florida by the mid-1970s and with that came lots of music consumers. I was surprised that Michelle's mom was okay with this particular choice of venue, however as soon as Nick had parked the car Ursula stepped out with raised her arms and shouted "let's dance!", leading us all inside.

Sure enough, the lead singer from Foghat was shouting out the chorus from one of their top radio songs in a raspy voice, "I just want to make...love to you!" They would be playing that song several more times during the evening, and the audience would get wilder every time they played it. The stage was standing in the back corner of the club with sound and light technicians stationed over in the opposite corner, operating the racks of colored lights, floods, and fog machines to make the stage come alive. The band members were modestly dressed in T-shirts and jeans, looking like they had to drive to another gig right after the show (which they probably did), their teased long hair the only clue to their rock status. But the sound was loud and tight; a significant improvement over the usual garage band rabble. We squeezed through the crowd, found an open table near the dance floor and ordered drinks, a J&B and water for Michelle and a gin and tonic for me. Ursula ordered a Mai Tai, her party drink. Nick and Annie ordered cokes. I was watching the sexy cocktail waitress walk back to the bar to get our drinks when Nick shouted "That's my mom!" Ursula was out on the dance floor with a good-looking guy in his early twenties who was clearly digging the way that she danced, nodding his head in approval. Then Nick covertly spiked his and Annie's cokes from a flask that he had smuggled into the club.

I took a big sip from my gin and tonic and asked Michelle to dance. To my relief, she took my hand. Ursula was dancing with a second young man when we made it out onto the dance floor. Upon seeing us she said "Hey you two," clapping her hands above her head as she swayed her hips.

"Hey Mrs. Wagner," I said stupidly. She turned her nose at that. Fortunately no one else seemed to have heard. "Ursula," she cautioned. "Oh, sorry," I said and we danced together for a moment to make it better. When I turned back to Michelle I was instantly captivated by the way that she moved her body, more fluid and sexy under the rotating colored lights than I had ever noticed before. It was hard to remember her aggressive stance playing table tennis a few days before. Michelle had been transformed by the dance floor, and I liked it.

We kept dancing through two more songs and finally took a break, weaving back through the crowd to our table. When our cocktail waitress returned, giving a sly wink to let me know that she had caught my wayward glance earlier, I ordered ice waters and several appetizers from the bar menu. The band took a break and house music came on, a DJ was directing it from a booth over to the right of the stage. Ursula returned to the table and gratefully accepted an ice water that I handed it to her. Nick and Annie returned a few minutes later. I hadn't seen them out on the dance floor. Evidently they had gone out to the car, and I was pretty sure what for based on their afterglow grins.

Michelle leaned over to me and said "let's go get some air." I followed her to the rear exit and we stepped outside to the back parking lot. A cool evening breeze swept by us, gently drying our skin. Other couples were walking out to their cars as well to have some privacy so I led Michelle over to a grassy area where a park bench had been conveniently stationed.

"I really love how you dance," I said after we sat down.

"You're not so bad yourself, once you loosen up," she teased.

A crescent moon emerged from behind the clouds; brightening her features just enough to give me pause. I took a breath and slowly let it out, composing my thoughts. "You're really beautiful," I said at last. Her relaxed smile showed me that everything was okay, for the moment. "I'm happy with you Brett," she said. I had heard that before.

"But…" I asked, unsure whether I wanted to hear the answer.

"But nothing," she said, putting her finger again to my mouth. When she dropped her hand I reached toward her, touching her hair and then sliding my hand around to bring her close. That kiss was long, peaceful, forgiving, and kind.

"I would do it all again," I said after a pause.

"What? Hitch across the country to see me? Haven't we had this conversation before?"

"Oh yeah," I said.

"Well the evening's not over yet Brett," she said. "Let's go back inside."

We returned to the club, ordered another drink and joined the crowd back on the dance floor. By that point I was feeling the music and matching Michelle's moves. She caught on to this and started matching mine. I reached over and took her hand, giving her a little spin which she seemed to enjoy.

"Hola Brett!" I heard from the girl next to me. It was Paola and she was dancing with Pete. She had on a form fitting dress that complimented her voluptuous figure, I tried not to look down. "Hey Paola," I shouted over the music, "Hey Pete!"

"We just got here," Pete said. "I had no idea Foghat would be playing here tonight. Pretty damned awesome!"

"Good to see you and Michelle together," Paola said, smiling and gesturing to us with her arms as though it were a blessing.

"Thanks!" I said, and focused back on Michelle before another guy could cut in. That was close, I thought to myself.

We had formed our own nuclear dance party by the time the band came back out for their encore, Michelle and I, Nick and Annie, and Paola and Pete. Seeing this, Ursula excused her final dance partner of the evening and joined us, still waving her arms with unbridled enthusiasm. Our skin was damp with sweat by the time the lights came on.

Ursula went back over to the table to pay our bill. I waited for her as the others queued outside. "Can I help with the tab?" I asked.

"No Brett, that was my treat," Ursula said. So I escorted her out to the car where the others were waiting.

Nick drove us back to their house. I thought the evening was ending as we pulled into the driveway, but Ursula had other plans for us. "Let's go skinny dipping in the pool!" she said, a little tipsy. Nick nodded to Annie and they headed into the house with Ursula close behind. I looked over to Michelle to see what she was thinking.

"Come on, the water will feel great after all that dancing," she said. I followed her through the back door of the garage into her bedroom to change. Michelle switched on a lava lamp over on her night stand and turned off the ceiling light. I took off my borrowed clothes and carefully folded them, placing them over next to the wall. I briefly considered whether to put on my bathing suit, but Michelle was already heading out to the patio and I could clearly see that she was naked. Then I heard a splash as she jumped into the pool. I collected myself for a moment, taking a few slow deep breaths until my heart rate dropped back down, and then decided that I was ready.

When I stepped out to the patio I saw that the pool light had been turned off, the only illumination coming from the proud crescent moon that had now reached its zenith in the evening sky. Nick and Annie were whispering softly on the other side of the pool and Ursula was swimming laps. I jumped in and swam over to Michelle who was leaning against the wall directly opposite from Nick and Annie. Ursula continued swimming by and I tried not to look, which caused Michelle to let out an easy laugh. I looked down at her in the water and watched her legs kicking slowly while she rested her arm on the ledge. Then, no longer able to help it, I looked up to her breasts suspended buoyantly in the water. They were even more beautiful that I had imagined them earlier in the day, when I had seen them from behind in the canoe. Then I willed myself to maintain eye contact, hoping that I wouldn't appear to be too excited, and trying to seem relaxed even though the sexual tension inside me was almost palpable.

"Hey again," she said as I reached my arm around to slip next to her, now resting it on the ledge behind her shoulders. I felt myself relax as our bodies touched.

"Want a beer?" Nick called out from the other side of the pool.

"I do!" said Michelle. I was certainly okay with that. "Yeah Nick, please bring us a couple if you don't mind," I said. Nick hoisted his body out of the pool with his back to us and walked with soggy feet into the kitchen to get the beers. He came back with an armful of cans, handing one to Annie and another to Ursula when she swam by. Then he set the rest on the ledge and jumped back in the pool with Annie, motioning for me to swim over to get mine. I tried not to look at Annie when I approached and she let out a giggle, clearly amused. "The water feels great after all that dancing, huh?" she said.

"Yeah, it sure does," I said. Nick gave me a sly wink.

"Thanks," I said, grabbing a beer with each hand and kicked off the side of the pool so that I could glide through the water back over to Michelle. I handed her a beer while again resting my other arm behind her on the pool ledge. This time I felt a new kind of warmth between us as we nestled together in the water sipping our beers. I looked up to the stars and studied them, thinking here I was back down on Earth, naked in a pool with a girl who I had travelled three thousand miles to see, to see about, what?

"I wish we could be together somehow," I said. I was not really sure what I meant by that but could find no other words just then. "I just wish we had more time."

"Maybe someday," she said.

"Yeah, maybe someday," I said, willing myself for it to be true. "But let's stop talking like that."

"Definitely," she said, smiling again.

I heard more whispers and another giggle from the other side of the pool. Nick hoisted himself out of the water again and went to get a beach towel, holding it up for Annie to climb out. He wrapped it around her and they went into the house together. I looked over and saw that Ursula was leaning against the back side of the pool, lost in her own thoughts. "Hey Mrs. Wagner," I said. "Thanks again for a nice evening."

"It was very nice to meet you Brett," she said in her German accent as she hoisted herself out of the pool, locating another beach towel to wrap around herself. "I'm going in now kids, I am very tired," she said as she walked over to the house. "Take all the time you want and have a nice flight home tomorrow Brett."

"Thanks," I said, not wanting to think about that just yet.

When it became quiet again, Michelle said "I'll be right back." She climbed out of the pool, found a towel and walked around to the kitchen to get something. She came back carrying an ice bucket.

"About done with the pool?" she asked.

"Yeah, I guess."

"Good, come on." She handed me a towel and carried the ice bucket back to her bedroom. I followed her in, having no fully formed idea what to expect. I certainly wasn't expecting to see her sitting on her bed when I came in, but there she was still naked and waiting for me. The champagne bottle was in the ice bucket.

I finished drying off and sat on the bed next to her. "Whoa," I said, letting out a breath. "You sure you want to do this?"

"Do what Brett?" she said teasingly.

"Oh come on, you know you've been thinking about it just like I have," she said when I didn't answer. "Did you bring any protection?"

And then I remembered. At the party, the night of my graduation, one of the football players had passed around a bowl of condoms. I had taken one and put it in my wallet. It was still there, I realized with a wave of relief. I went over to my pile of clothes and retrieved it from my pants, carrying the packet with me back over to the bed.

The only other time I had gotten this close to having sex was with my first girlfriend in the ninth grade. The girl's family was from Spain and Teresa had complimented me on my taste in Latin women. But we had been too young and it had ended our relationship. I wasn't sure whether or not I was doing the right thing just now.

"Let me see that," Michelle said, snatching it from me and inspecting the wrapper. She was humming a tauntingly silly tune and then she read the label out loud. "Textured for maximum pleasure," she said. "Hmmm." She looked down and could see that I was ready. "Stand up for a second," she said. I thought she was joking, but then I understood as she went to get a beach towel to spread out onto the bed.

"Not so fast," she said as we settled back down. I leaned over to kiss her soft lips. They parted and our tongues explored as the kissing became more passionate. Then she gave a throaty sigh as I began to explore her neck with more soft kisses, moving down to her breasts as her body accepted my touch. She put a hand on each of my shoulders and gently lifted up my head so that she could look at me. Her eyes looked happy but they were also a bit moist, as though she was struggling with her emotions.

"Okay, let's stop," I said, pushing myself up from the bed.

She reached out and gently pulled me back. "Lie down next to me," she said. I slid over and she repeated the favor, exploring my body with soft and gentle kisses. I never realized how sensitive my nipples could be, and it was definitely a new experience. I felt her warm breath against my belly as she continued to explore. And I heard the wrapper tear as she took out the condom and put it on me. Then she lay back next to me and slowly parted her legs. I could see that her knees were shaking, so I gently stroked her thighs, trying to reassure her and then felt her relax just a little.

"Go ahead," she said. "Please."

At first she was clenching and entry was not possible. "Are you sure you want to do this?" I said again.

"Yes, please keep going," she said, grabbing my buttocks and pulling me toward her. She yielded with a heavy sigh and I felt her whole body relax as I slid inside. We started moving together slowly. I could not have imagined a feeling quite like this, the warmth of our bodies, the feeling of trust and acceptance, and emerging passion. Gradually, her moans became more urgent and she dug her fingernails into my back.

Neither of us spoke when it was over. Michelle went over to get the bottle of champagne and brought it back to the bed, handing it to me. I hadn't really expected what had just happened between us, and I certainly wasn't prepared for anything as symbolic as this. Fortunately I was able to twist out the cork without making a mess of things. "Want to take the first sip?" I said, tentatively handing the bottle to her. "No, you go first," she said, holding the bottle to my mouth. For some reason, I felt reluctant to accept but took a small sip and felt the bubbles tickle down my throat as I swallowed.

"It's good," I said, exhaling.

"Yes it was," she said, "thank you Brett."

"What do you mean?" I asked, as she took a sip herself.

"For not rushing me," she said.

"You're welcome," I said. "I guess." She laughed. Her face was glowing, but the teary eyes had returned. Then she nodded with a serious expression.

"I think you should go now." I had heard that phrase before, but this time it was different. It was kind but firm, as though she wanted to make sure that she wouldn't change her mind. It felt like a closure, but I wanted it to be a beginning. She took another sip, setting the bottle on the night stand, and lay back on the bed, this time pulling a sheet over her.

"Look, maybe I should move out here with my dad, apply to the University of Florida and see if I can get in by spring semester. I could probably work for him until then."

"No Brett, I think that's a really bad and stupid idea."

"Why?"

"Because I'm just not ready…"

"But you were ready for that! Weren't you?"

"I thought I was… now I'm sure I'm not. Just go Brett!!"

I stood up to leave, walking over to my pile of clothes. She seemed to be getting angry and I had no idea why. It was the hardest thing to put my clothes back on.

"Put that record on," she said. Bowie's first album was on the turntable. I switched it on and carefully set down the needle. *Space Oddity* began to play.

"Goodbye Michelle," I said as I reached the door, "I'll come back when I can."

"Yes," she said, "maybe you will."

"Ground control to Major Tom" faded away as I shut the door carefully behind me.

Annie was sitting out there on the patio, waiting for me so that she could drive me home, for which I was quite grateful having not thought that far ahead.

"Well?" she said, teasingly.

"Well what?" I said, trying to regain my composure.

"You know," she said, teasing again.

"Gentlemen don't kiss and tell." I was hoping this attempt at levity would be the end of it.

"Yeah right," she laughed, and gave me a playful punch to the shoulder. "Come on, let's go."

The grandfather clock in my father's front hallway was just striking "one" when I entered the house. I felt my way down the hallway to my room, not wanting to turn on a light and risk waking anyone. I stripped naked again and slid between the cool sheets of my bed, trying to reimagine the sensations I had felt lying next to Michelle. Then I thought about how she had told me to go. It was the saddest feeling I had ever experienced.

CHAPTER SEVENTEEN

I SHOWERED EARLY the next morning and packed my things. My stepmother had left me a small carry-on bag for the additional clothes she had bought. I could tell by the smell of bacon and eggs that she was in the kitchen making breakfast.

"Your father left a while ago to check on his job sites," she said when she heard me coming. "He said that he would be back by seven thirty." He must have gotten up at the crack of dawn to get this done before driving me to the airport. She motioned for me to sit at the table where a place setting was waiting.

"Well I'm already packed," I said between sips of her fresh squeezed orange juice. "Thanks for the carry-on bag, and thanks so much for the clothes you bought. You always seem to know what I need before I do."

"Not a problem, Brett," she said in her lilting voice as she served the food. Then she busied herself with the dishwasher while I forked into my breakfast. When she was done she joined me at the table with a fresh cup of coffee. She took a sip.

"Brett, I understand that part of the reason you came out here was to see Michelle," she said. "I hope that went well for you. She's very nice."

"Yes, I think it did…" I said, nodding to myself. She let it pass.

"But I want you to know, it really meant a lot to your father that you came to stay with us again," she said after taking another pensive sip from her cup.

"It meant a lot to me as well. I really enjoyed spending time with my dad… And with you too," I added. I stood up to rinse off my plate and utensils and put them in the dishwasher, giving me time to think.

"It's been great having another opportunity to get to know you better," I said after returning to the table. "You've gone out of your way to embrace me as family, to make me feel welcome here. I guess I needed that! I feel really grateful. So thank you, I really appreciate it."

"You're always welcome here, Brett," she said. Her look told me that I had chosen the right words.

"Yeah, well I know my visit came unannounced. Sorry about that, by the way. I really should have called ahead. I know how busy you are."

"Just try to give us a little more notice next time, okay?"

"Yeah," I said, shrugging my shoulders and smiling, "I will."

"Well good," she emphasized the second word. Then she smiled.

My father pulled over at the curb in front of McCoy Airport to let me out. Just as I was about to open the door he reached over to shake my hand. "It's been great having you with us Brett," he said, pumping slowly.

"Yeah, I'm happy it worked out, that I actually made it here and all," I said. "I've especially enjoyed spending time with you Dad. I wish there had been more times like this when I was growing up. I'm glad I came." His eyes glistened as I reached over to give him a hug, which he returned, patting my back firmly to let me know that it was a man-hug. "Anyway, it really meant a lot to me," I said.

"Me too," he said.

I stepped out and got my backpack and carry-on bag from the back of the truck, standing by the curb to say one last goodbye.

"I'm really proud of you son," he said, beating me to the next sentence. I had never heard him say that before.

"Thank you Dad. I love you," I said.

"Love you too, son. Take care, Brett," he said, as he started the ignition. "And don't forget to write from college."

"I won't, Dad," I said, "And thanks again."

A Journey with Strangers

I watched him drive away and walked into the airport to find the ticket counter. I paid for the ticket, checked my backpack and walked over to the gate to wait for my flight departure, sitting down next to a plump middle-age woman who was busying herself with her knitting. She didn't seem interested in talking. I looked outside to see if my plane had arrived yet. It hadn't, but I could see that it was going to be another beautiful day here in Central Florida. I was going home.

It was a non-stop flight from Atlanta to Los Angeles and I had a window seat, so I spent most of my time looking out the window studying the changing landscape. Forests, lakes and open spaces rolled by quickly as we flew over Georgia and Alabama.

After about an hour the captain announced that we were passing over the Mississippi River. There it was, glimmering in the sunlight with a tiny steamboat headed down river. According to the map I had in the seat pocket in front of me, I was pretty sure that city down there was Vicksburg. I thought about Bubba, the self-proclaimed grand wizard of Vicksburg's Ku Klux Klan chapter. What would he be doing about now? Probably sitting on a bar stool at a local diner having lunch while chatting up some waitress who happened to be prettier than his wife. Was he happy, I wondered? I didn't think so.

The pilot came back on the mike and said we were now flying over the State of Texas. It had taken about two hours to get this far by plane, a distance that took me over two and a half days the week before.

"If you look to the right of the plane you can see that we are passing over the City of Dallas," the captain said. The memory of Kennedy's assassination came back to mind. Alan had let me off somewhere down there in Dealy Plaza where I had managed to find a flop house hotel to spend the night. He would be driving home in his Pontiac Firebird about now, probably blasting Hendrix from the stereo with a cold beer between his legs.

Plano was a suburb north of Dallas, according to the map. Cindy might be riding her horse. Maybe she was practicing her barrel racing. It made me smile.

It was difficult to comprehend how fast things were moving by as I watched the green farmland change to open prairie and then desert landscape. We were flying above it all at over 550 knots. It felt like I was studying a spinning globe of the Earth, or maybe like I was looking at one through a highly powered magnifying glass in slow motion.

Flying smoothly up here at 30,000 feet, I was feeling a bit disconnected from the ground. None of the other passengers were even looking out the window. It felt wrong somehow. It wasn't really possible to make out the intimate details anyway, no matter how hard I tried to imagine them. You had to experience them from the ground to truly appreciate their beauty, to understand their nuances, and to respect their hazards. It was difficult to appreciate things like that up here.

I remembered a family road trip that my stepdad had taken us on through the desert when I was 9 or 10 years old. He liked to stop in ghost towns and scavenge for relics. We had broken down at this truck stop and the car would no longer start, bad starter motor. He had to rebuild it out there on the hot asphalt because the guy who ran the truck stop didn't have all the right parts. Sweat was dripping down his nose onto the pavement as he struggled with the few mismatched tools he happened to have in the trunk. I watched him work while eating one of the Popsicles that my mother had bought to keep us kids busy. My Popsicle was drippy too. We would be okay, my mother said. We were. I remembered getting back in the car and accelerating onto the highway with all the windows rolled down. We had all cheered when we were back underway.

I had felt that way last week while hitching rides under the hot desert sun, with clouds forming on the horizon and threatening rain. Eventually a car would stop, sometimes with air conditioning, and everything would be fine. The open road was like that. You could

A Journey with Strangers

never be sure how the journey would go. And you had to be ready to improvise if things happened differently from what you were expecting, which could be fairly often.

Road travel could be a completely different time dimension for experiencing things. It was time enough to absorb the changing textures of the land, and to talk with people who had different opinions and beliefs along the way. I reflected on some of the things I had learned down there from people in cars. Although the Civil Rights Movement was supposedly behind us, racial prejudice still held a strong grip on the nation. I had experienced some of it first-hand. People had lots of different passions, and plenty of differences. And many folks were struggling with Vietnam's aftermath, what it all meant. Having listened to some of the young men who had fought over there and lived to come home, I had a keen desire to understand what really had happened and why. Even now, I choke up every time I walk down along the Vietnam War Memorial in Washington DC. I think of Bob, Baldy Bill and Alan, and about their friends who never came back.

I was thinking about the first Apollo moon landing and how it had unified the nation, if only for a moment. But the space race was over now, and the Cold War was still upon us. A president was being impeached. We were thinking differently about our leaders now. The social unrest of the 60's was not over, it seemed; there would be more to come.

Then my thoughts returned to Michelle. Wasn't she the key reason I had gone on this journey to begin with? It felt like too many things had been left unresolved between us. I had offered to move to Florida so that we could be together, but she had told me that I was being stupid. So did any of this matter? Did she want it to matter? Any future I might or might not have with her was still an open question. And for some reason, I felt at peace with myself just then.

What then had I learned about my father? I had taken a journey with strangers across this country and understood now that feelings of strangeness are only temporary. Strangers soon become real people when you allow yourself to talk to them. The same was true for my dad. He was no longer an abstract "father" to me, but a real person who cared about me. So did my stepmother apparently.

Another thing was surer to me now. I was about to spend two and a half months working in a wire mill and this was not something I wanted to do for the rest of my life. And I didn't want to wind up an insurance salesman like Alan down in Texas either. I had managed to get some of the uncertainty out of my system, to prove to myself that there were no immediate answers. The idea of college made more sense to me now. It was an open door, but not yet a path. That would come later.

The wheels touched down on the tarmac at Los Angeles International Airport and jolted me awake. I must have dozed off somewhere over Arizona. As we taxied over to our terminal I watched the landmark steel and glass dome pass by. I remembered seeing it for the first time when my stepfather had driven our family to LAX for what would be my first plane trip back in the early 1960's. We were flying to Ohio to see my grandparents. It had looked like a space station, and seeing it now, it still looked that way to me.

When the stewardess told us that we could unfasten our seatbelts and "de-plane" (my first time hearing this funny word), I retrieved my carry-on bag from the overhead rack and queued down the stairway with the rest of the passengers toward the terminal. The vast numbers of people moving about inside made it difficult to locate the signs that would direct me to baggage claim. I would need to retrieve my pack, figure out where I could catch a shuttle bus to the downtown station, and…

"Hello stranger!" I heard while watching the bags move by on the conveyor. It was Teresa, my raven haired goddess friend from high school.

"Hi Teresa!" I said, a bit stunned to see her. "What brings you here? Are you going somewhere?"

"No silly, I came here to get you," she said, punching me teasingly in the stomach and then giving me a hug. It felt good and I hugged her right back.

"How did you know I was here?" I asked, having trouble believing that she was actually standing there before me.

"I tried calling your house a bunch of times last week to see if you were okay but there was no answer until yesterday. Your mom had just read the note you left on the table and said you would be flying back today but she wasn't sure what time."

"Yeah, I knew she had just gotten back... I meant to call her yesterday but wasn't able to. I tried calling again this morning before I left for the airport. But I guess it was still too early..." She looked like she was about to scold me but fortunately she didn't.

"Well anyway, she gave me your father's number so I called him long distance and he told me what time you would be landing. I was worried about you Brett! You should have called me after the party." I shrugged, still somewhat embarrassed.

"Sorry about that. I was having a crummy week, and then I just got this incredible urge to go somewhere, you know?"

"Well you can tell me all about it later. Let's find your bag and get out of this terminal, away from all these people."

"Uh, you mean my backpack," I said. She looked perplexed. "I hitched across the country," I explained.

She smiled at this admission. "Don't worry, I won't tell," she said, "but I do want to hear all about it."

"Look, there it is." It was wrapped in plastic with airline tape. I took it off the conveyor, tore off the plastic, and shouldered my pack for the last time. I reached down and picked up my carry-on bag. All of me was back.

"Let's go," she said, clasping my hand as we walked out of the terminal.

I spied her red 1969 Camaro as we approached the parking lot. It was a car that I had greatly admired.

"Can I drive?" I asked. "Not yet..." she said. "I've got someplace to take you first. You can drive it later when we head back home."

It was still afternoon out here on the west coast and I wound my watch back three hours to make it official. We headed down Interstate 10 toward the coast, exited at Coast Highway and drove north to Will Rogers State Beach. Teresa pulled into the parking lot and gunned the engine one last time before shutting it down. It let out a throaty sigh. "Well?" she said, turning to me with a knowing smile. "From coast to coast and back again, huh? I thought you might like to stop at the beach first before going home."

The sun was still traveling on its way over the Pacific Ocean, and it was a beautiful summer day. Palm trees swayed in the gentle breeze. "Excellent plan," I said with a smile that I felt all over my face.

Teresa pointed to a public restroom with changing stalls next to the parking lot. "You think you can find a pair of swim trunks in that backpack of yours?" she asked.

"Actually, I do have a pair," I laughed. "My stepmother bought them for me when I was in Florida. They're in my carry-on bag."

"Well get them silly," she said. "Now would be a good time for them!"

"Okay, okay," I held up my palms in surrender.

She fetched a beach bag from the trunk and we walked over to the restrooms to change, returning with our street clothes back to the car. It felt good to walk barefoot with the sand between my toes as we weaved through clusters of people to locate a place where we could lay out our towels. I took in the sound of crashing waves and the sight of seagulls cruising over the water in formation. The air was warm but not humid like back in Florida. I felt like I could stay here forever. Looking out to the water, a surfer had just caught a wave and was sliding down into the curl. It looked like he might catch a tube ride if he was lucky. I was finally home.

Teresa pulled a Frisbee from her beach bag and motioned for me to walk down the beach a ways to receive the toss. She was wearing a cream white bikini now that complemented her tanned body perfectly. "Okay, let's see what you've got," I said once I had found a spot to position myself, digging both feet in the sand.

Standing up the beach with her legs slightly apart, Teresa was winding up for the toss. It was a perfect throw and was headed straight toward me. I bent my knees and twisted my feet sideways in the sand, reaching around for a behind the back grab.

About the author: Mark Reynolds grew up in Southern California and was an unapologetic teenager of the '70s. It was a time before cell phones, cable TV and internet when kids had to go out into the world to experience life. He has always wanted to write about that period and this book is his first such effort. In his professional life, he works in the biotechnology industry developing clinical diagnostic tests that improve a physician's ability to diagnose and treat their patients. He continues to be passionate about running, hiking, travel and music. He lives in Carlsbad, CA.